THE LAST PHARAOH
The Ten Faces of Farouk

THE LAST PHARAOH

The Ten Faces of Farouk

Hugh McLeave

LONDON

MICHAEL JOSEPH

First published in Great Britain by
MICHAEL JOSEPH LTD
52 Bedford Square
London, W.C.1
1969
© *1969 by Hugh McLeave*

7181 0569 9

Set and printed in Great Britain by
Tonbridge Printers Ltd, Peach Hall Works, Tonbridge, Kent
in Times ten on thirteen point, and bound by
James Burn at Esher, Surrey

ACKNOWLEDGEMENTS

My thanks are due to the following for permission to reproduce extracts from works in which they control the copyright: *Cassell and Company Limited*, History Of The Second World War, Vol. 3, The Grand Alliance p. 95 by Winston S. Churchill, and Memoirs of Sir Anthony Eden – Full Circle; *Collins Publishers*, Memoirs – Field Marshal Viscount Montgomery; *The Hamlyn Publishing Group Limited*, Revolt On The Nile by Anwar el-Sedat; *Victor Gollancz Limited*, Egypt's Destiny by General Neguib; and *Laurence Pollinger Limited*, Memoirs – the Aga Khan.

The following have also been kind enough to grant me permission to reproduce photographs in which they control the copyright: *Keystone Press Agency Limited*, 4 and 6; *The Associated Press Limited*, 3, 8, and 10; and *Mrs Ina Naylor*, 1, 2, 5 and 7.

ILLUSTRATIONS

1 Queen Nazli with four of her children   *facing* 64

2 Farouk as a young boy   65

3 Farouk and his four sisters on their arrival in England for the coronation of King George VI and Queen Elizabeth, 1937   96

4 Farouk at Saint Moritz   97

5 Farouk wearing the summer uniform of Field Marshal   97

6 Farouk and his first queen, Farida   128

7 Farouk driving his sports car   129

8 Duck shooting at Mansouria, near Cairo   129

9 Farouk, his second queen, Narriman and their infant son, Ahmed Fuad   160

10 Farouk at the opera in Monte Carlo in April 1956   160

BIBLIOGRAPHY

Arabic

AMIN, MOSTAPHA: *Layaleh Faruq.* Akhbar el-Yom, 1953

EL-TABEH, MOHAMED: *Secrets of Egyptian Politics and Politicians before the Revolution.* State Publication, Cairo, 1954

HAFIZ, SULEIMAN: *This is the Revolution.* Cairo, 1954

NEGUIB, GENERAL MOHAMED: *Story of the Abdication.* Al Ahram, 1953

English

AGA KHAN: *Memoirs.* Cassell, London, 1954

AVON, LORD (ANTHONY EDEN): *Full Circle.* Cassell, London, 1960

AYROUT, HENRY: *The Fellahin.* Schindler, Cairo, 1945

EL-BARAWY: *Military Coup in Egypt.* Renaissance Bookshop, Cairo, 1952

BLAND, JAMES: *Prince Ahmad of Egypt.* Stanley Paul, 1939

BLAXLAND, GREGORY: *Objective Egypt.* Muller, London, 1966

BRYANT, SIR ARTHUR: *The Turn of the Tide.* Collins, London, 1957

CHANDOS, LORD (OLIVER LYTTLETON): *Memoirs.* The Bodley Head, London, 1962

CHURCHILL, WINSTON S.: *The Second World War, Vol. III.* Cassell, London

COOPER, DIANA: *Trumpets from the Steep.* Rupert Hart-Davis, London, 1960

COWARD, NOËL: *Middle East Diary.* Heinemann, London, 1944

CROMER, LORD: *Modern Egypt.* Macmillan, London, 1908

DOUGLAS, SHOLTO: *The Years of Command.* Collins, London, 1966

HEYWORTH-DUNN, J.: *Religious and Political Trends in Modern Egypt.* Washington, 1948

HUSAINI, ISHAK, M.: *The Moslem Brethren.* Khayat, Beirut, 1956

ISSAWI, C.: *Egypt at Mid-Century.* Oxford University Press, 1954

JARVIS, H. W.: *Pharaoh to Farouk.* John Murray, London, 1955

KIRK, GEORGE, E.: *A Short History of the Middle East.* Methuen, London, 1948

LACOUTURE, J. AND S.: *Egypt in Transition.* Methuen, London, 1958

LANDES, DAVID S.: *Bankers and Pashas.* Heinemann, London, 1958

LITTLE, TOM: *Egypt.* Benn, London, 1958

LLOYD, LORD: *Egypt since Cromer.* Macmillan, London, 1933

LUGOL, J.: *Egypt and World War II: Société Orientale de Publicité.* Cairo, 1945

MANSFIELD, P.: *Nasser's Egypt.* Penguin Books, London, 1965

MARLOWE, JOHN: *Anglo-Egyptian Relations 1800–1953.* Cresset, London, 1954

MONTGOMERY OF ALAMEIN, FIELD MARSHAL VISCOUNT: *Memoirs.* Collins, London, 1958

NASSER, GAMAL ABDEL: *Philosophy of the Revolution.* National Publication House, London, 1954

NEGUIB, GENERAL MOHAMED: *Egypt's Destiny.* Gollancz, London, 1955

ROWLATT, M.: *Founders of Modern Egypt.* Asia Publishing House, Bombay, 1962

RUSSELL PASHA: *Egyptian Service 1902–1946.* John Murray, London, 1949

RUSSELL PASHA: *Ronald Seth.* William Kimber, London, 1966

EL-SADAT, ANWAR: *Revolt on the Nile.* Wingate, London, 1957

SANSOM, A. N.: *I Spied Spies.* G. Harrap, London

SHAH, IKBAL ALI: *Fuad King of Egypt.* Herbert Jenkins, London, 1936

STERN, M.: *Farouk.* Bantam Books, 1965

STEVENS, G. C.: *Egypt Yesterday and Today.* Holt, Rinehart and Winston, New York, 1963

STEWART, DESMOND: *Young Egypt.* Wingate, London, 1958

TUGAY, EMINE FOAT: *Three Centuries, Family Chronicles of Turkey and Egypt.* Oxford University Press, London, 1963

TULLY, A.: *Central Intelligence Agency, The Inside Story.* Arthur Barker, London, 1962

VATIKIOTIS, P. J.: *The Egyptian Army in Politics.* Indiana University Press, Bloomington, 1961

WHEELOCK, K.: *Nasser's New Egypt.* Atlantic Books, Stevens, London, 1960

WHITE, A. SILVA: *The Expansion of Egypt.* Methuen, London, 1899

WILLIAMS, FRANCIS: *A Prime Minister Remembers.* Heinemann, London, 1961

WILSON OF LIBYA, LORD: *Eight Years Overseas.* Hutchinson

GREAT BRITAIN IN EGYPT: *Information Paper No. 19.* Royal Institute of International Affairs, London, 1952

PRESIDENT'S PROPOSAL ON THE MIDDLE EAST: *85th U.S. Congress Hearings.* Pub; 1957

THE PALACE COLLECTIONS OF EGYPT: Sotheby and Company, 1953

THE KORAN

French

ABDUL FATH, AHMED: *L'Affaire Nasser.* Plon, Paris, 1962

BERNARD-DEROSNE, JEAN: *La Déchéance d'un Roi.* Editions Francaises d'Amsterdam, 1953

LIVRE D'OR: *La Réforme Illustrée.* Alexandria, 1945

THABET, KAREM: *Memoirs.* Journal d'Alexandrie, 1955

THE MOHAMED ALI DYNASTY 1805–1953

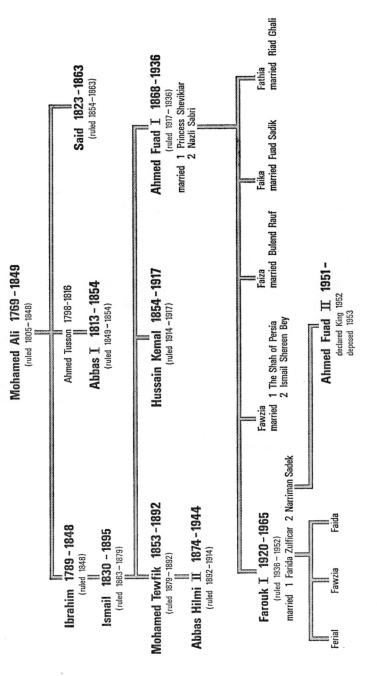

Mohamed Ali 1769–1849
(ruled 1805–1848)

Ahmed Tusson 1798–1816

Said 1823–1863
(ruled 1854–1863)

Abbas I 1813–1854
(ruled 1849–1854)

Ibrahim 1789–1848
(ruled 1848)

Ismail 1830–1895
(ruled 1863–1879)

Hussain Kemal 1854–1917
(ruled 1914–1917)

Ahmed Fuad I 1868–1936
(ruled 1917–1936)
married 1 Princess Shevikiar
2 Nazli Sabri

Mohamed Tewfik 1853–1892
(ruled 1879–1892)

Abbas Hilmi II 1874–1944
(ruled 1892–1914)

Fawzia
married 1 The Shah of Persia
2 Ismail Shereen Bey

Faiza
married Bulend Rauf

Faika
married Fuad Sadik

Fathia
married Riad Ghali

Ahmed Fuad II 1951 –
declared King 1952
deposed 1953

Farouk I 1920–1965
(ruled 1936–1952)
married 1 Farida Zulficar 2 Narriman Sadek

Ferial   Fawzia   Faida

CHAPTER ONE

*And who speaketh fairer to thee than he who biddeth to
God and doth the thing that is right, and saith, 'I for my part
am of the Muslims'.*   (Koran XLI: 33)

NO-ONE could have said that horse and rider behaved like a team
as they leapt the set of low jumps in Richmond Park on that
muggy, overcast day in April 1936. The fault did not lie with the
bay which might have cantered over the course blindfolded with a
dead weight on its back; no, it was the boy who was trying its
douce temperament as he checked and wrong-footed it before a
jump, jerked on the reins in mid-air or dug his heels into its flanks
to urge it to greater efforts. Naturally, the horse reacted by
attempting to jump away from the boy, forcing him to cling on
more by spirit than skill and bringing a scowl to his handsome
face which was set determinedly under the thatch of golden hair.
On horseback by his side, his instructor, Sir Louis Greig, shouted
advice though this seemed to go unheeded.

Engrossed in their lesson, neither noticed the Daimler
approaching Thatched House Lodge. From the bonnet flew the
Islamic green pennon of Egypt with its crescent and three five-
pointed stars. The car halted near the makeshift course and out
stepped a man wearing a black frock-coat and a red tarbush; in
his mid-forties, he had a long, lugubrious face and a slow,
dignified stride. Almost hesitant. Both riders spotted him and
reined in their horses. He walked towards the boy and
bowed.

'Your Majesty,' he began. 'I have sad news for you . . .'

'My father is dead.'

'I regret, His Majesty King Fuad died at 1.30 this afternoon.
Your name was the last word on his lips. Her Majesty, Queen
Nazli, wishes you to call her, and there is a message for you from
the Prime Minister at Kenry House.'

13

For some weeks they had known that the boy's father, Fuad the First, King of Egypt, was lying critically ill in the vast, yellow palace of Kubbah on the outskirts of Cairo; four days ago news had reached them that the doctors gave him no chance. Now he was dead. To his son, Farouk, that meant he was ruler of the most ancient kingdom in the world; it meant, too, that for the second time since Tutankamen, three thousand three hundred years in the past, a boy sat on the throne of Upper and Lower Egypt, sovereign of Nubia and the Sudan provinces, Kordofan and Darfur. The two men watched him, observing his reaction, waiting for his response. The courtier, Ahmed Mohamed Hassanain bey, his tutor, a minister pleni-potentiary and a renowned explorer, had served father and son; Sir Louis Greig, Deputy Ranger of Richmond Park, had once acted as tutor and companion to the Duke of York, later George the Sixth.

Farouk appeared unimpressed; he glanced at them, reining his horse away. 'I'll just do three more rounds of jumps then I shall return with you,' he said.

Hassanain made no comment, no sign. But Sir Louis caught hold of the reins. 'Sir,' he said. 'You'll do nothing of the sort. Get down off that horse.' Farouk started to scowl, then grinned and dismounted. As an aside to Hassanain, Sir Louis muttered, 'We can't have two kings of Egypt dying on the same day.' He had seen Farouk fall too often and had little faith in his judgement or riding ability.

'He didn't mean it,' Hassanain replied, not for the first time having to find an excuse for Farouk's conduct. Later, when asked by friends if the young prince had really shown such a callous and capricious reaction to his father's death, he would ward them off diplomatically. 'It was a poor joke at my expense. He was only sixteen.' To his more intimate circle he confessed his astonishment at Farouk's attitude; it proved what he had often suspected, that the boy truly feared his father.

The flag flew at half-mast over Kenry House, the grey-stucco mansion among the rhododendrons and rose gardens on Kingston Hill which Farouk and his retinue had occupied for seven

14

months while he studied for entrance to the Royal Military Academy at Woolwich. The telegram from the Prime Minister, Ali Maher pasha, requested him on behalf of the government to leave for Egypt as soon as possible; his mother reinforced the suggestion with a tearful and urgent plea for his return when he telephoned her. She told him that, though still a minor, they had proclaimed him king until his constitutional powers were handed over to a regency council.

Hassanain proposed that they should leave the following day and Farouk agreed. England he disliked. Here, he was merely Prince Freddie, a homesick exile slogging at maths and gym, resenting the prospect of another two years in spartan cadet quarters being drilled as a future king. Yet, in his last years he would rhapsodise about its rain and fog, his hard days at The Shop, his nights in Piccadilly and his teas at Buckingham Palace as if he had known no other childhood.

Farouk had the madcap notion of travelling home disguised. Hassanain scotched this on the grounds that the formalities of the departure and the news that his father had died ruled out secrecy; he also rejected the idea of flying home as too hazardous. The new king would return incognito by ship even though it meant missing his father's funeral.

Next day, hundreds of messages of commiseration and goodwill arrived at Kenry House, including one from King Edward the Eighth who had befriended Farouk and taken him to football and rugby matches. He would like to see King Farouk before he left. So, on the way to Victoria Station, Farouk called at Buckingham Palace and spent half an hour chatting informally with Edward who, within eight months would have renounced his throne. The King of England offered to lend him a warship for his journey to Egypt, but Farouk declined on Hassanain's shrewd advice. To begin his reign by stepping off a British gunboat would hardly appeal to the people of a country which had spent half a century trying to get rid of British troops. At Victoria, the Duke of Kent and Mr Anthony Eden, the Foreign Secretary, said farewell; at Dover the Seaforth Highlanders paraded in his honour, piping him on board the French packet-boat, Côte d'Azur; at

15

Marseilles he slipped, almost unobserved, on to the Viceroy of India for home.

Had anyone ever received such a welcome in Egypt? From first light on the glowing morning of the sixth of May, crowds had begun to throng into Alexandria. Thousands had marched through the night, thousands more rode in on donkeys, in gharis, on camels or in ramshackle buses; fellahin with their veiled women-folk and children followed the multitude, jostling their way into the Mohamed Ali Square or squatting in groups round the Western Harbour where their boy Malik would land. The long rays of the sun were beginning to warm them when the guns announced the king's arrival; they thumped rhythmically from the British and Egyptian warships in the harbour, from the ancient Kait Bey fortress and the coastal batteries along the corniche as the king transferred from the liner to the royal yacht Mahroussa. There he spent some minutes meeting the Prime Minister and his cabinet before embarking in a launch which brought him to the jetty of Ras el-Tin Palace. The slight figure, in black frock-coat, white shirt, black tie and red tarbush, crossed the gangway and stepped on to Egyptian soil. The boyish face smiled. A sad smile. His hand rose in salute. A half salute. The roar swelled, obliterating the wailing sirens and the clamour of the guns. *Yahia, Malik Farouk,* – Long live King Farouk – they screamed. *Allah-ho-Akhbar,* – None is greater than Allah. One by one, his own cabinet bowed to the king; most of them kissed his hand; a few went through the ritual of gathering the dust on which his feet had trodden and anointing their heads with it.

Among the mass of peasants and fishermen, shopkeepers and factory workers, schoolboys and girls, stood a young man in his twenties who had also come to cheer his king. Haz Khittab, a worker on Fuad's estates, could not then know that he would be the last man on earth ever to see this king, when they buried him like a thief and his reign had become a by-word for corruption and depravity. Now, however, he was shouting *Yahia, Farouk* with half a million other voices.

16

'Aeewah, that was a sight. Had anyone ever been more hand-some than that boy Malik? To us he was a young god. Have you seen thousands of beggars cheering, and the fellahin giving up a day's work in their fields for a king? They did on that day, for-getting their misery and their hunger and the poverty in the villages. We even forgave Fuad, the hated, the *naashif* (tight-fisted) and cruel for such a son, such a king. Aeewah, with this one we could do anything. Did he not speak our language and share our feelings. Pashas would no longer wring money from their fellahin, the *omdas* (village headmen) would no longer whip their tongues into obedience on voting days, the poor would no longer go hungry and the beggars no longer need to beg. And the *Inglesi*? He would take them and all other infidels off our backs. Aeewah Farouk. That day – his day – we felt was the first day of our freedom.'

The royal procession moved off at walking pace through the city, towards Ramilly Station. Standing erect in the back of an open Rolls-Royce, the boy king acknowledged the cheering crowds surging behind Egyptian and British troops who flanked the streets; to greet their Chief thousands of Boy Scouts had paraded and with them young Blue Shirts from the nationalist party and Green Shirts from the Young Egypt movement. Their shrill voices rose above the din; youth seemed to be calling to youth. Women and girls strewed piles of hibiscus, jacaranda and desert blossoms in front of the car. Many knelt to kiss the ground over which it had passed.

From the great Mediterranean port the news fanned out to the cities of the Delta; east to Rosetta and Damietta and Port Said; south-west to Tanta and Zagazig and Suez; west to the desert towns of Alamein and Matruh; south to the lonely oasis of Siwa. Up the Nile it ran to Cairo where markets emptied and the streets thickened between the main station and Abdin Palace. Radio carried it into villages bracketing the eight hundred miles of the Egyptian Nile. There, even the *fellahin* straightened their backs over their hoes, ploughs and primordial water wheels and listened to the jubilant echo from the other end of the country. Not much touched these people in their cotton fields, their plantations of beet

17

and sugar cane, their clover and rice fields, their orange and mango groves. This moment did. Many of them quit their toil in the Delta to climb on to the mud roofs of their huts, to cling to palm trees, to line the railway track and perhaps catch a glimpse of the king as his train passed on its way to Cairo.

Through the greatest day of his life, Farouk moved with the poise of someone born to the role; the slim, straight-backed figure had the right, pensive smile as he responded to the Cairo crowd or met the three thousand dignitaries who greeted him at the station. Government officials, ambassadors and the foreign colony all commented on his bearing and assurance. From this exhausting welcome he drove straight to El Rifai Mosque on the city perimeter to pray before his father's tomb. The *sheikhs* and the *ulema*, keepers of the Islamic faith, murmured their approval as he removed his shoes and entered the mosque to kneel and intone part of the Koran. For a boy of sixteen the whole of that day had been an impressive performance.

On the eighth of May, two days after his arrival, Farouk broadcast to his eighteen million subjects, the first king ever to speak directly to them and the first time a monarch had addressed them in their own tongue, Arabic. The speech he wrote himself with some help from Hassanain and Ali Maher. In Cairo, Alexandria and other cities people filled every café owning a radio; in the villages, loudspeakers relayed the king's voice. They heard him say he had left the country seven months ago at his father's wish, to study Western culture and democracy, to prepare himself for kingship. His greatest wish would have been to continue this training at his father's side.

'But the supreme will of Allah has denied me the happiness of seeing my father again; it has deprived me of realising the great hopes which I placed on his beloved person and his happy reign...' His voice had a deep, musical timbre. His Arabic? Maybe the purists tut-tutted, but who understood classic Arabic? To the crowds, hearing their king speak came as a revelation. He went on: 'I start my new life with a good heart and a strong will. With you as a witness, I promise to devote my life and my being to your good, to bend all my efforts to create your happiness. I have seen at first hand your attachment to me, your affection for me. I declare it my duty to work with you for the good of our beloved Egypt. For I believe that the glory of the king comes from the glory of his people ... I pray to Allah to help me make the nation happy, to achieve for it all the greatness which I wish. With all the will I possess, I shall seek to reform the country. Allah is my strength.'

Farouk believed the promises he had given the nation; so, in fact, did Hassanain and other courtiers to whom the king spoke his mind. The despotism of his father had ended and with it the political and social evils that enslaved the people. He would abolish the feudal system binding peasant to pasha; he would rid the country of usury; he would purge corruption in the palace and government. And by chasing the British out he would give Egypt back to the Egyptians.

CHAPTER TWO

'Deal calmly therefore with the infidels; leave them awhile,
alone.' (LXXXVI: 17)

As a boy, Farouk betrayed no interest in history, earning a re-
proof from some of the less sychophantic tutors for his scant
attention to his own ancestry and the development of modern
Egypt. One master, Ahmed Yussef, wrote in the prince's notebook, 'It is regrettable that you do not know the history of your
forebears.' Had the Emir es-Said, Prince of Upper Egypt, spent
less of his boyhood careering aimlessly round the royal estates in
his car and racketing wildly through palaces he might have discovered much about his own heredity and character. For he
descended from one of the most eccentric dynasties in history,
from a class of adventurer in whom madness and genius blended
strangely. The line which ended with Farouk's son began with
Mohamed Ali who kept the Middle East in ferment for nearly half
a century.

Mohamed Ali was born in 1769 at Cavalla, on the frontiers of
Thrace and Macedonia. His father, a Turkish farmer, left him
orphaned; his uncle, military commander of the town, took him
under his protection. Before long Mohamed Ali had become ringleader of the town's hotheads which forced his uncle to enrol him
in the *gendarmerie* and keep his fighting within the law. A few
years later he married Amine Hanim, daughter of the Turkish
provincial governor, and was threatening to usurp his uncle in
Cavalla. So, when the Turks started recruiting *Bashi-Bazuks*
(volunteers) to fight against Napoleon in Egypt, the uncle intrigued to have his nephew appointed force commander.
Mohamed Ali sailed as second-in-command in July 1799. In the
first engagement at Abukir Bay, the French pushed him and his
men into the sea where Mohamed Ali would have drowned had a
sailor in the British admiral's gig not pulled him to safety. That

unknown rating transformed Middle East history. When they had thrust the French out of Egypt, the British expeditionary units departed. Mohamed Ali stayed on with his regiment.

By the beginning of the nineteenth century the miraculous, ancient civilisation had slid backwards into a starving, ignorant land of two million five hundred thousand people, whereas thirty dynasties of pharaohs and three thousand years of recorded history had populated it with three times this number. In 525 B.C. Pharaoh ceded to Persian, and he in turn to Alexander the Great in 332 B.C. For three hundred years Ptolemaic kings, descended from one of Alexander's generals, ruled the country until Mark Antony and Cleopatra died and the Romans arrived. In A.D. 639, the Arabs seized Egypt and governed until the end of the twelfth century when Saladin the Great overthrew them, leaving his Mameluke mercenaries to run the country for the next four hundred years. In 1517, came Turks who used the Mamelukes as petty tyrants and tax collectors and turned Egypt into an economic and cultural wilderness with oppression and misrule.

Yet no powerful country could ignore Egypt, this country which amounted to no more than a fertile strip between two deserts, owing its existence to the river wedged like an enormous nail throughout its length. It hinged Africa to Asia and could bar the route between Europe and India. To the strategist, Napoleon, it seemed the key to the destruction of British mercantile power and to world conquest. His invasion not only stirred the somnolent culture of Egypt; by breaking Mameluke supremacy he virtually created anarchy. The Mamelukes, a wild military caste of mixed Turk, Mongol and Circassian blood, had subdued the country with sword and lash; now they were warring with their Turkish overlord and had found an ally in the Albanian contingent and its commander, Tahir Pasha. These troops rebelled against the Turkish governor of Egypt, Mohamed Khosrev, demanding their pay; he turned his guns on them and they retaliated by storming the Citadel dominating Cairo. Khosrev fled, but Tahir lasted only twenty-three days before falling to an assassin. The sheikhs of Cairo turned to the man they believed could keep the peace: Mohamed Ali.

21

He and his Albanian guard had sat aloof from the bickering. Now he played cat and mouse, siding with the Mamelukes until they grew too powerful, then throwing in his lot with the Sultan. This shrewdness persuaded the sheikhs to name him Pasha of Egypt. The Sultan confirmed the title, and as part payment Mohamed Ali lured a hundred Mamelukes into the city and butchered them. Even so the unwary Mamelukes joined him against the British force which came to reinstate them in 1807 and celebrated their victory by parading hundreds of British heads on stakes through Cairo. The British defeat quashed their own future; four years later Mohamed Ali schemed their extermination, even rehearsing this mass slaughter on his own Albanian guard. Again, this force had rebelled over pay so their leader, warned by his cousin, the military treasurer, summoned them to parade in his own courtyard to receive their money. The Citadel guns annihilated them, cousin and all.

The Mamelukes fell into a similar trap. Knowing their weakness for military pomp, the Pasha invited them to the Jewel Palace in the Citadel to fête the departure of an expedition to Arabia. Resplendent in their martial robes, four hundred and seventy warrior chiefs rode in. Food, music and dancing distracted them so that they did not notice the guards had shut every gate in the fortress. As they rose from their banquet the guards began to chop them down while musketeers on the battlements finished the task. Blood gushing from the marble fountain covered the courtyard. The Pasha's son, Ibrahim, completed this grisly genocide in the provinces. An atrocious crime, wrote Sir Charles Murray, the British Consul-general. But, he added, a necessary prelude to all subsequent reforms.

What reforms? Mohamed Ali had one aim: to create an army and navy which would make the Middle East his. He began with Egypt. By confiscation and meagre compensation he grabbed almost the whole country; he granted the fellahin some measure of leasehold over their land, then employed Turks to beat taxes out of them with the *courbash* (rhino whip). More than twenty thousand fellahin perished in the forced-labour gangs which constructed the canal linking Alexandria with the Nile. Similarly, the factories which the Pasha established on European models ran at a loss which he made good out of his land profits. To confiscation he coupled monopoly; nothing changed hands without his sanction.

Credit him, none the less, with introducing long-staple cotton to the Nile Valley and rendering Egypt safe for travellers by disarming turbulent tribesmen. Cairo he transformed into a centre for foreign trade, Alexandria a prosperous port and Egypt the route to India and the Far East.

Power obsessed him. Peasants mutilated themselves in thousands to escape conscription but he drilled them into the best fighting force in the Middle East. To train troops and naval men France sent officers, among them a Colonel Joseph Sève who became a Moslem and changed his name to Suleiman pasha. This soldier, to whom even the fanatical Ibrahim submitted as a recruit, was an ancestor of Farouk on his mother's side. Within ten years Mohamed Ali had enough negro and fellahin soldiers to crush the Sultan and the strongest navy in the eastern Mediterranean. Ismail, another son, conquered the Sudan with its ivory and gold, spices and slaves, while Ibrahim helped his father's Turkish master in Greece. In 1831, however, when Mohamed Ali tilted at his overlord and extended his territory from the Sudan to the Taurus Mountains, Britain, France and Russia decided this enlightened villain had gone far enough, that the dismemberment of the Ottoman Empire might destroy the political balance of the Near East; they forced the Pasha to limit his army to eighteen thousand men, dismantle his navy and confine his conquests to Egypt, the Sinai Peninsula, the Sudan and some parts of Arabia. He bargained for and secured the succession of his family as pashas of Egypt, thus founding the dynasty.

We can almost visualise the ageing Lion of the Levant scanning the school reports of his favourite son, Said, interesting himself more in the boy's weight and fitness than in his mental prowess. Or contemptuously dismissing the clerk who was reading Machiavelli's *The Prince*, saying, 'I think I could teach him something.' Or splitting a French geography book in three with a scimitar so that it could be translated three times quicker. Or growling when they dissuaded him from demolishing the Pyramids to use their stones on the new barrage at the head of the Nile Delta.

At seventy-nine Mohamed Ali's brain went soft and he handed over to Ibrahim as regent; the son was to die in 1848 a few months before his father who died in 1849. Short, grossly fat and scarred by smallpox, Ibrahim suffered from a mad streak. Lord Cromer described him as a distinguished soldier and a man of great personal courage. 'It must be added that he was a half-lunatic savage,' he commented. He lopped off a relation's head when the man implied that the heavy-handed Pasha was cutting his horse's mouth with the bit. Ibrahim died as dramatically as he had lived. Following army manoeuvres he emptied a beaker filled with two bottles of iced champagne to cool himself; he developed pneumonia and this, coupled with a present from his mother of a young Circassian slave girl, proved too much for him. He was fifty-nine.

Abbas, grandson of Mohamed Ali lasted six years before two Mameluke slaves stabbed him. A cruel, sullen, saturnine recluse he undid most of his grandfather's work; he closed schools, factories, disbanded all but nine thousand men of the magnificent army and expelled all but a few foreigners.

In 1854, after his accession, Said re-opened the factories and in-vited the foreigners back, among them the friend of his youth, Ferdinand de Lesseps. For years this diplomat had dreamed of cutting a channel through the Suez isthmus to join the Mediter-ranean with the Red Sea. Some months after becoming Pasha, Said granted de Lesseps the right to make such a canal. His scribbled signature over the unread document had disastrous effects for Egypt; it gave the shareholders three-quarters of the profits, the promoters a tenth and Egypt something between a sixth and seventh. How could Said have foreseen that this canal would bring Britain into the area to protect her route to India, or that it would end the profitable overland traffic across the

24

isthmus? Said started something else: the national debt. He borrowed more than three million pounds from European bankers and ran up an overdraft of ten millions before he died in 1863.

Compared with Ismail Said ranks as no more than a minor spend-thrift. Ibrahim's second son, who acceded on Said's death, regarded Egypt as a vast estate with himself sole proprietor. As a young man in the courts of Rome, Paris and Constantinople he had established new records in prodigality; he returned to Egypt with marvellous notions to lift the country out of its feudal past into the nineteenth century, to model it on Europe. *'L'Égypte fait partie de l'Europe,'* he was fond of saying. Ismail first persuaded the Sultan to scrap the edict granting the succession to the eldest prince of the dynasty; henceforth, the law of primogeniture would apply and Ismail's sons would rule as khedives, the sultan's vice-roys in Egypt.

Ismail was Farouk's grandfather and we can catch echoes of the character of one in the other. Certainly Farouk was drawn to Ismail's life and personality and took more interest in him than any other ancestor; many people who knew Farouk well maintain that he attempted to emulate his grandfather in some of his be-haviour. If so, he succeeded only partially, for Ismail was one of the most bewildering personalities in history. Lord Milner saw him as a depraved ogre whereas Judge Crabitès portrayed him as a maligned but enlightened spirit. But then Ismail was one huge contradiction, a mixture of barbarism and good breeding, refine-ment and despotism, brilliance and ignorance. His fellahin he had flogged as never before to extort their last piastre in tax; yet they could go to schools he had ordered to combat their illiteracy. He used forced labour throughout his vast royal estates, though he mounted expeditions by Sir Samuel Baker and General 'Chinese' Gordon to put down the slave trade in the Sudan. He could drink tea with Queen Victoria or champagne with the Empress Eugénie of France but have his own finance minister strangled when the poisoned coffee he had offered him did not act quickly enough. His character was a bizarre amalgam of the Oriental potentate, European tycoon and Russian impressario; he always had a head full of projects which he barked at three secretaries transcribing them simultaneously in Turkish, Arabic and French.

Ismail, the visionary, imagined an African empire filled with the trappings of European civilisation; Ismail, the impractical, did not realise this would take a century instead of a few years. The cotton boom created by the American Civil War had filled his treasury; he emptied it just as quickly by laying one thousand miles of railway, eight thousand miles of irrigation canals and five thousand miles of telegraph lines. He raised the arable area of the country from about four million to five and a half million acres. Under him, the post office and customs were remodelled and new industries set up. Palaces sprang up in Cairo; in the centre Abdin Palace took on something of the shape of Buckingham Palace with five hundred rooms and grounds stretching over twenty-five acres of demolished housing; on the outskirts, Kubbah Palace, a country mansion inflated to four hundred rooms with more than seventy acres of gardens; at Zaafaran and Inchass he built two more palaces and scattered pavilions around the country.

He lost count of the number of mistresses he had and what he paid them. They often queued up outside his apartments, sent by princes and heads of state. One lady came to him from the King of Italy and found him occupied. To placate her Ismail said, 'Give her twenty-four locomotives.' The astounded demi-mondaine walked out with a contract to supply that number of railway engines to the Egyptian state. The same man could nevertheless quibble about tipping a Paris page-boy a few centimes, or spend half the day quarrelling with his gardener over a few piastres.

In business he could display great shrewdness. He duped Disraeli (who never let on) into paying a quarter of a million pounds over the odds for forty per cent of the canal shares, without voting rights; he forced the canal company to scrap concessions wheedled out of Said. And he revelled in the preparations for the opening of the canal on the sixteenth of November, 1869. He invited royalty from all over Europe, the diva of the spectacle being the Empress Eugénie, his great friend – mistress, some said. In the French imperial yacht, Aigle, she led the procession of sixty-eight ships through the new canal; the stately convoy slid through as though gliding over the sand, spent a couple of days carousing at Ismailia and reached Suez on the twentieth. Ismail had even commissioned Aida, a new opera by Verdi, for his sumptuous Opera House in Cairo; the building was finished, but not the opera and his guests heard Rigoletto instead.

The canal did nothing to solve Egypt's growing financial crisis. With his fantastic schemes and *quixotic* personal spending, Ismail had attracted swarms of European speculators, had leaned on European banks. Selling his canal shares in 1875 to Britain, his profits to France let him breathe again for a few months and dream of outwitting the finance houses. Could not one overdraft be met with another? He overlooked the elementary principle that each loan attracted higher interest rates until Egypt's debts stood at more than one hundred million pounds. Charitable critics claim that his personal extravagance accounted for no more than fifteen million pounds of this. Yet another inspiration struck him; he offered landlords life remission of half their taxes if they paid six years in advance. He forgot, he had bled them dry.

Alarmed by the tottering economy, Britain and France had to act; in 1879 they forced Ismail to nationalise his vast dominions, act as a constitutional sovereign and accept two British and French experts as finance and public works ministers. Ismail played his last card. He secretly organised a military riot in Cairo, seizing the pretext to sack his cabinet and restore his autocratic rule. Britain and France appealed to the Sultan of Turkey who was delighted to assert his authority; on the twenty-sixth of June, 1879, he sent two telegrams, addressing one to Ismail as the 'former Khedive', the other to his son, Tewfik, as Khedive. Four days later, Ismail left in the Royal yacht, Mahroussa; he was still babbling about returning to Egypt when he died, gross and dropsical, sixteen years later at Emirghian on the Bosphorus. Salih Magdi, the poet, apostrophised him thus :

> Your country has been hurled into the abyss,
> And why?
> To amuse Jusban.

Your money is squandered on pimps and prostitutes.
Normal men take a woman for a wife.
He wants a million wives.
Normal men take a house for living;
He takes ninety.
O Egyptians, there is disgrace all round;
Awake, Awake.

At twenty-seven, Tewfik the weakling, inherited chaos; foreign concession hunters and shady entrepreneurs preyed on the country, operating behind the Mixed Courts which protected them from Egyptian law. The new Khedive had to clear the debt. And Colonel Arabi now threatened a full-scale revolt.

Arabi, a Delta peasant, had seen his own army promotion stifled by the Turkish and Circassian officer élite; he was now contesting cuts in the army and a new law which gave the ruling clique more authority. Backed by troops, he compelled the dismissal of the Circassian war minister and demanded complete army reform. On September the ninth, 1881, he ringed Abdin Palace with two thousand troops and guns and cried to the trembling Khedive, 'We are no longer slaves. We shall not be handed from one master to another.' So began an army uprising – it has some strange parallels with the revolution which ousted Farouk seventy years later – and Arabi's attempt to take over the government.

Had Britain not intervened, Arabi would have succeeded. The Royal Navy bombarded Alexandria on the eleventh of July 1882 and several weeks later a force defeated Arabi at Tel el-Kebir, sending him into exile. Now the British had committed themselves to setting Egypt right. As Sir Evelyn Baring put it when he returned the following year as British agent and consul-general, 'The Englishman came not as a conqueror but in the familiar garb of a saviour of society.'

Baring, who had begun his career as a gunnery officer, knew Egypt's problems better than anyone; he had served on the dual control commission and had drafted a report on Ismail's eccentric budgeting. The government in London handed him a curt brief:

28

balance the books and get the troops out. But who could accomplish this without changing the tax system, lifting the burden on the fellahin, tempering the hand of the khedive and the pashas, rebuilding the country's industries? Behind the bayonet came the bureaucrat and the dam-builder. Britain had expected to withdraw in a few years; she stayed for three-quarters of a century.

In 1883, the capricious tyranny of Mohamed Ali and his clan still fresh in their minds, the Egyptians welcomed the new pasha, though his colleagues found him hard to take at times. One wrote:

> The virtues of patience are known.
> But I think when put to the touch,
> The people of Egypt will own with a groan,
> There's an evil in Baring too much.

The fellahin have cause to remember the Great Lord with gratitude. He abolished the *corvée* (forced labour) and the *courbash*, salt taxes, customs duties, bridge and lock dues; he paid the national debt and invested a million pounds in irrigation schemes. British engineers cleared the canals and built a dam at Aswan; the fellahin responded by trebling the cotton yield and boosting sugar production. In his twenty-four years as consul-general, Baring (later the Earl of Cromer) gave Egypt a political stability and prosperity such as she had never known. He created the machinery of Modern Egypt.

Two questions blighted his term of office: the Sudan and Denshawi.

Since Mohamed Ali's expeditions in the 1820's, Egypt had considered the Sudan part of her territory. In the early 70's, Ismail had sent Charles George Gordon to open it up and repress the slave trade, appointing him governor-general. 'Chinese' Gordon – so-called for his exploits in China – a bizarre Old Testament figure, left the Sudan in 1879. In 1883, Mohamed Ahmed, a religious fanatic calling himself the Mahdi (guide) of Islam, rose in revolt and annihilated an Egyptian force of ten thousand men under Colonel William Hicks. Next year, the British government sent Gordon back with orders to cope with the revolt and evacuate Egyptians from the Sudan. Despite Baring's opposition to British intervention and to the appointment of Gordon, he made his way to Khartum, the last real stronghold. Within a month the Mahdi had isolated and besieged him. London and Cairo dithered until British public opinion, fired by the Gordon legend, forced Gladstone to send a relief expedition. It arrived two days after Gordon's head had been borne as a trophy to the Mahdi.

Baring accepted some responsibility for Gordon's death, though he pointed out that such an incongruous character had no business in the Sudan. Not until 1899 did British and Egyptian troops reconquer the Sudan and sign the Anglo-Egyptian Condominium giving both countries equal share in administering the Sudan.

Cromer suffered more from the Denshawi incident since it occurred at the end of his period as pro-consul. On the fourteenth of June 1906 several British officers were shooting pigeons at the invitation of the omda of Denshawi village in the Delta; near the firing butts a cornfield began to blaze, provoking peasants to attack the officers. A shot was fired and a village woman fell dead; the crowd then beat up the officers, killing a Captain Bull and wounding two others. For this, an Egyptian court condemned four villagers to be hanged on the site of the incident, twelve others were flogged and imprisoned. Denshawi, the worst blunder Britain committed in Egypt, raised an outcry against Cromer who was absent in London at the time but lent his authority to the sentences. Poets immortalised it; nationalists like Mustafa Kamel inflamed anti-British feeling by citing it; even the fellahin refused to forget it. The Lord drove through the silent streets of Cairo when he retired the next year.

Nationalism had never bothered him much; he dismissed it as an intellectual eddy which barely disturbed the Nile. Before he left, he warned the fellahin against the pseudo-representatives who would dupe and mislead them and 'without the shadow of real authority, credit them with ideas which they neither entertain nor fully comprehend ...' In the same speech he said, 'I shall deprecate any brisk change and any violent new departure. More especially, should it be necessary, I shall urge that this wholly spurious, manufactured movement in favour of parliamentary institutions should be treated for what it is worth; and, gentlemen, let me add that it is worth very little.' Cromer must have smiled at Shawki's verses celebrating his going:

> How shall we name this era, after you or Ismail?
> Were you born Pharaoh to govern the Nile?
> Or despot by conquest of the land of Egypt,
> Deferring to no one, never answerable?
> Master by might of our necks in servitude,
> Did you try the path to our hearts meanwhile?
> At your departure the land gasped in thankfulness,
> Freed from a pestilence too nearly fatal . . .

Tewfik had died in 1892 and his son, Abbas Hilmi, the new Khedive, began to intrigue secretly with the nationalist movement of Mustafa Kamel, imagining he might restore himself to full authority. Sir Eldon Gorst, who succeeded Cromer, gave the nationalists their head and they gathered round a young lawyer named Saad Zaghlul whom Cromer had appointed Minister of Education and who was now Minister of Justice. Lord Kitchener, who took over in 1911, realised the khedive was not only sponsoring the nationalists but encouraging the Turks to stir up trouble in Egypt. He must toe the line, or go. The outbreak of the 1914–18 war found Abbas visiting Constantinople; Turkey had come into the war on the German side which meant her vassal, Egypt, might technically be considered at war with the allies. On the eighteenth of December 1914, the Foreign Office issued the following statement: 'In view of the state of war arising out of the action of Turkey, Egypt is placed under the protection of His Majesty and will henceforth constitute a British protectorate. The suzerainty of Turkey over Egypt is thus terminated and His Majesty's Government will adopt all measures necessary for the defence of Egypt and protect its inhabitants and interests.' The following day another proclamation deposed Abbas for making common cause with the king's enemies; his uncle, Husain

Kemal, second son of Ismail, assumed power with the new title of Sultan.

Husain Kemal reigned for three years, dying in October 1917; his son, Kemal el-Din, should have succeeded but, thinking the Germans would win the war, he handed his father a letter renouncing the title several days before his death. As he lay dying, Sultan Husain Kemal sent for his cousin, Prince Yussef Kemal, and whispered to him, 'Yussef, don't let the British choose my brother, Ahmed Fuad. My son doesn't want the title because he thinks the Turks will shoot him when the Germans win. The British won't have you or Prince Omar Tussun. They're going to offer it to Fuad. If they do it's the end of the dynasty.'

However, Fuad it was. To the British, the sixth son of Ismail seemed the least offensive member of the ruling family. Indeed, he impressed them. While other members of the Mohamed Ali fraternity talked revolt, got drunk, disgraced themselves with women, Fuad busied himself with his Presidency of the Red Crescent Society, founded handicraft industries for women, built schools and hospitals and shared the British obsession for hygiene. Sir Reginald Wingate, the new High Commissioner, thought it no disqualification that the rest of the ruling family appeared to hate and distrust Fuad. On the contrary.

CHAPTER THREE

'And speak to the believing women that they refrain their
eyes, and observe continence; and that they display not their
ornaments, except those which are external; and that they
throw their veils over their bosoms and display not their
ornaments except to their husbands or their fathers, or their
husbands' fathers, or their sons, or their husbands' sons, or
their brothers, or their brothers' sons, or their sisters' sons,
or their women or their slaves, or male domestics who have no
natural force, or to children who note not women's
nakedness.' (XXIV: 31)

In 1917 the more eligible members of the royal family might
cast an apprehensive eye at Berlin, Vienna and Constantinople
and tell the British to look elsewhere. Fuad held no such doubts.
For him, the sultanate came as the fulfilment of his destiny; the
strange chance that had brought him the throne of Egypt after
two brothers and a nephew had occupied it merely confirmed
his faith in the mystical purpose of his life. Had his favourite
Indian seer not predicted it twenty years before? So Fuad
accepted the throne and, for nineteen years, ruled Egypt with as
much despotism as the British and the nationalists would permit.
He became adept at playing the British off against the nationalists,
the nationalists against the British; but he could contend that the
three sides took part in the same game. 'Were I not a conjuror, I
would have lost my throne twenty times,' he confided to the
German ambassador, Dr Eberhard von Stöhrer. This atmosphere
of palace autocracy and backstairs intrigue were his political testament to Farouk, something the son believed he understood. What
Farouk comprehended dimly, if at all, was the personal legacy of
his father and the set of events which shaped his life long before
he became sultan.

As a boy of eleven, Prince Ahmed Fuad sailed into exile with
his father Ismail. Determined that he would have a European

education, his father sent him first to the Tudicum Institute in Geneva and, at eighteen, enrolled him in the Military Academy at Turin from which he joined the Italian army as an artillery officer. For a year he acted as aide-de-camp of the Sultan of Turkey at the court of Vienna, creating such an impression that his nephew, Khedive Abbas, recalled him to Cairo as his personal ADC. Those years proved the most frustrating of his life, since Abbas first rejected his advice then his services. Although Cairo society lay open to a prince of the dynasty Fuad could not enjoy it; he had no money and depended on his pay and small allowance from the khedive. The Italian army had also schooled him in drinking and gambling, two things which relieved his frustrations but landed him in debt. At one time he could hardly count his creditors among club boabs (porters), barmen and tailors. For a penniless prince there was, however, one solution: marriage. Fuad's eye fell on his cousin, Princess Shevikiar, not only a beautiful girl but one of the richest women in the country.

Had he not been killed in a train crash, Shevikiar's grandfather, Prince Ahmed, would have been khedive, since he was older than Ismail. Her father, Prince Ahmed Fehmi had two other children, Mohamed Ibrahim and Ahmed Seif ed-Din. It was to the prince's pink-and-grey palace behind the British Residency that Fuad came to smoke and grumble to Prince Ahmed about the court squabbles. And there he proposed to Shevikiar. He was twenty-eight and she was nineteen.

Their marriage was a disaster. Shevikiar found herself living with a martinet who had fixed, outdated ideas about the status of women, decreeing they should be penned in the harem and should abide by Koranic law. She discovered he had a violent temper and ran his palace like a guards' mess. He made personal inspections of the kitchen, especially since he had come upon a servant making his tea by dousing the leaves in an old sock. A bad smell and he would chase round the palace armed with an eau-de-cologne spray until he located and smothered it. His obsession with cleanliness dated, so people said, from the day he was walking through the Khan el-Khalili, Cairo's bazaar area, and someone threw a bucket of slops on his head. Shevikiar also found it hard to get used to someone who leapt out of bed at five o'clock as though answering some inaudible trumpet call, and spent half an hour doing physical jerks in front of a mirror. She thought, and others agreed, that Prince Ahmed Fuad did not really care for women.

She, too, had her foibles. In a society not easily shocked her family caused talk. Over the Residency wall British diplomats watched, fascinated, as the two boys chased each other with revolvers charged with live ammunition. Stories filtered through to Cromer and his staff that the younger boy and his sister were lovers; but then, incest did not raise much of an eyebrow in those circles. Shevikiar was wilful and Seif ed-Din, even then, was considered slightly mad.

Up to a point, Fuad overlooked his wife's behaviour; her brothers came and went freely in Zaafaran Palace. Nine months after their marriage they had a son whom he named Ismail for his father; the child lived only nine months. This tragedy drove Fuad to his fortune teller, for he would believe the words of any seer. The man, an Indian, told him: 'I see a crown, great wealth and influence over millions of people. One day you will be a king.' He added, 'The letter F is lucky for you.' Fuad was persuaded; from that moment he scattered the letter F throughout his rooms and gave all his subsequent children names beginning with F.

By now his marriage was foundering; Shevikiar was accusing him of having married her for her fortune; they quarrelled and Shevikiar drove to her old home in Kasr el-Dubara. Fuad followed with police, caught her after a chase round the garden and locked her up in his palace. She managed to write to young Seif ed-Din, saying Fuad was going to divorce her and thus ruin her reputation. The young hothead swore to avenge his sister.

On the seventh of May 1898, as he drove past the Khedivial Club in Cairo whom should Seif ed-Din observe on its balcony but the hated brother-in-law. Rage possessed him. He leapt from his carriage. Up the steps. Past the Syrian boab on the door. Round another servant on the stairs. Through the door and into the Silence Room. There stood Fuad talking to another member.

At that moment Fuad turned and saw the young man, a mad light in his face, a revolver in his hand. Round the table he sprinted with Seif ed-Din after him, firing as he went. Firing until the gun was empty. The first bullet hit Fuad on the left side, below the heart; another struck him in the throat; a third lodged in his thigh. Two pashas had dived under the leather sofas, the Russian minister made for the lavatory and the war minister climbed the curtains. Fuad dropped to the floor. Seif ed-Din, his brainstorm spent, was walking slowly down the steps. The British oriental secretary, Harry Boyle, called the porter who summoned a corporal from the staff officer's house to arrest the prince.

Fuad could not be moved. His doctors decided to operate on the floor. With a lifelong dread of anaesthetics he refused chloroform and they removed the bullet from his left side while he was still conscious. The one in his throat lay too near an artery so they left that. His mother, Princess Ferial, fainted as they probed for the third bullet in the thigh. Later, Fuad told Queen Nazli how he had smelled death all round him. As he recovered consciousness a nightingale perched on the window of the Silence Room. It was an omen. 'If it sings three times, I shall live,' he said to himself. The bird sang three times.

Cromer refused to hush up the affair. There must be a trial to demonstrate to the royal family that they were not above the law. It was memorable for the statement by the guard corporal who had been warned he was giving evidence about two dynastic princes. 'Hearing sounds of gunfire, I turned out a file of the guard and proceeded to investigate. I saw the nigger standing at the top of the marble steps and closed with him and overpowered him.' Had they declared Seif ed-Din insane, his estates which were worth fifty thousand pounds a year in income, would have passed under the khedive's trust. Instead, they sentenced him to five years' hard labour. He broke rocks in the Turah quarries and did prison carpentry until his written threats to kill the khedive and other princes convinced doctors that he was mad. There was no suitable mental home in Egypt, so Cromer suggested an asylum run by a Dr Newington at Ticehurst, near Tunbridge Wells. It seemed the end of the affair.

However, like some evil jinn, the Shevikiar family haunted Fuad, and later Farouk. Fuad could never forget the incident. The bullet in his throat affected his speech and every few minutes caused him to utter something between a bark and a yelp. He developed such a complex about his bark that those who did not pretend it was not there never graced his presence more than once. One diplomat's wife, whom no one had briefed, was literally bowled over backwards by the high, metallic sound. That bullet would finally kill him.

After the Seif ed-Din affair and his divorce from Shevikiar, Fuad turned his back on the court, the nationalist movements and the emerging political parties. Unlike Abbas, he saw that the British had too many guns to be nudged out of Egypt by romantics like Mustafa Kamel; that the People's Party commanded little support from people or pashas; that poets wrote fiery verse and sheikhs preached holy strife with little impact on events. Fuad busied himself with the country's institutions. 'It is nothing to be a prince. It is something to be useful.' He acted out his dictum; the portly figure, the jowly face, the moustache, waxed and turned up like an Italian bandsman's – these could be seen everywhere. He created a new university with European professors, he threw his weight behind the Red Crescent, the new public assistance scheme, the tourist association, the political economy society; he sponsored Egyptology and exploration, sending Ahmed Mohamed Hassanain to open up the route to Darfur and Siwa oases and launching him on the career which would make him a power in Egypt.

In those days Fuad was really training to be a king. But king of whom and what? He tried for the Albanian throne but failed; a year later, the world war changed the situation and made the seer's words come true.

But a Sultan chosen by the alien British who had to settle his card debts and household expenses and back him with their guns! A Sultan who scorned the ladies of his own circle, preferring Italian mistresses! A Sultan whose bark frightened the servants and whose attempts at Arabic made them sneer! Those who did not despise him disliked or distrusted him. Fuad responded characteristically by immuring himself in Abdin or Kubbah and working all hours to consolidate his rule. Rarely did the palace gates open to Mohamed Ali's family who had spurned the obscure prince. When they hinted that he needed a wife and should choose one of his relatives, he rasped, 'It was enough to have married Shevikiar. I finished with several bullets in me.' None the less, he did want to marry and assure his line.

One day, in a theatre, he noticed a tall girl sitting in a box with three other ladies. No one could tell him if she was married, if she was Turkish or Egyptian. Several weeks later he was having dinner with Lady Graham, wife of the First Secretary of the Residency, and confided that he was looking for a wife. She scoffed, saying that no prince who had flitted from one affair to another for twenty years could hope to marry and settle down. Yes, he insisted. He had a girl in mind. When he described her Lady Graham left the table and returned with a photograph. 'That's the girl,' Fuad cried. Her name was Nazli Sabri, daughter of Abdel-Rahim Sabri pasha, Minister of Agriculture. Would she marry him? And would Lady Graham ask her father's blessing? She did, but came back to announce that Nazli had refused point-blank; she did not hurt his feelings by revealing that the girl had laughed at the idea of marrying someone thirty years older. The snub did not deter Fuad; like a youth he hung around her house, 'phoning her until she spoke to him and agreed to meet him at Lady Graham's. To her surprise she found him gentle and charming. They were married at a simple ceremony in Bustan Palace on the twenty-fourth of May 1919.

The marriage sent Fuad's royal relations into a huff. Nazli was not a royal princess but someone who traced her descent from Suleiman Pasha, the Frenchman. And was she not also a friend of Saad Zaghlul, the nationalist leader who was fomenting trouble for the British and the Palace? In fact she had leaned heavily on Zaghlul's wife, Safia, because she had lost her own mother as a child. Madam Zaghlul had advised her to marry Fuad, though the nationalist leader, who hated Fuad, had opposed the marriage.

Happy with his new bride, Fuad was overjoyed when his physician, Dr Mohamed Shahin, announced that the Sultana was expecting a baby; he spent more time with her than at his desk in Abdin Palace; her whims (it took six months to get her special hair-combs from Paris) had the force of royal commands; he prayed for a boy. 'If Allah will give us a son I promise to stop drinking and gambling,' he declared. As ever, he consulted his oracles. One morning he was sitting with Nazli at Bustan Palace when a white nightingale alighted on the window. He then told her the story of such a bird when his brother-in-law had shot him. 'If this bird sings three times you will deliver a boy child,' he said. The bird obliged, and Fuad danced ecstatically round the room clapping his hands.

But Egypt, being a land of myth and legend, people began to gossip about this unborn child. (They would never cease during his life, and even after his death.) The rumour started among the discarded royal line and spread through the Mohamed Ali Club to the foreign community. When the Sultan strolled into one of his clubs, the rustle of newspapers, the conversational whispers embarrassed him; when it echoed back from the mouski (bazaar) he realised he would have to scotch the talk.

Farouk, the gossips said, has already been born. Nazli has been his mistress for more than a year and when she became pregnant the Sultan thought that if it were a boy he would marry her, if not he would reward her with a handsome present. They are married, therefore it must be a boy.

Knowing the Egyptian capacity for myth-making and twisted logic Fuad grew concerned about the story. It worried him even more when his Italian obstetrician told him that Nazli had gone into labour nearly two months prematurely. This was enough, he realised, to turn the myth into truth. On the evening of the eleventh of February 1920 the Sultan summoned Miss Lucy Sergeant from Kasr el-Aini Hospital to act as midwife; that same evening he ordered all the leading members of the cabinet of Yussef Wahba Pasha to report to Abdin Palace and when they arrived he escorted them to the wing where the Sultana was lying in labour.

'I know all about the gossip,' he told them. 'So that no one will believe ill of me, my wife or this child you will see it at the same moment as I do.' So, like a gathering of would-be fathers, the Sultan and half a dozen of his cabinet ministers paced up and down the waiting room. At about ten o'clock the door opened and Dr Mohamed Shahin appeared with a baby in his arms. 'Sire,' he said. 'Allah has blessed you with a son.' Fuad took the infant and handed it round to each of the ministers. The Sultan's child looked so tiny, so fragile that they wondered if it would survive. Fuad had made his point and the myth was muted. However, some people in Egypt still cling to it.

The baby arrived two months before its time. For once, Fuad forgot his tight-fistedness, doling out ten thousand pounds to the poor, one thousand pounds to Dr Shahin and eight hundred to the mosques, for which he had little time. Next day, Cairo and Alexandria teemed with people celebrating the birth of an heir; animals were sacrificed for evening feasts and dancing went on through the night; from the barracks at Abbasiah and the Citadel, British and Egyptian eighteen-pounders boomed in salute; from five hundred minarets the muezzins called the faithful to prayer for the boy in Abdin Palace.

Fuad had already chosen his name, beginning of course with the letter F. It was Farouk, an appellation of the Caliph, Omar. In Arabic it meant, One Who Knows Right from Wrong.

CHAPTER FOUR

'And call to mind when the unbelievers plotted against thee, to detain thee prisoner, or to kill thee, or to banish thee; they plotted – but God plotted: and of plotters is God the best!' (VIII: 30)

With Fuad everything was calculation. He had chosen his wife and had his son, Farouk, now approved as heir by the British. It remained for him to restore the power of the palace. The Sultan really believed Egypt to belong to the descendants of Mohamed Ali by the divine right of conquest. His father, Ismail, had temporarily lost it to the foreigners through gambling. Tewfik and Abbas he dismissed as marionettes keeping step to a British army march; Husain Kemal, the bucolic innocent, had been a cypher. He, Fuad, might also have to bow and scrape to the British. For a while at least. Until he had strengthened his own hand and recovered some or all of the Nile Valley. Fuad's style of government by intrigue, his desire to rule as an autocrat and his squabble with the nationalists set the pattern of Farouk's reign and left the boy king a legacy of ill-will.

The Sultan's first crisis came not from the British but the Egyptian nationalists who had discovered a new leader with a scrawny figure, a venerable face and the tongue of a demagogue. Saad Zaghlul was of *fellahin* stock in the Delta. His talent as a lawyer and administrator raised him to the ministries of education and justice; his fire-and-brimstone oratory made him the idol of the masses who had been reared on the Koran. He had friends among the ruling dynasty as well as the support of his old religious teachers at Al Azhar, the oldest of Islam's universities. In his way, he typified Egyptian nationalism with its two broad concepts: independence and Islam. The first implied the ejection of foreign troops and the establishment of constitutional government; the second trend, Islam, had wider overtones. Late nineteenth-century sheikhs disagreed about its place in government. The xenophobic Sheikh Jamal el-Afghani would have based authority firmly on the Koran and treated Western culture as a menace; the more moderate Sheikh Mohamed Abdu considered religion as one of the props of constitutional government. Zaghlul leaned towards Abdu's teaching, though Islam meant less to him than self-determination. He incorporated a third element in his nationalism: the unity of Egypt with its old provinces in the Sudan. His predecessor, Mustafa Kamel, had whipped up fear among the *fellahin* that the British might cut the water of the Nile, their lifeline; the demagogue, Zaghlul, adopted this rallying cry.

The end of the war seemed his moment. Egypt had grumblingly accepted the protectorate as an emergency measure. Four years of martial law had, however, eroded confidence in British administration. As always, the *fellahin* rebelled against conscription; they complained, too, about the requisition of their land, their crops and animals. The pashas had made fortunes out of them while the omdas seized the chance of avenging themselves on rivals by drafting them into the army. Some of the wrath fell on the British High Commissioner, Sir Reginald Wingate.

> Woe on us, Wingate,
> Who has carried off corn,
> Carried off cattle,
> Carried off children,
> Leaving only our lives.
> For the love of Allah, now let us alone.

On the thirteenth of November 1918, two days after the Armistice, Zaghlul and two collaborators presented themselves as a delegation (*Wafd*, in Arabic) to Wingate, who listened sympathetically to their demand that Egypt should be represented at the Peace Conference to plead for independence. London, however, would have none of it. By now, Zaghlul had the country behind him and a *Wafd* was elected to go to Paris. On the eighth of March, Zaghlul was arrested and deported to Malta with three of his supporters, Ismail Sidki, Mohamed Mahmud and Hamid el-Bassal.

Violence exploded in Cairo where hysterical mobs attacked British troops and public buildings; in the Delta and Upper Egypt mobs blockaded foreign colonies, tore up railway lines and demolished buildings. At Dairut, in Upper Egypt, a British prison inspector, two officers and five other ranks were brutally clubbed to death by a frenzied crowd. Troops had to quell the riots; but Egypt still simmered even after Lord Allenby, the commander-in-chief in Egypt, had been appointed High Commissioner and had ordered Zaghlul's release. In December, Britain sent out Lord Milner with a mission to inquire into the unrest; it met a boycott from the politicians, passive resistance from the people and riots in areas it investigated. Despite this, Milner collected his evidence and the Government invited Zaghlul and seven associates to London for discussions. The Milner-Zaghlul memorandum made sweeping concessions: Egyptian independence with a British right to station forces under a treaty; the abolition of the Mixed Courts which protected foreigners; the right to foreign representation. But negotiations foundered when Zaghlul held out for an end to the protectorate. There was deadlock, and only one man who might resolve it: Fuad.

From Abdin, the Sultan had watched the British and *Wafd* tussle as his ancestor had the Turks and Mamelukes. Maybe the British had given ground, but they still held real power. Fuad became a constant visitor to the Residency and kept his austere study door in Abdin always open to Lord Allenby. He also noted a schism in the *Wafd*. For some old associates Zaghlul was becoming too dangerous and intransigent. The Sultan might use those disaffected *Wafd*ists. Allenby soon gave him the chance by writing this letter:

His Majesty's Government, after a study of the proposals made by Lord Milner, have arrived at the conclusion that the status of the Protectorate is not a satisfactory relation in which Egypt should continue to stand to Great Britain. While they have not reached a final decision with regard to Lord Milner's recommendations, they desire to confer regarding them with a delegation nominated by Your Highness, with a view, if possible, to substitute for the Protectorate a relationship which would, while securing the special interests of Great Britain and enabling her to offer adequate guarantees to foreign powers, meet the legitimate aspirations of the Egyptian people.

On the eighteenth of May 1921 the Sultan picked his delegation, led by the prime minister, Adli Yeghen pasha. Zaghlul reacted naturally by boycotting the delegation and inflaming a mob to besiege Abdin Palace and hurl abuse at Fuad. At this the Sultan raged, 'I work all hours of the day. I work harder than any fellah, and this is the result.' From those riots sprang the feud between Fuad and the *Wafd,* now a political party. The Palace, the *Wafd* and the British grouped themselves into a triangle of forces which dictated the government of Egypt for the next thirty years. When the London talks between Lord Curzon and Adli pasha broke down, the *Wafd* leader again stirred up riots; this time he was deported to the Seychelles and with him went the *Wafd* secretary-general, another firebrand named Mustapha el-Nahas.

Allenby recognised the need for independence. After secret negotiations with the prime minister, Abdel Khalek Sarwat, he left for London with joint proposals, and his own resignation, already written to lend them weight. On the twenty-seventh of February 1922 he was back, and the following day, issued this declaration:

1. The British Protectorate over Egypt is terminated and Egypt is declared to be an independent sovereign state.

2. So soon as the Government of High Highness shall pass an Act of Indemnity with application to all inhabitants of Egypt, martial law as proclaimed on November 2, 1914 shall be withdrawn.

3. The following matters are absolutely reserved to the discretion of His Majesty's Government until such time as it may be possible by free discussion and friendly accommodation on

both sides to conclude agreements in regard thereto between His Majesty's Government and the Government of Egypt.

(a) the security of the communications of the British Empire in Egypt;

(b) the defence of Egypt against all foreign aggression or interference direct or indirect;

(c) the protection of foreign residents in Egypt and the protection of minorities;

(d) the Sudan;

Pending the conclusion of such agreements, the *status quo* in all these matters shall remain intact.

This declaration made Fuad King of Egypt; the seer had been right. His royal rescript said the country would have a constitutional government on modern lines. He hinted, though, that he did not envisage himself in the role of a democratic king. He began to style himself King of Egypt and the Sudan, but Allenby firmly quashed this idea. The constitution gave him power to appoint two-fifths of the senate, and dissolve parliament and order elections. He let Zaghlul fret in exile while the constitution was drafted; by the time the *Wafd* leader returned Fuad had become the most powerful figure in Egyptian politics. He had weaned away two powerful *Wafd*ists, Ismail Sidki and Mohamed Mahmud and had formed the Palace party; he also had his Royal Cabinet which could make and break politicians in government.

Zaghlul had the popular vote and the first elections gave him all but twenty-four of the two hundred and fourteen seats. With this backing he felt he could take on Fuad and the British; if they failed to meet his demands he could always let the Cairo or Alexandria mobs loose. But could he control them? When the British ignored his demands for complete evacuation and sovereignty over the Sudan, he provoked riots which ended tragically. On the nineteenth of November 1924, at 1.30, a gang of men sprang out at Sirdar Sir Lee Stack, governor-general of the Sudan and head of the Egyptian army; they threw a grenade at his car and fired twenty revolver shots at him. Sir Lee died the next day.

45

The evening of the funeral, Lord Allenby surrounded Zahlul's office with two hundred and fifty cavalrymen. The prime minister could hardly credit his demands: a full apology and punishment of the criminals; a ban on political demonstrations; a fine of £500,000; immediate withdrawal of Egyptian troops from the Sudan; an increase in the irrigated area of the Sudan. Zaghlul had to resign, broken by the violence he had inspired. He knew that two of his henchmen, Ahmed Maher and Mohamed Fahmy el-Nokrashi, were implicated with other *Wafd*ists. Though seven men were hanged for this crime, these two were acquitted and this caused the British tribunal judge to resign in protest as well as a Foreign Office refusal to accept the verdict. Maher and Nokrashi both became prime ministers under Farouk; both died, ironically, at the hands of assassins.

From all this, Fuad emerged master of Egypt. His private cabinet created and dismissed governments, made and unmade prime ministers; he, himself, cynically manipulated politicians through palace patronage and the buying and selling of titles. When the *Wafd* grew vociferous, he brought in Sidki, then Mahmud to amend the constitution, to modify the electoral law. There were ways of preventing the *Wafd* winning elections. The government appointed the village omdas and they told the *fellahin* how to vote, reinforcing their advice with the *courbash*. Villagers were bundled into trucks and taken to the polls where the police, who also owed their patronage to the government, stood guard. The fellah who dared to utter the wrong name found himself suddenly popular. 'Aeewah, a man of rare courage. Good for you.' The policeman would slap him on the shoulder, leaving a white chalk mark which told those outside that the poor peasant had to be thrashed. A few were given half a ten-piastre note – two days' pay – with the promise of the other half when they voted. Lord Lloyd, who replaced Allenby, was horrified to discover one of his own servants who had voted fourteen times. What did it matter to the *fellahin*? Were not all governments alike?

With the death of Zaghlul in 1927 Fuad thought he could control the *Wafd* at last. The king had a hand in choosing his successor, Nahas, an amenable man and no politician. No one could foresee then that Nahas would cause him and Farouk much more trouble than Zaghlul. One of Zaghlul's original band, Nahas hailed from Samanoud in the Delta where he had worked as a telegraph operator while studying law. He was as ugly as a camel, with a mesmeric outward squint which gave people the impression he was staring past each of their ears. 'Keeping an eye on Upper and Lower Egypt,' ran the caption to a caricature when he was appointed Minister of Communications. But he had a way with peasants. One man asked Dr Mohamed Kamel Husain how people could possibly prefer a vulgar character like Nahas to Ismail Sidki. 'Everybody in Egypt has an uncle like Nahas,' replied the doctor. 'Who in Egypt has an uncle like Sidki?' Soon, Nahas had Fuad regretting his error of judgement. The new *Wafd* leader could rouse a mob like Zaghlul, and he believed, too, in keeping the king in his place.

When Nahas became prime minister in March 1928, he made it clear that he expected Fuad to observe the constitution; the king looked round for a pretext to dismiss the *Wafd* government. Of all unlikely people, the man who brought down the Nahas government was Prince Ahmed Seif ed-Din, the cousin who had shot Fuad thirty years before.

For twenty-six years, Seif ed-Din had lived in his asylum near Tunbridge Wells. At the beginning of September 1925 came news that he had escaped, aided by two attendants, John Bastone and William Pilbeam. He was making for Egypt, they said. Fuad believed Seif ed-Din had broken out of his asylum to come and kill him; so did the British who alerted every embassy and consulate with orders to stop him. Several weeks later, the prince turned up in Constantinople and claimed the fortune which Fuad had administered since becoming Sultan. In 1927, Seif ed-Din's mother engaged three leading Egyptian lawyers to attempt to break the king's hold on her son's millions. They were all *Wafd*ists: Nahas, Wissa Wassef bey and Gaafer Fakhry bey. They knew Fuad was reliving the most traumatic moment of his life, but did not spare his feelings.

The case was dragging through the Royal Court Council when

47

Fuad gave it a dramatic twist, which demonstrated his genius for intrigue, and turned the affair to his advantage. For years he had painstakingly built up his intelligence service, recruiting club and hotel porters, journalists, Egyptian and British civil servants. Now his spies brought him two pieces of news: one of the counsel had written to Seif ed-Din's mother, saying that if necessary they would bring parliamentary pressure to bear to win the case: secondly, the fees promised the three lawyers amounted to no less than one hundred and thirty thousand pounds. The next day, the Press had the story and Nahas was out of office, even though he and the others later answered the charges completely.

Only Lord Lloyd, another autocrat, stood between the king and absolute rule. Fuad cried on the Aga Khan's shoulder about the High Commissioner. 'Lloyd pulls the strings while the marionettes dance. Cromer turned Abbas Hilmi into a puppet. Lloyd is turning me into a corpse.' Was Lloyd so wrong? He once took a young British diplomat to a banquet at Abdin where they watched Fuad shaking hands with his cabinet ministers then calling for a silver bowl full of eau-de-cologne water. As he washed his hands, the king growled loudly several times, *Canaille*. He once had to choose between Ismail Sidki and Mohamed Mahmud as prime ministers; he wanted Sidki, his cabinet chief Mahmud. Fuad the gambler, took a ten-piastre silver piece out of his pocket and asked the man to call. He chose heads and the king spun the coin which fell with his own face upwards. 'You've lost,' he said blandly; the cabinet chief agreed.

He despised Egyptians. 'Don't ever expect good faith of the Egyptians. They don't understand what it is.' Who could tell what effect this attitude had on the young Farouk when he heard his father speaking thus?

Between 1917 and 1936 Fuad built up a fortune which people could only guess at, none compute. As Sultan, he summoned one pasha with several thousand acres of Delta land, the richest in the world. 'How much do you want for your land?' he asked. The pasha mentioned the market price, five hundred pounds an acre. 'Ridiculous,' Fuad snorted. 'You're disloyal to your Sultan. I shall send the government valuer.' The civil servant arrived at a

48

figure he thought would please the Sultan – twenty-eight pounds an acre. Fuad generously paid the astonished pasha thirty pounds. By this form of legal confiscation he acquired thousands of acres, in fact one seventh of the cultivable land of Egypt. Where a pasha resisted he would discover that the government surveyors had thought fit to divert the irrigation channels away from his land. Dozens of landowners exchanged their land for titles, others a mere decoration. As the vast royal estates grew, Fuad had to ensure a market for his produce. It was simple; his officials and the police made arrangements to stop all other fruit and vegetable lorries on the road to the big cities until the king's goods had been sold. His workers got two piastres a day when the rate was five or more. General Mohamed Neguib has told the story of how he had ordered the flogging of a guard for picking some dates from a tree in Bustan Palace garden; he also abolished the free rations which had been a privilege of the royal guard for years.

He died the most powerful and the richest man in Egypt. And the most hated.

Such a man was Farouk's father.

CHAPTER FIVE

'They desire thee to deal smoothly with them: then would they be smooth as oil with thee.' (LXVIII: 9)

HAD the walls of Kubbah Palace been a foot or two higher it might have passed for a prison rather than a king's residence. For six miles they stretched, with driveways running more than a mile to the sprawling, yellow buildings. Within those walls were grounds full of exotic trees, flower gardens and artificial ponds, forming a moat round the palace. In fact, everything seemed designed to prevent the prying eye, the unwanted visitor, to insulate the buildings from the north-east Cairo suburb in which they stood.

Here, in Kubbah, Farouk spent most of his boyhood and adolescence; he roamed its four hundred rooms, its seventy acres of enchanted gardens. It was his nursery, his school, his play-ground. Every boyhood relationship, every contact with life took place within those walls. There was Abdin, in Cairo, Ras el-Tin and Montazah in Alexandria where he spent some of the year. But still the same high walls, the same extensive grounds, shutting him off. For a boy he had everything: a pool and a lake for swimming and boating, tennis and squash courts, horses and camels in the stables, cars when he grew old enough to drive them, rooms full of toys and gadgets. And yet, if the boy wanted to amuse himself with children of his own age he had only his four younger sisters, Fawzia, Faiza, Faika and Fathia. He saw no boys; indeed, he met hardly anyone outside his parents, their staff and the tutors who would walk or bicycle the long road from the huddle of slums beyond the walls.

On the rare visits from royal relations the boy was out of sight. Egyptians? Fuad would never have dreamed of contaminating his son by contact with them. So Farouk's horizons remained the pine forests of Montazah and the ornamental grounds of Kubbah;

as a prince he ventured beyond the palace walls no more than half a dozen times. Before he became king he had seen nothing, had not even visited the Pyramids twelve miles from Abdin. No wonder, on meeting his English governess for the first time at the age of three, he rebuked her for trying to take his picture. 'I'm not like other boys,' he said. She assured him he was.

Mrs Ina Naylor, widow of a Yorkshire doctor, had been summoned in 1923 to come out to Egypt and look after the royal children. Farouk became her special charge until his father died. Fuad instructed her that his son should be brought up in the British way and, so far as she could, she gave him the right background. But how could she succeed? She protested he should be allowed to meet and compete with boys of his own age, but Fuad was adamant. She objected that the staff spoiled him; if he played football they would run and place the ball at his feet with a bow; if he swam, an escort of sailors from the Mahroussa would appear at his side. The day he fell off his horse and Ninzi, as they called Mrs Naylor, ordered him to remount at once, the horrified whisper carried all the way to Fuad's study. The king believed, however, in setting Farouk a tough curriculum. In his own day as king, Farouk once said to the wife of the American Judge, Jasper Brinton, 'I was brought up the hard way.' Like so many of his confessions it was a half-truth.

When he reached five years of age, Farouk had to rise at just after six and turn out for an hour of gym with a French physical instructor; he rode for about an hour during the day and had fencing lessons several times a week with an English instructor. With one break of two hours at midday, the young prince was kept studying until six in the evening. He had tutors in English, French and Arabic; he read the Koran; at his mother's insistence he practised the piano despite being tone-deaf. The boy had a quick mind, perhaps too quick for his tutors; he picked up languages easily, though his grasp was more colloquial than literary. The drill laid down by Fuad should have given him a grounding for the future. But his unfortunate tutors could make nothing out of him; the young prince had their measure early on and knew he could treat the Egyptians among them as he liked.

51

They had an eye to the future and that meant Farouk would one day lord it over them. Did they not say that his father could not last very long? Farouk played on their servility. 'Just you wait until I'm king . . .' he would mutter if they displeased him. Of course they seldom did. He once wrote an Arabic composition of about a hundred words which evoked this eulogy from his tutor. 'Excellent. A brilliant future awaits you in the world of literature.' There happened to be no fewer than seven elementary spelling errors in the paper. Ahmed Yussef, alone, took him to task for his failings in history, and scrawled in his notebook, 'Improve your handwriting and pay attention to the cleanliness of your notebook.'

With his complex about his short, stubby figure and pendulous stomach which his five o'clock exercises could not refine, Fuad had decided that his son would stay slim. His tutors would ensure that Farouk did not drink water, or eat anything during his classes. Queen Nazli's lady-in-waiting, Madam Zeinab Zulficar, remembers the boy bursting out of his classroom, sprinting to the haramlek and his mother's refrigerator. He would gulp down a bottle of lemonade, play for a few minutes then swallow a second bottle. He would turn to the larder, looting it and stuffing himself with cream cakes. Watching him, his mother would cry to Madam Zulficar, 'What is Fuad doing? He's making a martyr out of the boy.'

Whatever fun the children had was organised by Fuad. Treasure hunts through the grounds of Kubbah; paper chases in which they used his favourite eau-de-cologne to help them find the trail. Within his lights he tried to give them a happy childhood. It was no fault of his that he scared them with his fierce figure, his ungovernable rages and the metallic squawk he emitted. Farouk no less than his sisters. More than once, visiting diplomats caught a glimpse of the prince and princesses scurrying into hiding as they heard the raucous approach of their father.

Fuad gave his son more of a start than most oriental monarchs; if he loaded his curriculum with languages, mathematics and applied science, he did so from the conviction that Farouk should set an example to the rest of the nation. At times, however, he must have wondered what sort of king his son would make, for he often came near to breaking his vow never to punish the boy physically. Farouk often found himself on the carpet, with Fuad shouting and barking at him for some misdemeanour. He once made a wait-till-I'm-king threat to a gardener who had rebuked him for trampling over the flower beds in Abdin. That earned him half an hour of his father's most violent temper. On another occasion, with an air gun presented by Mrs Naylor, he smashed every ground-floor window in Kubbah and wound up with gun and slugs confiscated. He once pointed a camera at his father and, as the smiling Fuad waited for the click, out popped a long, green snake. Perhaps the nearest Fuad ever came to striking Farouk was the day Queen Nazli was entertaining the Queen of Rumania in the haramlek. Farouk asked if Queen Marie would like to see his horses, Sammy and Silvertail. 'Bring them up,' she said, little thinking that the young prince would. In a few minutes Farouk was leading Silvertail round the salon while the two queens laughed. Not for long. The apoplectic voice of Fuad came on the telephone from Abdin to order the horse out of the palace and Farouk to his room for the rest of the day.

Preoccupied with political upheavals, Fuad had little time to spend with his son; in any case, lessons in kingship hardly figured in eastern tradition. He had manoeuvred himself into a position of leverage between the British and the *Wafd* and he tried to dun this policy into Farouk. 'Always take the stick by the middle,' he would say. When Zaghlul came to the palace in 1925, Fuad took the opportunity to introduce him to Farouk. 'Do you know, Saad pasha, who cheers you when you come to the palace? Farouk. From behind the curtain he sees your car arriving, then runs down to the head of the crowd and shouts, "Vive Saad!"' Farouk was summoned, shook Saad's hand and watched the old man shuffling up the marble staircase, pausing twice to get his breath. Zaghlul was one of the rare figures to meet Farouk; the diplomats who came and went seldom saw the boy, let alone met him.

However, he did make two public appearances before Fuad's death and his own accession. When his father fell sick, he had to open the international postal congress in Cairo and give a short address in French. Then, when he became Chief Scout of Egypt, he exhorted the parade of Scouts at Abdin with these words: 'Young men! Young Scouts! It is our task to bring our bodies into subjugation to our wills.' Those who watched him saw a handsome schoolboy on his best behaviour, seeming less concerned with his role as a prince than with pleasing his governess. 'Papa, I think Mrs Naylor is pleased,' he said when he had finished the scout ceremony. Ninzi's approbation meant a lot to him in those days. She would find crude notes on her pillow. 'I'm sorry I told that lie today, Naylor.' Also, 'I will try to be a better boy to-morrow'. At an official tea-party the British High Commissioner, Sir Percy Lorraine, knowing his fondness for cakes, pressed him to eat some more. 'No thank you, Mrs Naylor told me to leave some for the poor,' he said.

Even then, the contradictions which baffled those who attempted to assess his character later in life began to emerge. The boy who could seize a stick from a servant who was beating a donkey at Montazah and thrash the man with it could also turn on his fencing master and strike him painfully on the arm with his foil; the child who cried inconsolably when a hawk swooped and killed a pet rabbit could grab a cat by the tail and dash its brains out against a wall; he played up his tutors mercilessly, knowing they feared him, yet had the sensitivity to tell the priests not to slaughter sacrificial bullocks until his sisters had passed on ceremonial occasions. Stories infiltrated the city beyond the palace walls about his behaviour, and the upper classes told their children, 'Don't be like that wicked boy in the palace.' Still, Farouk gave almost half his pocket money of five pounds a month to buy books for poor children; he kept the family of a groom who had gone to prison for stealing his diamond tie-pin. And, at six o'clock in the morning, he would creep through the Montazah gardens with Mrs Naylor to free quail which had been trapped by the nets his father's gamekeepers had rigged to catch them.

When the tedium or the discipline of the classroom oppressed him, he had his sanctuaries – the haramlek and the servants' quarters. The luxurious trappings of his mother's drawing-room with its Second Empire furnishings, Turkish rugs and Italian paintings, the bedroom with its sumptuous bed covered with a silk canopy, its walls a mass of colours – this breathed luxury in contrast to the austerity of the rest of the palace, peace and security compared with the ritual and ceremony elsewhere. Here, he was petted and pampered by his mother and her ladies-in-waiting who allowed him to do what he liked, up to a point. Nazli often grew impatient with his practical jokes, once writing to Mrs Naylor:

'I am trying to punish Farouk for his impertinence and arrogance to me lately. He is impossible – as soon as he comes to my rooms it is to tease the maids. He will not let them work, locking them up everywhere and taking away the key. Every day it is the same. I said if he were to go on like that he had better not come into my rooms at all. He immediately said, "All right, I will not come". He does not seem to mind anything or anybody, and is getting more selfish every day.

'When I said to him that I wished he were like the girls who are always so sweet and never say unkind words, you know what he had the cheek to say? – "You should come and see what they say against your back and the way they talk about you sometimes at table." I want you to help me and show him what he is doing to his mother, just how very wrong it is – and please don't send him to me unless you see that he is sorry, which I don't believe he can ever be. Anyhow, let me know please by a few words when you think it is time for him to come.'

But Nazli could never exist long without her darling. What else did she have in the vacuum which Fuad had constructed round them? Fuad had abolished the veil in 1927. Not, however, in his own palace. Turkish manners ruled, with rigid separation of men and women. His queen and her retinue were virtually prisoners. If the foreign community and all but a few Egyptians caught a fleeting sight of Farouk, they never saw Nazli. A white veil fluttering at the window of a car or in a theatre box, a silhouette at the trellised window of the harem: that was the queen. If Fuad trusted Nazli, and many felt he did not, he took no chances; she saw only her father and brothers; the entrance to the haramlek was guarded by six Nubian eunuchs.

We can imagine Nazli's reactions. She was a young woman who had revelled in the gay life of Cairo, meeting young friends, attending dances and seeing every new show. Then, immured in the palace, she had produced a son and four daughters one after another. Once she had shown a flair for painting and played the piano well. Now she had to suffer the enforced idleness of the harem as well as its atmosphere of captivity. It hardly consoled her that Fuad treated her well, dining with her every night at eight and escorting her to the vast, gilded theatre in Abdin several nights a week. But she could not get used to a husband who forbade her to see her friends, who even monitored phone calls to her in the palace. It was true. Several of her women friends rang her to find themselves listening to the rasping voice of Fuad and submitting to an interrogation on how they had the queen's private number. 'Why does he shut me up like this?' Nazli would wail to her ladies-in-waiting.

And what importance did she have? Why, even the Circassian slave who slept on a mattress on the floor at Fuad's feet had more influence than she. That slave knew all the king's secrets, had his trust, kept the keys of every room in the palace and gave orders as though she were the real queen. Fuad would not even let her go abroad for the operation she needed. Nazli suffered from kidney trouble which nearly killed her twenty years later. But the king insisted that she stay in Egypt and ordered his doctors to convince her she was healthy. This they did in a characteristic Egyptian fashion. Dr Mohamed Shahin approached an English woman working in the palace, asking her if she minded having an X-ray taken. 'If there's anything wrong with the queen we shall show her your X-ray,' he said. She refused.

So Nazli fretted her youth away. Not surprisingly, Farouk became the centre of her life. She spoiled him outrageously. If he got into trouble with Fuad there was always the harem and its women to fawn on him. When Fuad, after his illness, was persuaded that Farouk should go abroad to finish his studies, that he should enrol at an English prep. school and attend university, Nazli would not hear of the suggestion. Farouk stayed.

More so even than the superstitious Fuad, the queen would hang on the prophecies of any sorcerer or soothsayer. When she was expecting one of her children she sent Mrs Naylor to every mosque with a donation, hoping they would pray for a son. 'Majesty,' said Mrs Naylor, 'you cannot bribe God – everybody in the palace perhaps. But not God.' Nazli then persuaded her to consult an old fortune-teller who squatted near the Sphinx. She returned with distressing news. 'He says there will be eight girls in that family before there are any boys.' The queen even kept an old woman soothsayer in the palace and consulted her every night. Farouk was dragged along to these sessions in which the old woman would weave spells and babble incantations into the small hours. On the nerves of a weary, sensitive boy, these seances had a disastrous effect and he went off his sleep. This insomnia never left him and he acquired the habit of sleeping in the morning and staying awake until late at night.

Farouk's other hiding-place in the palace was the servants' quarters. Dead against Fuad's wishes, he spent hours there and picked up Turkish from one group of servants, Italian from the other. The Italians had entrenched themselves strongly in the royal household, having been imported by Fuad who spoke their language fluently and had close ties with the Italian royal family. He also had a penchant for Italian mistresses which made his Italian servants especially useful. One of them had immense power, a man named Ernesto Verrucci whom the king had known for thirty years, whom he had styled a bey and made architect for the royal palaces. Verrucci, a bearded, bespectacled Roman ensured that the king's private affairs never provoked any scandal. Soon, he had built up a clique of Italians: the barber, Caro; the assistant-barber, Pietro; the kennelman, Cafazzi; the electrician, Francesco.

One day, when he was a boy of nine, Farouk's electric train broke down; he rang for Francesco, but instead a youth he had never met before appeared and fixed the train in a few minutes. Thus began a friendship between the prince and a palace servant which lasted twenty-six years and made the young electrician, Antonio Pulli, one of the most powerful men in Egypt. Pulli, nephew of Francesco, had not long before quit an Italian ship to join Fuad's service. From Lecce, in the heel of Italy, he was a quiet, serious young man who spent patient hours repairing Farouk's library of toys and gadgets. Now, when the prince escaped from his tutors he could stow away in the servants' quarters and have fun with Pulli and the others. With his quick gift for mimickry he picked up Italian; he also listened to these men talking about things he had never known, about men and women and how they behaved, things his parents, his tutors, his governess would never have dared discuss.

Such were the compass points of the prince's young life: the discipline of the classroom and the playground which he identified with some irksome duty he owed his father; the love which the women of the harem and his governess showed him and seemed his by right, like his title; the pleasure he experienced in the servants' quarters where no one scolded or criticised, where everyone deferred.

Something happened to shatter the pattern of this life, to breach the palace walls, to fix him in a different orbit. In July 1934, Fuad returned from an open-air reception, his bark hoarsened by a cough; in a few days this fever had developed and he lay in a coma. Through his bedroom at Kubbah went his own doctors, followed by specialists flown from England; they all left shaking their heads. Fuad, they said, had six weeks to live at the most. Like any secret in Egypt the Khan el-Khallili was whispering it within an hour; from there it gathered speed and substance and cities and villages digested it. Since the palace issued no bulletins everyone was soon convinced that the king was dead.

From behind the curtains of his room, Farouk watched the comings and goings; the staff of the British Residency entered and quit the royal cabinet offices; the inconspicuous figure of Abdel Fattah Yehia, the Prime Minister, arrived to talk with his father's cabinet chief, Said Zulficar pasha. He, Farouk, was the subject. What happened if Fuad died and a boy of fourteen was left to rule?

As the statesmen deliberated, Fuad began to recover slowly. His *baraka* (good fortune) had not deserted him. For months he had to keep to his bedroom in the palace, putting in only one public appearance to disprove bazaar gossip that he was dead. The *Wafd* and the British needed no such sign; Fuad was pulling the strings as astutely as ever. None the less, the illness had scared him into deciding about Farouk's education. The new British High Commissioner, Sir Miles Wedderburn Lampson, was insisting on an English school and, despite Nazli's protestations, Fuad agreed. For Lampson it was a triumph, since Italy had been coaxing Fuad to send his son to his old military academy.

So avidly had his tutors extolled Farouk's scholarship that it shocked Fuad when the headmaster of Eton rejected the Prince of Upper Egypt; he fell far below the school's academic requirements and had no Latin. He must therefore go straight to the Royal Military Academy.

Farouk accepted his exile as tearfully as his mother. Before he said farewell to Nazli at Montazah, he rang Madam Zulficar. 'Would you come and sit with my mother tonight? She will be very lonely,' he said. At the quay, as he boarded the launch taking him to the British cruiser Devonshire, the High Commissioner said, 'You'll soon be back, Farouk.' Choked with emotion, he held up two fingers of his right hand – two years! – and ran across the gangway.

He had a mission of twenty courtiers, tutors and servants to supervise his stay in England. In September 1935 they took over Kenry House, an eighteen-roomed mansion with four acres of gardens on Kingston Hill overlooking the Surrey Hills. There, he installed himself with his tutors, his professor of Moslem religion, his physician and servants.

Fuad had taken considerable pains to choose the staff of the mission. Its leader he found in his own palace: Ahmed Mohamed Hassanain bey. This enigmatic character, who played such an influential role in Farouk's life, was Egyptian though he had blue eyes and a light complexion. Ability had won him a place at Balliol College from which he graduated after the 1914–18 war, and became secretary to General Sir John Maxwell, commander of the British forces in Egypt. Fuad noticed him in the early twenties, sponsoring his expeditions to the Libyan oases of Darfur and Siwa which made him the only Egyptian to hold the gold medal of the Royal Geographical Society, then picked him as one of his palace advisers. He was married to Lutfia, daughter of Princess Shevikiar, the king's first wife, by a subsequent husband.

Few people ever fathomed Hassanain; he seemed a strange amalgam of conflicting thought and passion, a man of two cultures. Something of a dreamer and a mystic, more at home in the desert than a cabinet office, he none the less became one of the most able diplomats in Egypt. As an Oxford product he admired the British for their transparent honesty and integrity; yet he could act as deviously as a bazaar merchant on behalf of Egypt. He had a long, lugubrious face, as though the clash of cultures had bleached it of expression. When approached to act as Farouk's mentor he welcomed the change of masters. Publicly, he gave his loyalty to Fuad; personally, he detested the political intrigue and corruption which the king operated.

With Hassanain went General Azziz el-Masri, a wiry little firebrand trained by the Turks and Germans, who hated everything British. He might have headed the mission had the king not mentioned this fact to Mrs Naylor. 'Majesty,' she said, 'you cannot possibly send a man with manners like that as head of the mission. He would only be received once at Buckingham Palace.' Events proved her right. During the war, General el-Masri collaborated with the Axis Powers, passing British secrets to them and attempting to escape and aid them; when Farouk was deposed, the revolutionists asked what should be done with him. El-Masri replied, 'A head only interests me after it has fallen.'

With two such men guiding him, Farouk heard two versions of almost everything, until el-Masri resigned and returned to Egypt. Within weeks of his son's arrival, Fuad received another blow: Farouk had failed the entrance exam for Woolwich and could only enrol as a Gentleman Cadet when he had passed in maths and science. During the entrance exam, the prince had sat nibbling his pencil, waiting for someone to supply the answers, the procedure which held good at Kubbah and accounted for his distinctions in every subject he studied there. Soon, reports began to percolate back to Fuad that all was far from well at Kenry House. From Hassanain he would read that Farouk was working well and would soon pass into the academy; from el-Masri he heard they were turning his son into a softie, teaching him to drink and go the rounds of night clubs. The truth lay somewhere between those accounts. Hassanain saw that Farouk attended The Shop three times a week, and accompanied him while he studied science, did some boxing, fencing (at which Hassanain had gained a Blue) and squash. He realised, nevertheless, that a boy who had spent fifteen years in isolation had to enjoy himself, so he arranged several expeditions into London. When Fuad accepted Hassanain's version, el-Masri resigned; he carried back tales that Farouk was gambling, drinking and even had a *garconnière* in Mayfair, provided for him by one of his countrymen. None of these stories was true. At that time, the idea of gambling revolted the young prince; he drank nothing stronger than lemonade, for they discovered early that he had an allergy to alcohol which produced a rash on his hands and body and left him feeling sick. The *garconnière* was probably a club where Egyptians gathered in Baker Street.

However, Hassanain did confess to British friends that the prince's conduct sometimes worried him. He had tried to prevent him from ordering piles of rubbishy articles from London shops and stores, from buying expensive jewellery to send home to his mother and sisters; he had caught him slipping off on his own to the West End when he should have been in bed. And, at times, the future king behaved very badly. Once, in the Baker Street club he was sitting with some young Egyptians when he beckoned negligently to Hassanain and handed him the stub of the cigarette he was smoking. 'My manservant, you know,' he cried. Of course, it raised a laugh.

He had a schoolboy adulation of George the Fifth and Edward, Prince of Wales. Edward took him to the Britain-New Zealand rugby match at Twickenham and met him once or twice at Buckingham Palace. Farouk was later to boast, 'You know that I taught Edward English slang...' No one was fooled; his own slang was twenty years behind the times. Of the lunch he had at Buckingham Palace, he wrote to Mrs Naylor: 'By the way, we did not have macaroni for lunch with King George. The king and queen were very nice, so also was the Duke of Gloucestshire' (sic). She had chided him one day when he was slopping over macaroni and warned him not to eat it like that at Buckingham Palace. At that lunch, King George commented on the fact that the Egyptian royal family had a weakness for the letter F. 'Why is it so important?' he queried. How could Farouk confess his father's superstition? Or his own? He thought quickly, and replied, 'For economy, your Majesty.'

On the 20th of January, 1936, three months after he arrived, King George died. Conspicuous in his bright red tarbush among royalty from all over the world, Farouk walked in the funeral procession which he described in these terms to his governess. 'Wasn't it sweet of Papa to have given me that lovely decoration? I do hope I will be worthy of it. I wore it in the funeral procession and at the dinner given at Buckingham Palace. There I saw five kings and many more princes. My greatest friend there, though, was Prince Felix, Duke of Luxemburg. I felt a bit stif (sic) the day after the funeral through having to walk so slowly. We walked the nine miles in two hours and then at Windsor we walked for another half hour. The Duke of Gloucestshire (sic) just missed fainting. There were thousands lining the streets. Windows sold at as much as one hundred and fifty pounds apiece.'

Though he did not care for England, some things he liked. 'I love all the rain and fog,' he wrote home. 'I think that is the best part of this country.' He enjoyed browsing around shops and stuffing himself in tea-shops. People around Kingston grew accustomed to seeing him riding his bicycle through the town or sending another batch of delivery boys to Kenry House. Prince Freddie they called him. At The Shop, in Woolwich, they thought him a fine boy. Major-General A. A. Goschen, Commandant of the Royal Military Academy, looked on him as a bright young man, lacking formal education rather than intelligence, good-natured, with a keen sense of competition and the will to take on any chore – even cutting up marmalade oranges for General Goschen's wife. Sergeant Parker, the PT instructor, treated him like any other young gentleman, cuffing elementary boxing lessons into him and putting him through an hour's gym, army-fashion.

Later in life he would talk British diplomats and senior officers to sleep with his reminiscences of The Shop, at which he spent too little time. The sessions of sweating at games with other cadets, lunches in the mess, the grinding tuition in maths, physics and chemistry, the extra drill incurred by the droop of an eyelid – all this he magnified in the telling as though he were searching for some purpose in his adolescence. Like almost everything Farouk said or did, it had a strong touch of fantasy. He wanted to belong, but the truth was that he never shared the harsh discipline of the academy. The 1936 report of the RMA commented: 'His return to Egypt has left us with the feeling that The Shop has missed much in not having him as a Gentleman Cadet.'

Farouk was the real loser. Two years at Woolwich would have given him the sense of duty and discipline which he could never acquire in Egypt. Competing with an élite of officer cadets would have sharpened his intelligence and developed the personality which life in the palaces of Cairo and Alexandria had stifled. Lastly, it would have kept the young king away from Egyptian courtiers and politicians at an age when they felt they could take advantage of his inexperience. Those, like the *Wafd* leaders, who had suffered under Fuad saw the chance, with this callow boy on the throne, to redeem their authority; the palace clique hoped they could persuade the son to finish the work of breaking the *Wafd* which his father had begun. And the *fellahin*, that anonymous voice like the chorus in some Greek tragedy? – perhaps they expected too much of their boy malik.

63

CHAPTER SIX

God loveth not the presumptuous, the boaster.   (LVII: 23)

FAROUK remained king for only ten days before the cabinet transferred his powers to a Regency Council until the twenty-ninth of July 1937 when he would reach his majority – eighteen years reckoned by the Moslem or lunar calendar. His uncle, Prince Mohamed Ali, also his heir, was an automatic choice as a regent. More British in outlook than Sir Miles Lampson, the prince suffered from epilepsy which had prevented him from marrying. Handsome, dandified, with a tarbush steeply angled on his white head, he lived among his banyan trees and tropical gardens at Manial Palace on Roda Island. When Fuad died, the prince had pressed strongly to keep Farouk in England for two years; the dead king, ever suspicious, had briefed Ali Maher to recall Farouk on his death and ensure the succession in case Mohamed Ali made a bid for the throne with the aid of Nahas. Maher's government appointed two other regents: the soldierly, monocled figure of Abdel-Aziz Ezzat pasha, and Cherif Sabri pasha, brother of Nazli.

Both Regency Council and government had to turn to the unfinished business of the previous reign. Fuad had initiated negotiations between Egypt and Britain to resolve the four contentious points of the 1922 Declaration. But other events compelled both countries to reach a fresh compromise. The Fascist dictators were re-arming in Europe, and Mussolini, his eyes on North Africa as part of his new Roman Empire, had invaded Ethiopia. Britain and Egypt would now have to look over their right shoulder at a further threat to the Canal. In May 1936, Ali Maher disbanded his interim cabinet and Nahas became prime minister for the third time. Lampson convinced him to sign the treaty quickly and identify the other political parties with it so that they could not repudiate it later. In August

Queen Nazli with four of her children

Farouk as a young boy

a delegation of thirteen – Nahas, six *Wafd*ists and six opposition leaders – arrived in London.

For a *Wafd* prime minister the treaty constituted little advance on the 1922 Declaration. Its first clause did, however, terminate the occupation of Egypt by British forces. The treaty also reduced the status of the High Commissioner to Ambassador and gave Egypt representation at the League of Nations and in other countries. Nevertheless, it bound Egypt to take Britain's part in any hostilities and conceded the right of Britain to station up to ten thousand troops, four hundred pilots and their ancillaries in the Canal Zone. Egypt could well have objected to such conditions, but such was the power and personality of Nahas that he returned to a hero's welcome; parliament ratified the treaty by two hundred and two votes to eleven, and the Senate also approved with only a few dissidents. Nahas called it a 'treaty of honour and independence', though it had decided neither evacuation nor the Sudan problem, the twin commandments of the *Wafd*. Another question was resolved: the capitulations which indemnified foreigners in Egypt. At Montreux, on Lake Geneva, Nahas sighed a convention with the capitulatory powers which abolished the conventions and made foreigners amenable to Egyptian law.

Meanwhile, Farouk was enjoying his new freedom. At last the palace gates had opened and he had become his own master. By any reckoning he had immense power and wealth. He owned five palaces and vast horizons of the richest land in Egypt, estimated at one tenth of all the cultivable land. Fuad, the penurious prince, had died possessing twenty-eight thousand acres, and forty-five thousand more which he supervised; he had invested more than fifteen million pounds in European banks and had twice as much in Egypt. All this came to Farouk and his family; with it, two sea-going yachts, the Mahroussa and the Fakr el-Behar, which had once belonged to the Kaiser; his royal villas and rest-houses were scattered from the Mediterranean to the Sudan; he had more than a hundred cars, including ten Rolls-Royces; a squadron of royal aircraft stood by for his orders. His omniscient authority embraced everything from national policy to trifling everyday matters. The King of Egypt could erase anything which displeased him on the cabinet agenda; he approved the appointments of ministers, magistrates, civil servants, doctors and staffs of embassies. No member of the royal family could leave the country without his consent. Even the date the police changed from summer to winter uniform had to be agreed with the king.

Sovereignty brought other boons. No longer did he have to bother about tutors or about pleasing Mrs Naylor who had left the palace just when her influence might have helped the young ruler. In her last days there she noticed two curious incidents: the picture of Farouk in his scout uniform suddenly dropped on the floor and its glass smashed; a day or two later the portrait de Lazlo had painted twisted on its cord and hung upside down. 'It sounds ridiculous,' said Mrs Naylor, 'but I remember thinking, "He'll never die a king".'

Farouk did not begin much like a king. Freedom appeared to go to his head. At any hour of the day or night he would jump into one of his cars and drive madly along the Cairo-Alexandria road, or out to Ismailia on the Canal. People learned to leap for their lives when they spotted a royal car. He had every car in his garages painted pillar-box red to prevent the police from stopping him and had even ordered a ban on this colour for other people. One newspaper editor was jailed for printing a story that Farouk's car was followed by an ambulance to pick up the casualties. In the palace they waited for the inevitable crash. Of course it came. In a red MG sports car he hit a tree outside Cairo and, although both he and his ADC, Colonel Omar Fathi bey, escaped injury, the car was beyond repair. One thing only scared Farouk: what would Queen Nazli say? She had often warned him about his crazy speeding. He must get another car, which was not easy since hardly anyone had a red car, let alone an MG. However, the Cairo police remembered a British resident in Alexandria with the same make of car and the same colour. They located him. Would he drive at once to Cairo? His Majesty, the king, wanted to see him. The man reported to Abdin Palace, Farouk paid him for his car, and Nazli remained ignorant of the accident. The Egyptians smiled indulgently at the pranks of their young king. Even when he began to shoot at the tyres of cars which were trying to pass him they dismissed it as high spirits. Better than the wooden-faced Fuad, they said.

Some people took a more serious view of Farouk's bizarre conduct. The three regents, for example. He came to them saying he did not like the station at Montazah; they should build a new one for him. The council agreed, even if the royal train stopped there only twice a year when it carried the royal family for its annual holiday and brought them back. When Farouk returned with his plan, drafted by Ernesto Verrucci, the council demurred at the cost, thirty thousand pounds. They would construct their own station for two thousand five hundred pounds they insisted. That day, Farouk led a convoy of lorries to Montazah, demolished the station and built the new one himself.

At this time he also began the collections which became such an obsession that his friends feared he had kleptomania and hid their prize possessions. Pulli, the timid young electrician, became the keeper of a strange museum of bric-à-brac in his own room at the servants' lodge. Anything his eye lighted on Farouk seized. There never seemed any question of aesthetic or rarity value, of cost or interest. So Pulli piled up the beer-bottle tops, the razor blades, the match boxes, cigarette and playing cards, miniature figures in wood and clay. Farouk would grow excited as the indiscriminate junk grew, then he would become bored and Pulli would have to titillate him with some new collector's item.

Obviously, Farouk needed guidance and a firm hand. Or so it appeared to Sir Miles Lampson who took the chance, while in London for the treaty negotiations, to speak again to the headmaster of Eton. 'We must do something about young Farouk,' he said. 'He lies in bed all morning and runs wild the rest of the day. He needs one of your masters to put him on the right lines.' The head recommended Edward Ford (later Sir Edward Ford, private secretary to King George the Sixth and Queen Elizabeth). They wanted him quickly so he flew out in August 1937, only to kick his heels for a week in a hotel until

Hassanain met him. The chamberlain, now a pasha, explained his difficulty: the king was still under the influence of his mother who did not wish anyone else to gain a hold over him. They would therefore have to ease the tutor in gradually. Ford suggested a programme of general education to which Hassanain agreed. Farouk, however, had other ideas. No sooner would they sit down to a lesson than he would press a button under his desk and a servant would appear carrying a platter of sweet drinks. Would Mr Ford like to see his collection of firearms? Another button, and another tray of revolvers. Farouk's obsession at that time and always. Shall we go for a drive? They would take the Opel or MG and spin, without purpose, through the grounds of Kubbah or Montazah. A swim? The tutor soon realised Farouk liked nothing better than playing a hose on people while they were dressing. For every session he had a hundred diversions.

He had no past to talk about, so he would invent one: a transparent mixture of fantasy and falsehood. Noticing some silver trophies on a palace table one day, Ford asked about them. 'A few trophies I won at sport when I was young,' said Farouk. This from a boy of sixteen who had hardly put a foot outside the palace. The tutor picked them up, spotted the price tags. Farouk had to confess they had come from a jeweller so that he could choose one to present to the Alexandria Yacht Club. 'I nearly had you there,' he laughed.

'Have you ever seen anyone shot?' he asked Ford, who had to admit he had not. 'Well, I have,' Farouk said. 'Poor little fellow. Very messy.'

This boasting had its sinister side. Cairo newspapers, quoting a palace spokesman, reported that King Farouk had brought down two hundred and eight birds on his first duck shoot. This was more than anyone else had bagged, including Sir Miles Lampson, a first-class gun. Ford taxed the king about these reports, and Farouk replied, blandly, that he had certainly shot two hundred birds with his own gun. He could not vouch for the other eight! The tutor found out that Farouk had shot very well for a beginner, accounting for forty to fifty ducks; other members of the party had slipped the rest into his bag. Ford pointed out that, sooner or later, a bubble reputation like this would burst.

Perhaps Farouk resented anyone who gave him advice; perhaps he really believed the notion that his tutor was no more than a British spy planted on him by Lampson. Tuition periods were reduced to twice a week, and later it became difficult for the tutor to penetrate the oriental screen around the king. Ford did, however, accompany the royal party when they toured Upper Egypt to allow people to meet their boy malik and give Farouk some idea of the country he would rule. On the second of January 1937, four paddle steamers and two launches sailed from Helwan Quay with the royal family, the regents and members of the court on board. On either side of the Nile, tribesmen on arab horses, on camels and on foot loped alongside the flotilla; at the main villages, the boats anchored and the king was received with great ceremony by provincial governors, sheikhs, omdas. He watched games and dancing, afterwards presiding over a feast for which the pashas had sacrificed bullocks in his honour.

Edward Ford, who kept a diary of this and the subsequent trip to Europe, noted something of the strange quality of Farouk's character, also the genesis of the palace clique which would have such a baleful effect on his career. Of the courtiers, he wrote, 'Their minds are filled with few thoughts except those of preferment, and the main, if not the sole, preoccupation of those Court officials is that they shall not do, nor seem to do, anything which could possibly offend His Majesty. Few of them have much work to do, and still fewer have any recreation or hobby. They are very courteous, at least to those who have any chance of being useful to them. The sycophancy that is the order of the day is repugnant to a European; but with them it is almost a necessity. This accounts for the loathsome familiarity of the King's personal servants.'

At times, though, Farouk could act like a king. Sheikh Mustapha el-Maraghi, Rector of Al Azhar University and leader of the Islamic priesthood, extolled his zeal and devotion. In fact, Farouk seemed to take his religious responsibilities seriously, carrying a Koran in his pocket and quoting from it. The dignity and simplicity of his responses to readings from the Koran impressed the sheikhs and the townspeople wherever they stopped. Even in his own circle he would tolerate no breach of the faith. At Aswan, as far south as the royal flotilla went, he strode into the harem boat where Queen Nazli's ladies-in-waiting were passing the time with cards.

'What are you playing?' he asked.

'Poker, Your Majesty,' one of them said.

'And is this a game you play for money?'

'For a few piastres only, Your Majesty.'

'Then it is a *haram* (sin) against our religion,' Farouk retorted. He swept the cloth, and cards and money, off the table and stalked out.

But soon he would have lapsed once more into adolescence, uttering appalling and childish puns at lunch on the boat and embarrassing his elders. Ford noted: 'Towards the end of the meal, in boyish mood, he made Murad Mohsen (Keeper of the Privy Purse) turn away from him on some pretext, and then picked the handkerchief out of his pocket.' Ford spoke to Hassanain about the young king's shortcomings, his unpunctuality, his error in creating false impressions. 'Hassanain seemed to approve what I had said, though he suggested that it was no good talking like that to His Majesty now. His Majesty *was* King, and must be coaxed and wheedled: one must appeal to his pride, to his good sense, rather than reprove or admonish him. The pasha had sometimes had to do so, but he had now found "a more excellent way". The pasha himself was insecure of his position: he thought it likely that His Majesty would reject one who had to act, so to speak, as his schoolmaster, especially when the inevitable intrigues started. The King, he told me, was very elusive, and often could not be found even in the palace. He received most of his information and gossip, even on political matters, from his Berberine servants. He was no longer a boy, and had become a King. And he had the idea that a King must be perfect: therefore he must not be "found out". That is why he must have the reputation of doing everything. His people expected that. No one must be allowed to prick the bubble.'

So this was why Farouk wanted to avoid his tutors, and later his cabinet ministers; they knew too much for his comfort. The sense of inferiority, of incompleteness which made him shun his advisers also hampered the development of his intellect and his personality. From this moment, his favourite retort to anyone on any subject was, 'I know.' He thought those two words hid his ignorance, his inferiority when in fact they closed his mind. Ali Maher, the Black Eminence of his court, described Farouk as a know-all who knew nothing. Yet, he had intelligence – enough to appreciate how little he understood and how much he had to disguise his lack of education. But this complex forced him to escape from those courtiers, ministers, diplomats in whose presence he felt diffident and uneasy. There were others who admitted his superiority, his infallibility even. The servants. They might bow and scrape, tell him only what would please him, but they made no demands on his intelligence, and never criticised. With Pulli, Pietro, Caro, Mohamed and the others he really felt like a king.

What more excellent way had Hassanain explored? The courtier had gained influence with the one person to whom Farouk still deferred: his mother. Like her son, Queen Nazli had her freedom at last; for her, too, Fuad's death had thrown the gates open. On the tour of Upper Egypt she danced on the boat every night; she looked radiant and happy; her illness no longer troubled her and she seemed better than at any time since her marriage. Everyone knew the reason. During the month they spent in Upper Egypt her escort was her son's chamberlain, Ahmed Mohamed Hassanain pasha. She had fallen in love with him and refused to keep the fact secret. Did Hassanain love her? No one ever penetrated that tortuous and obtuse mind to answer that question. However, he returned from the Nile trip one of the most powerful people in Egypt. As Nazli commented much later, she gave the king Hassanain, and while he remained nothing much could go wrong. She was right.

To help Farouk meet friends of his own standing and overcome his shyness, Hassanain and Nazli threw several parties at the palaces in Cairo and Alexandria. At one of these parties he approached his mother's friend and lady-in-waiting, Madam Zulficar.

'That girl in blue over there. Who is she?'

'You don't know?' He shook his head. Madam Zulficar laughed. 'You really don't know?' she asked again. 'That's my daughter, Safinaz.' Farouk made no move to introduce himself but merely glanced at the girl and walked away. Madam Zulficar thought no more of the incident; after all, Safinaz was only fifteen and Farouk eighteen months older. He must have seen her several times with his own sisters.

Some of the best families in Egypt offered their daughters for the king's approval, but Hassanain discouraged them. Farouk would not marry for several years, he said. He failed to take the king's own emotions into account. In the spring of 1937, when he had just turned seventeen, he fell in love. Several times he had seen the girl, though every time he approached her she would evade him. This behaviour only fired Farouk's ardour further, until he realised that he loved this girl. Well then, he would go to her and propose. How could she refuse to become Queen of Egypt! With his ADC, the impassive Omar Fathi bey, he drove to her house in Giza and knocked on the door. An upper window opened and the girl looked out. 'What do you want?' she asked.

'Open the door.'

The girl did not budge. 'My father and mother are away and I could not see you without their permission.' She closed the window in the face of Farouk and his ADC.

Farouk jumped into his car and raged all the way back to Abdin. To Omar Fathi he said, 'She did not shut the window in my face, she shut it on her happiness. I wanted that girl to become Queen of Egypt but she has lost her chance.'

The rebuff had shaken his vanity. Imagine a girl rejecting him, a king idolised by everyone, sought after by the best families! It hurt his ego. At Kubbah he locked himself in his room, full of shame and anger at the insult. Finally, his mother drew the secret out of him. She would try, she said, to change the girl's mind, even invite her on their forthcoming trip to Europe. Nazli had no more success than her son; she could only comfort him and hope he would forget. He never did. In nostalgic moments he would chuckle and joke about the girl who had spurned him to marry some obscure university professor in Cairo and live as a suburban housewife. It was mirthless laughter. The scar remained.

Another girl came into his thoughts, the friend of Fawzia, the girl in blue he had seen at his first party, Safinaz, daughter of Yussef Zulficar, vice-president of the Appeal Court in Alexandria, and Zeinab, his mother's lady-in-waiting. On the twenty-fourth of February, three days before their boat sailed for his trip to Europe, he and his mother were discussing the list of guests accompanying them. It was two o'clock in the morning, not unusually late for either of them. Suddenly Farouk said, 'We must take Safinaz.'

Nazli knew he had never spoken to the girl, or even mentioned her. 'Is this love at first sight?' she asked.

Farouk shook his head. 'I just want her to be with us.' He picked up the telephone, demanded her number in Alexandria and handed the instrument to his mother with the instruction to invite Safinaz. The sleepy voice of Zeinab answered.

'Is anything wrong?' she asked.

'Nothing,' Nazli replied. 'We just want to take Safinaz with us on the tour of Europe.'

'That is impossible. Safinaz is preparing for her baccalaureat and must attend school.'

'She must come,' Nazli insisted. 'The princesses say she must come with us.'

'But she has no clothes for such a trip.'

'She can buy those in Europe.'

'She cannot get a passport in three days,' the mother persisted.

'That will take three minutes.'

'I shall have to ask her father,' Zeinab said, dubiously.

'You can tell him that it is a royal decree.'

Madam Zulficar woke her husband, repeated the conversation

to him; the judge listened and said, No, his daughter could not go.

Again the telephone rang. By now it was three o'clock. 'What have you decided?' the queen mother asked.

'My husband says that Safinaz may not go until she has finished her studies.'

'You can tell him that this is a royal command,' Nazli said.

They woke Safinaz who was astonished at the request but wished to go; she had no idea that Farouk had insisted that she join the royal party; she went believing the queen mother's story that she would act as a companion to the princesses.

The party of thirty-two sailed on the Viceroy of India, taking with them two hundred and fifty pieces of luggage weighing seven tons. The newspaper, Al Misri, sent its leading writer, Mohamed el-Tabeh, to cover the king's tour. Though a friend of Hassanain he had never suspected any relationship between the courtier and the queen. As he wandered the deck waiting for the ship to sail, he noticed two figures leaning over the rail, silhouetted against the lights of Port Said. The man had his arm round the woman's shoulder. They were Hassanain and Nazli.

On the voyage to Marseilles, Farouk had the captain's quarters and made the most of the three days. The Egyptian journalist discovered that he breakfasted on caviar, digging it out of a tin with a soup spoon, then followed this with twice the normal breakfast. He never missed a dance on the first-class or the tourist decks.

At St Moritz, they booked into Suvretta House where Farouk decreed that all journalists should be excluded, something the management could hardly do. Winter sports did not interest him. His new skis never lost their varnish and he shrugged his skating instructor aside. Tuition was an insult to the perfect young monarch, who made an exhibition of himself scooting around on one skate. During the day he bombarded Hassanain, his sisters, servants and Swiss officials with snowballs; in the evening he peppered the guests on the dance-floor with puff-balls which were distributed during Gala-nights, and flirted with the occasional girl. Rarely did he rise before midday, and he breakfasted when everyone else was having lunch. His afternoons he spent shopping for watches and gold coins which he collected by the hundred. He played pin-table machines, investing so heavily that his shelves sagged under the trashy gifts he won. He frittered away his days in St Moritz, Berne, Geneva and Zurich, leaving behind him a reputation for frivolity, irresponsibility and unpunctuality. Why, Swiss officials demanded, did a man with such a passion for watches never turn up on time? He cancelled a visit to a chocolate factory, pretending tiredness; he appeared hours late for two other official receptions; he kept the Swiss cavalry school standing forty minutes in the cold though they had the last laugh: they repeated the Egyptian national anthem five times forcing Farouk to keep at attention for a good fifteen minutes.

Sometimes, in the afternoons, he would come and watch his sisters skating on the lake behind the hotel. One day Safinaz fell, twisting her ankle and crying out with the pain. Farouk darted across the ice, yelling to his sisters that Allah had punished them for skating. 'I will order her to do no more skating,' he said. The girls protested, so he went to his mother and gave the order.

'But this has nothing to do with you,' Nazli said.

'It has. I don't want her to fall and die.'

'Is it because you love her?'

Farouk did not reply; he blushed, turned and walked away. His mother had guessed the truth; she noticed that when their eyes met they both blushed, and that Farouk now spent more time with his sisters. That way he could stay near Safinaz.

At the beginning of May, not long before the coronation of King George the Sixth, the Egyptian party arrived in England. To give Farouk some general idea of Britain, Edward Ford had mapped out his programme: lunch at Buckingham Palace and Marlborough House; the cup final between Sunderland and Preston North End with the King and Queen; the House of Commons and the Lords; meetings with politicians, university heads, theatre personalities; week-ends with the nobility. Before long, Farouk had wrecked the agenda and turned the tour into something of a fiasco. At Boughton, as a guest of the Duke and Duchess of Buccleuch, he kept the dinner guests, including the Foreign Secretary, Anthony Eden, kicking their heels for an hour and a half because he suddenly decided, at eight o'clock, to drive twelve miles and have a swim; the vice-chancellor of Cambridge University marked time for an hour and three-quarters, in full regalia, to greet the king who had squandered that time buying puppies; as an official guest at the Naval Review he delayed dinner by a quarter of an hour before a servant arrived with a note saying the king would eat in his cabin. An unofficial visitor, he could play no part in the Coronation; this sent him into such a huff that he packed up his whole entourage and sulked for a week in Paris.

Edward Ford not only had to deal with the king's foibles. One experience with Queen Nazli unnerved him. Travelling to Cambridge together in a first-class compartment, she launched abruptly into her confessions: she had been unhappy; Fuad had picked her from a photograph and kept her locked up. 'My life? I was always having babies.' Then Ford, by now slightly alarmed at this emotional outburst, heard her cry, 'Do you think I shall ever know the love of a man?' Some people felt she was making strenuous efforts. She had quit Kenry House, to which Farouk had returned, and taken a suite at Claridges. Every other night she had a box reserved at a theatre, and of course could not go unescorted. Invariably, she summoned the elegant and sophisticated Hassanain, who found himself more committed to the queen mother than to the king.

From the diaries which Edward Ford wrote at the time we get remarkably prescient assessments of Farouk's failings. Then and now, Ford judged his mission as fruitless and felt he had done too little for the young king. How could he have done more when Farouk's sycophants were whispering to him to beware of the British spy? Ford had, however, an almost prophetic insight into the character defects which, in the boy, made him vulnerable to intrigue, to flattery, to self-indulgence; which, in the man, would crystallise into corruption, despotism and moral corrosion. That ambivalence he had noted in Egypt became more marked in the king's contacts with people in Britain. One moment the earnest young ruler with a perceptive, inquiring mind; the next, a schoolboy indulging in pranks with courtiers and servants. The heads of universities, even the great Lord Rutherford, would overlook his late arrival as he turned on his charm, leaving them the impression of a cultured, intelligent young man; he had a talent for seizing on the precise point of a conversation, for posing the awkward question, for halting at the most interesting exhibit in a museum or science lab. He might then spoil the impression by making some ridiculous pun. And the pretence. 'Ha,' he cried on seeing the undergraduate rooms at Cambridge, 'very comfortable, nothing like the bare rooms we lived in at Woolwich.'

Ford observed two traits in Farouk: one was his careless indifference to his mother, who doted on him. Nazli seemed determined that no one but she would possess or influence him. Not even Hassanain. The chamberlain thus faced the task of serving two masters at once. The second shortcoming was Farouk's preference for servants. Hassanain reported to Ford that he had challenged the king with passing too much time in their company and had been rebuffed. 'They don't nag me,' Farouk had snapped.

'It was a repellent sight,' Ford noted, 'to see him slapping his Italian valets on the back, or to find them meekly submitting to have their tongues painted with black ink before going in fancy dress to a servants' ball at Kingston. And I determined on a suitable occasion to tell him of the dangers of encouraging those who might try to exert influence without having any responsibility. At the moment, it is probably true to say that he enjoys himself more in his rooms and with his books (though he doesn't read them) and medals, and in the company of his servants than in that of his family or his chosen advisers.'

With equals he appeared uneasy. He did not, Ford commented, seem to have the capacity for making friends; nor did he appreciate that friendship involved give-and-take. To create an impression he would take refuge in fantasies about his non-existent exploits which had the Munchausen ring even if they lacked the Baron's original touch.

The time had come for Farouk to leave England for Europe and home. Within a few weeks he would be King of Egypt in name as well as in fact. In the thirteen months since his father died he had learned little. The boy who wanted to become the Perfect King had, in that time, revealed profound weaknesses of character which troubled his immediate circle of advisers. How long before the people found out?

CHAPTER SEVEN

Woe to those who pray,
But in their prayers are careless;
Who make a show of devotion,
But refuse to help the needy.

(CVII: 4 to 8)

A GOOD day's march away in the desert, tribesmen could marvel at the splash of light over Cairo; the drums carried miles from teeming streets where crowds danced throughout the night. Tomorrow, the twenty-ninth of July 1937, the first king of an independent Egypt would ascend the throne and the million people of his first city were already caught up in the excitement of the coronation. Two million more were arriving to swell the population; on cheap excursion trains, on camels and donkeys, by Nile steamer and felucca. Fellahin and their children jumped clear as frenzied horsemen careered through the bazaars and shopping centres firing their carbines in the air; they gawped at the fireworks and the huge triumphal arches erected outside Abdin Palace and on the route to the parliament buildings; they squatted in the streets, feasting on free mutton which they washed down with lemonade; at dawn they answered the call from the minarets, knelt to the east and prayed for their king.

The roll of cannon from Abdin and Abbassiah announced that the king had left his palace; the roar of the crowd reverberated down the city streets as the procession edged towards the Chamber of Deputies. In a resplendent white coat, green sash, red tarbush, Farouk greeted the crowds from his gilded coach. Flowers and palm leaves fluttered at the feet of the six grey horses which drew the carriage. By the king's side sat his prime minister, Mustapha el-Nahas pasha, his craggy face impassive. This was Farouk's day.

At the Chamber of Deputies, the king mounted the dais to the throne seat, draped with a red velvet canopy. In his left hand he grasped a sceptre, the right he placed on the Koran. The assembled senators heard him intone clearly, in Arabic, 'I swear by Allah that I will respect the constitution, the laws of the Egyptian nation, and will uphold the independence of the country and safeguard her land.' Applause burst from the crowded chamber; in the royal box, above and to his left, Nazli and her daughters smiled at him as he glanced up nervously. The queen mother had dared to appear in public for the first time in a half-veil.

The simple dignity of his speech moved many of the deputies. 'I shall have the interests of the country at heart before all other matters. We are all children of Egypt and we all belong to the country. We are all her soldiers and her servants, and the king is the first servant of the country. I believe that the greatness of a king can come only from the greatness of his people. And the king must have faith in this and be ready to sacrifice for this. The poor are not responsible for their poverty, but rather the wealthy. Give to the poor what they merit without their asking. A king is a good king when the poor of the land have the right to live, when the sick have the right to be healed, when the timid have the right to be tranquil, and when the ignorant have the right to learn.'

For three days and nights Cairo forgot everything but its new monarch; suddenly they had a man who spoke for the people. Farouk was everywhere; waving from Abdin Palace balcony to thousands sweltering under parasols; reviewing the army; receiving leaders of the foreign community; leading prayers at different mosques. On a shining bay, dressed in field marshal's uniform, he took the oath of allegiance from a hundred and twenty-seven officers and two thousand three hundred soldiers in Abdin Square. While he saluted, they recited this text: 'I swear three times on Allah, his sacred book and his prophets, on my honour and faith as an officer, to be the loyal, faithful servant of His Majesty, King Farouk I, and of his government, to obey all his august commands and all his orders that will be transmitted to me by superiors, to execute on land, sea and air and beyond the borders of the Nile Valley, to be against those who oppose him, and to defend the rights of his country, and not to abandon my arms until death.'

Cairo might have done him proud. But what was Cairo? The diamond stud in the fan handle of Egypt, a patchwork of East and West, a cosmopolis of Moslem, Copt and Christian, of Egyptians, Syrians, Lebanese, of British, French and Italian, of store tycoons and stall-owners, of government palaces and rat-run slums, of rich foreign bankers and beggars crying backsheesh, of pashas making free with the rents and profits from their lands along the Nile and peasants existing on a handful of beans a day. Peasants had no place in Cairo and the capital soon emptied of them, with their gallabiyas and head-cloths, their feet bare and hands encrusted with river mud. They had to get back to their land, for it was the *Wefa el-Nil* (Nile floods). Their crops could not wait.

Yet these men were the land which Farouk ruled. They constituted nine out of every ten people who worked. As though rooted and growing in the Nile slime, they went on using immemorial techniques like the primitive *saquia* (water wheel), the Archimedian Screw, or a wooden lever to bleed water from the river into their fields of cotton, wheat and maize. It cost a pasha seven pounds a year for each fellah, so muscle-power came cheaper than machines or even farm animals. Only his *gamoosa* (buffalo), or his donkey lent their weight to his. If the rhythm of his life had to keep pace with the slow coming and going of the river its fabric had been woven in Cairo by some landowner he had probably never seen. The flimsy lease on his land had more than a hundred different clauses which he could not read let alone comprehend. They meant that high-water, low-water, high prices, low prices, lean and fat years, he, the fellah, got no more than seven pounds a year. A cotton boom – the pasha would exercise his option on the crop. A slump – he would exact the money in rent. For the reluctant fellah there was always the *nabbut* (stave) or the *courbash*.

Of politics the fellah knew and cared nothing. Poets in Cairo and Alexandria might rhapsodise about his misery, glorify his

81

aspirations, portray him as a nationalist ablaze with the idea of liberty. What did freedom represent to men living in mud huts, toiling from sun-up to sunset, feeding their families on beans except during feast days? The same as democracy? That, he did know, meant the omda had written his name on the *Wafd* list and the *nabbut* and *courbash* would fall on him if he voted any other way.

Of the sixteen million people in Egypt when Farouk mounted the throne, only two million could read and write. Outside the cities literacy was as rare as a white camel. Yet, the fellah made good educational material; up to fifteen he quickly learned the ways and traditions of the village, the skills his father taught him; after this, grey mud and silted water seemed to become part of his soul, the monotony of his toil and the village life dulled his mind. Superstition governed his existence. Hardly any of the villages had drinking water in 1937 because the fellah believed the Nile to be male, alive and to bring fertility; his wife would eat a handful of river mud when she was expecting a child, for this reason. And who needed medicine when mud and water had such magical properties? So, few villages boasted a doctor; most of the three thousand practitioners never left the cities.

Disease was the other enemy. In the thirties, Egypt had the highest infant mortality rate in the world, one in four of its children dying in the first days of life. The man who reached sixty could consider himself fortunate, or perhaps not. He would have probably survived the epidemic diseases like malaria, typhus and cholera which scavenged the Nile Valley every few years; he would have been the one in ten lucky enough to escape *bilharzia,* the debilitating parasite which breeds in the stagnant slime; he would have also avoided hook-worm and tunnel-worm, those slow killers. No traveller in Egypt can fail to notice the blind and partially blind. Three out of every five people suffered from eye disease, aggravated by the glare, the dust and sandstorms. In some villages scarcely anyone was untouched by corneal opacity, cataracts, glaucoma or trachoma.

These peasants had as much say in their own survival and welfare as the beasts which helped them; in their simple proverbs the word patience occurred inevitably; their hopes and sorrows were expressed in the ritual phrase, *Insha Allah* (if God wills) which pervaded every thought and decision. Even their gestures appeared to have petrified like those on the wall paintings of the Tomb of Ti at Sakkara, or Tutankamen in the Valley of the Kings.

Elsewhere in Egypt things were changing, though perhaps only the prescient few could decipher the signs.

Not long after Farouk returned from Europe, he received a long letter; copies of this document also went to Nahas and other government leaders. Its message was unequivocal; it called on the king and his government to abjure western decadence and return to the path of Islam. In Koranic prose, it urged them to be 'the first to offer in the name of the Prophet the vial of medicine from the medical art of the Holy Book in order to save the ailing world'. Its fifty clauses declared how Islam must redeem the country and reform its society. Frankly xenophobic, it insisted not only on the expulsion of the British but every other foreigner. It advocated the abolition of political parties and the union of all politicians behind Islam. 'In this world,' ran the letter to Farouk, 'there is no system which supplies the awakening nation with the organisation, foundation, feelings and sympathies as does the system of Islam.'

In practice what did it all mean? Egypt would not only return to the teaching of Mohamed but to his way of life. With western culture would go cinemas, bars, night-clubs, gambling houses, racetracks; outside their homes, men and women would not mix, especially at parties where drinking took place; women would walk around veiled in drab colours of Egyptian make; the newspapers would cease to publish their pictures. Only Arabic, the language of Mohamed, would be spoken; only Egyptian articles would be bought; only Egyptians could be hired. In fact, the letter demanded a retreat of fourteen centuries to a primeval theocracy which would have obliterated most Egyptian institutions, destroyed its commerce, transformed its society and culture from top to bottom.

Reading the letter, Farouk dismissed its writer as a crank, the type of religious fanatic common in Egypt and the Middle East. So did Nahas and Hassanain. Not, however, Ali Maher. The singer, he knew, was greater than the song in this case.

The writer was called Hasan el-Banna, a thirty-year-old schoolmaster who marched around Cairo with light, tripping steps, dressed in a flowing white cloak, tasselled turban and the slippers of a Meccan pilgrim. He preached in mosques, cafés, village schools and halls. And always the same message: base your whole life on the Koran. El-Banna came from a Delta village where his father repaired watches for a living and read the lesson from the Koran on Fridays. Like most others, the boy learned his first words from the Moslem bible – only they struck deeper into his soul. At twelve he was fasting for three months instead of the one Ramadan month; as the Koran decreed, he prayed long and devoutly five times a day, and to ensure others did not backslide he made the rounds before the muezzin had mounted the minaret at dawn and knocked on doors with the shout that it was prayer time; he posted notices on mosque doors exhorting people to shun silk clothes and jewellery; in his spare time, he formed half a dozen religious societies such as the Society for the Prevention of Sin. At thirteen he was yelling for Zaghlul and independence, since this meant freedom from the infidel.

Not until 1928, when he was twenty-two, did el-Banna found the society that would spread its influence through Egypt and the Arab world, that would graduate from religious fervour to violence and fanaticism. His first posting as a schoolteacher took him to Ismailia. There, British troops controlled the base, the French the Canal. El-Banna clutched his Koran more tightly and muttered longer prayers through his black beard as he noted their western sin taking hold on the town. He resented the British guns, though the French with their smart clothes, their jewels, their cocktail parties in smart villas disgusted him equally. Yet no one reacted: the leaders of *Al Azhar*, the king, the politicians all remained mute.

He would act. He gathered several young sheikhs and students and proclaimed the new movement, the Moslem Brethren. He

84

and his followers travelled Egypt during their week-ends, preaching, recruiting disciples and members. Somehow his message penetrated the inertia and apathy of the villages and the Delta towns. By 1937 he had established more than a hundred branches in Egypt and had made himself something of a political reputation by helping the aggressive Grand Mufti of Jerusalem with the problem of the Palestine Arabs. This work brought him into contact with Ali Maher who realised he might fashion el-Banna's movement into a politicial lever for himself. Maher, then chief of the royal cabinet, foresaw war between the British and the Germans; he knew that the Moslem Brethren were forming para-military phalanxes, initiated on Koran and sword, to liberate the country from the British as well as cleanse it morally. If war did break out, the militant arm of such a movement might become decisive; a prime minister might even deploy it as a counter-weight to the *Wafd* if that body took the wrong side. Ali Maher had another vision. He saw Egypt as the leader of the Arab world, its young king as Caliph of the Moslems, Protector of the Faith, its prime minister (himself, of course) as a figure in world politics. So, while others smiled sceptically at el-Banna's bizarre notions, Ali Maher kept in secret touch with the movement, acting as its protector and advocate at the court.

Farouk and his advisers might have observed a transformation in another institution closer to the palace and the government. Until 1936 the Egyptian army had drawn its officers from the aristocracy and therefore mostly from the Turkish élite. Now the *Wafd* had signed a treaty of independence with the promise of a British withdrawal to the Canal Base; this, and its desire to make a show of democracy, forced it to open the Egyptian Royal Military Academy to boys of every class, regardless of their wealth or position. Late in 1936 and early in 1937, the first intakes of cadets started training at Abbassiah. Among them, and counting himself fortunate, was the eighteen-year-old son of an Alexandrian postmaster. Gamal Abdel Nasser looked inconspicuous, except perhaps for the crescent-shaped cicatrice on his brow, a legacy from anti-British demonstrations with fascist greenshirts in Alexandria. With Nasser went seven other cadets who would later collaborate with him in the revolutionary movement; they included Abdel Hakim Amer, Anwar el-Sadat, Zakariah Moheddin and Salah Salem. Who could predict that, with men like these, the army might cease to consider itself a praetorian guard around the king, instead an instrument of the people?

The *Wafd* as well had altered since the days of Zaghlul. Privilege, patronage and corruption had diluted its authority. No longer did it attract the thrusting professional man who shouted his demands over the heads of the king, the British and the pashas to the man in the market place and the fields. The pashas had joined the party; even the British threw it their support when it suited them. Only Farouk found it impossible to compromise with the men who had flouted his father's authority so often, whom he believed were tilting at him. Nor can we say that the *Wafd* shared the national delirium over Farouk's accession. Yes, they said. He promises allegiance to the constitution, better education, better medicine, better conditions. So did his father!

The party itself had come under attack, mainly for corruption. Such a word rang perhaps less harshly in the ears of an Egyptian politician than elsewhere; to most, political office meant a percentage of state building projects, the chance to buy cheap land in the track of an irrigation scheme, the acceptance of an oriental gift for securing some contract. Everyone who mattered in Egypt knew that *Wafd* corruption began at the top. Not with Nahas, whose honesty people never doubted. With the beautiful young wife he had married in his fifties. Thirty years younger than her husband, Zeinab el-Wakil flaunted her political fortune-hunting; she sold political office as cynically as a carpet hawker; a pashalik added up to so many acres of good Delta land; a minor favour equalled a house, furs or jewels; a good word in Nahas's ear and she augmented her collection of hundreds of gold cigarette cases.

Ignorant of the jobbery his wife was practising, Nahas worried more about the increasing power and prestige of the palace. The sins of his own party had to wait. First he had to limit the king's authority, to contest every action of the palace, to weaken Farouk's popularity wherever he could. In small as well as big issues the two men demonstrated their mutual distrust. At meetings with cabinet ministers, the king would sit with a bored, negligent look until some question arose for which he knew Nahas had no answer; he would then embarrass the prime minister by insisting on discussing it. Their attempts to score off each other were typified by the story of alterations to Abdin Palace. Farouk complained he had to work in a marble furnace, to which Nahas blandly suggested installing air conditioning. The king checked on the premier's scheme and discovered it would cost more than a million pounds; his advisers urged caution. 'The *Wafd* will say the king is living in luxury while the poor fellahin are dying in the heat,' they said. The plan came to nothing. The bickering continued.

At the beginning, Nahas had urged Farouk's return from England as fervently as Ali Maher and Nazli. Fuad had stifled the *Wafd*; now its leader thought he might recoup some of the lost influence by gaining a hold over the young king and the palace party. But the *Wafd* relied heavily on the masses; Nahas could not allow the king to win them over at his expense. The triumphal return from England, the successful tour of Upper Egypt were seen by Nahas as a challenge to *Wafd* authority. '*Le roi regne, il ne gouverne pas*,' was one of his favourite catch-phrases. Before the king took the oath of office he meant him to understand this. Their first clash came over the choice of the mosque at which the sovereign would hold Friday prayers. Farouk elected Al Azhar since Sheikh el-Maraghi acted as his religious preceptor; Nahas affirmed it should be Al-Husain. Farouk then decided he would visit a different mosque each Friday and the *Wafd* leader observed, with some dismay, that crowds followed him, chanting 'Yahia Farouk'. Through palace informants, Nahas discovered which mosque the king intended to visit and took himself to one nearby hoping that 'Yahia Nahas' would drown the cheers for Farouk.

Farouk expressed his wish to Nahas that he should be the first Egyptian monarch to wear a crown. The President of the Senate should place it on his head to make it appear that the people had crowned him. Nahas would have none of it, so some of Farouk's supporters began a collection among the people for a crown. At this the *Wafd* started a whispering campaign that the king was extorting money from the poor fellahin. Ali Maher forced Farouk to discard the project.

They quarrelled, too, over the army oath of allegiance. The officers should give their allegiance to the king, as head of the army. No, argued Nahas; they first owed loyalty to the constitution then the government, lastly the king.

Nahas thought up other ways of reducing the power and status of the monarch. In parliament he raised the question of the Italians in the palace. Since the government paid them it must have the right to appoint and dismiss them. Farouk could not bear to see his Italians insulted, refused to give ground and paid them out of the privy purse. This allowance then became the subject of another dispute which ended with Farouk cutting the money voted from two hundred and fifty thousand pounds a year to one hundred and fifty thousand pounds. When Nahas suggested another sacrifice of fifty thousand pounds Farouk stormed that he had gone far enough. No one would tamper with his money or tell him how to spend it.

The young king now regarded the *Wafd* leader as a threat to his authority, if not his throne. Nahas drove the final wedge between them when he attempted to dictate Farouk's choice of his royal cabinet chief by sending a list of the candidates he approved. The king had no doubt about his man: Ali Maher pasha, the politician his father had picked. If Farouk had sought a head-on clash with Nahas, he could not have made it plainer. The *Wafd* chief and Ali Maher detested each other, even though they had once shared a law office at the beginning of the century. Temperamentally, they had nothing in common. Nahas was an impulsive creature whose emotions often over-ruled his reason, who seemed more at home with peasants than with pashas; Ali Maher, a devious character, never allowed his scruples to interfere with his ambition. He was a dandy, from the tassel on his tarbush through his pearl tie-pin to his patent shoes, while Nahas always looked crumpled, even in his brocaded dress uniform.

He had few friends, this smooth-tongued lawyer who had

wormed his way into the palace. The British Residency disliked him; Cromer had kicked his father out for his intriguing and bad advice; his brother, Ahmed Maher, still remained suspect for his part in the murder of Sir Lee Stack. Few politicians trusted this man whom Fuad had nominated a senator and who had no party. Yet Farouk provoked a crisis by choosing this man to teach him the constitution. Now he wanted him as his chief counsellor.

The king understood little enough of the written constitution; he did not know that Fuad had largely ignored it, seizing on one precedent after another to frame his own unwritten constitution. Ali Maher taught the king how he, too, could manipulate the constitution in this way. He then waited for the inevitable collision between the king and his premier. It came over the appointment of an electrical engineer to the palace staff. The man was Italian. Nahas objected that the appointment had not been submitted to the finance minister; when Ali Maher stood firm, Nahas went to the king. He tried persuasion. It was not that he objected to the man, merely to the fact that constitutional procedure had not been followed. Farouk made no comment, so Nahas resorted to conciliation. 'Be sure, Sir, that I am speaking to you like a father and wish you well.'

Farouk rounded on him. 'Pasha, watch your language.' He would not be placated. 'The government has more to do than interfere in the choice of my barber or my hairdresser,' he growled.

This quarrel Ali Maher used to poison Farouk's judgement. The government had contested his coronation, his allowance, the oath, his choice of mosque. Now they were trying to appoint his staff. Why? To take advantage of his youth and inexperience, his ignorance of his rights, and undermine him. Ali Maher left the king's study with the promise that he would confront Nahas at every point. Maher was revelling in the situation; he had helped to draft the constitution. Now that Farouk, worried by *Wafd* tactics, was listening to him he could deal with Nahas. He saw the fulfilment of his own ambitions. The royal cabinet did not interest him. He had his eye on the prime minister's office, and now that the king realised he could dismiss ministers, dissolve and convene parliament, the door to that lay open. It did not matter to Ali Maher that he was giving Farouk lessons in despotism.

By the end of the autumn of 1937, the king and his prime minister were hardly speaking to each other. The rift deepened over the formation of the *Wafd* Blue Shirts which were Nahas's answer to the Green Shirts, a militant youth movement copied from the Hitler Youth. *Wafd* boys drilled like troops, saluting with a smart slap on their chests, and held political rallies. Though only an off-shoot of the main argument, Farouk protested that this organisation was acting as a rival to his own Boy Scouts. He forced Nahas to disband the movement and amalgamate Blue Shirts and Boy Scouts.

It was their last quarrel. Nahas made an attempt to solve their constitutional wrangle by appointing a commission, the membership of which he sent to the palace for approval. On the thirtieth of December he had his reply – a royal rescript dismissing him and his cabinet. Obviously prepared by Ali Maher, the rescript stated that the people 'no longer supported the methods of government practised by the cabinet, which it reproached for misunderstanding the spirit of the constitution and failing to respect and protect public liberties'.

Farouk had determined to rule as well as reign. From now on he would choose his prime ministers and their cabinets. Mohamed Mahmud, the strong man in Fuad's day, formed a coalition of minority parties on New Year's Day 1938. Ali Maher had sown the seeds of the autocracy which led to dictatorship, the cunning which bred corruption; he had planted them in a fertile mind.

In more than one way it was a fateful year for the young king. At his mother's behest, he leaned more and more on Hassanain, the one sane adviser in his court. When they returned from Europe he invited the chamberlain to live in the palace and moved him into a room in the royal wing, near Fuad's old bedroom. Nazli had come to depend as much on Hassanain as her son; now they saw each other every day, and her love for him grew. Far from disguising her fondness for him, the queen mother let her ladies-in-waiting know, and even members of the court. She confessed, too, that Hassanain was reluctant to return her love. When this gossip reached Farouk, through his constant companions, the servants, he became angry. On several occasions, servants and courtiers heard him shout that he would shoot the chamberlain; but the next day they would find him laughing and joking with him. For Farouk sensed that he could at least trust Hassanain; moreover, that the chamberlain might help to keep his mother in her place. This bond between the gay, pleasure-seeking queen and the placid, scholarly courtier puzzled so many people. What did they have in common? No doubt Nazli was attracted by Hassanain's elegant good looks, the polished manner; but perhaps just as much by his integrity, that rare component in Egyptian officials and politicians. For his part, Hassanain, however, unwilling to become the queen's lover, saw that he might exercise power over the son through her.

Both Farouk and Nazli kept late hours; often they might prowl through the labyrinthine palace well after midnight, though normally they kept to their own wings. Only the king had the right to enter the haramlek. Early one morning, a servant came and whispered to Farouk that Hassanain was in his mother's room. The king decided he would catch them both in the act. Along the broad corridor, flanked by busts of Napoleon, the great hero of Mohamed Ali, and his own ancestors, he padded up to the door of his mother's room. It was unlocked. Quietly he opened it and went in. He got two shocks: Hassanain was there, in the forbidden part of the palace. But the renaissance bed, with its pink silk drapes, had not been slept in. The chamberlain and his mother were sitting like a religious teacher and his pupil. He was reading her extracts from the Koran! In Farouk's own account of the scene he made no mention of Hassanain; he said he had found his mother with her lover, brandished a revolver at both and threatened to kill them if they carried on their affair.

Here, again, Farouk was confusing fact and fantasy. (How often revolvers cropped up in these myths like some Freudian virility symbol!) Farouk realised he could do nothing to stop his mother, who still treated him as a boy rather than a king; he knew, furthermore, that he needed Hassanain both in the role of adviser and because he had won his mother's love. Nevertheless, the boy of seventeen was stunned by this confrontation. Gossip was one thing, proof another. At that hour of the night he ran to the garage and jumped into a car, any car. No one ever discovered how or where he spent those hours. He returned next morning, his car covered in sand, as though he had driven across the desert; he flopped out on his bed and slept the rest of the day. That experience affected the young king profoundly. He had not surprised his mother and Hassanain in each other's arms, but he did not doubt now that they were lovers. His mother he loved as much as he could love anyone; Hassanain he idolised. He felt betrayed, humiliated. Whom could he trust now?

Later, he gave permission for Hassanain to marry his mother, but secretly with two witnesses he could count on from his own staff – Murad Mohsen pasha, and Suleiman Naguib bey.

His own thoughts were turning to marriage and to the girl whom he had invited on the European trip. One day in August 1937 he made an unexpected call on Safinaz Zulficar, and said to her, 'There is a girl I love and want to marry. How should I approach her?' The girl, then sixteen, did not know what to make of his obtuse question; she spoke to her father, who caught the implication. 'My advice to you is not to marry him,' the judge said. 'There are millions of reasons why not. You are free to do as you like, but I have to advise against it.' When she insisted on hearing the reasons, her father shrugged. 'I cannot say anything, but I do not want to bear the responsibility of this marriage before God.'

'But if he loves me?'

'You are still too young and he is too young. I cannot approve of this marriage.'

Farouk spoke once again to Safinaz who avoided replying. On the twenty-first of August he summoned his ADC, the stolid Omar Fathi. 'We are going to Alexandria,' he announced. Driving along the Delta highway, scattering men, women and animals, he turned to the ADC. 'Aren't you going to ask me why we are going to Alexandria?'

'I do not interfere with what Your Majesty does.'

'We are going to the most important meeting of my life,' Farouk said.

At Judge Zulficar's house, he left the ADC in the car and knocked on the door; a servant told him Safinaz was upstairs though the judge and his wife had gone out. By now the girl stood on the stairs. Farouk hesitated a moment, then pleaded with her to marry him. 'I have no father, and no one to look after me. You will be everything to me,' he stammered.

'This is a great honour for me, Your Majesty,' Safinaz said.

'Then you will marry me?'

'I approve,' she said, dubiously. 'But . . .'

'But what?'

'I must first ask my parents.'

Her father, she explained, had sailed that day for a two-week holiday in the Lebanon; her mother was visiting Madam Husain Sabri in Alexandria.

'But I cannot wait two weeks,' Farouk cried. He hurried to the car and whispered instructions to Omar Fathi who went off to fetch Madam Zulficar. Farouk himself put through a call to the police chief in Alexandria.

At Port Said, Judge Zulficar was saying goodbye to some friends on the ship he had taken for Beirut when a squad of uniformed police marched on board. Their lieutenant had a few words with the British captain, then confronted the astounded judge with an order for his detention. No charge, no explanation, no notice of his protests. Like some criminal, the distinguished jurist was hustled off the ship with passengers crowding the rails to watch the arrest. Meanwhile, Omar Fathi had escorted his wife out of her party in the same mysterious way; she returned home, asking, 'Why has Omar Fathi arrested me?'

When she heard the news of the king's proposal, she kissed Safinaz and gave her consent. Later that night, Judge Zulficar, still complaining that they had treated him like some thief, was summoned to Montazah Palace where he reluctantly agreed to the marriage. However, they should wait for several years, he insisted.

'We shall marry later this year,' Farouk announced, over-ruling him. Judge Zulficar did manage to fix the date as far forward as he could. The wedding would take place on the twelfth of January 1938.

Still, Nazli had not been informed. Not till Farouk had returned to Kubbah and woke her, did she learn about his engagement. It annoyed her that other people knew about her son's marriage before she did. But she objected on different grounds: Farouk and Safinaz were marrying far too young. 'I would prefer you to wait until you are thirty before getting married,' she said.

'Then you do not approve of this marriage?'

'I do not disapprove. Safinaz is a fine girl, better than you a thousand times. But neither of you is ready for marriage. You may be a king in the eyes of your people, but to me you are still a small boy. Marriage is the end of youth and the beginning of manhood, and you are not yet a man. The tastes of a boy, as far as women are concerned, change a hundred times before he reaches manhood. You have no experience, and I don't wish you to marry this girl and then desert her without any fault on her part.'

Farouk promised he would never look at other women; he would remain faithful to Safinaz all his life. In any case, he added, his courtiers had advised him to marry as quickly as possible.

'Your court does not know you as well as I do,' his mother retorted. 'You have been a prisoner in the palace all your life. You saw the Pyramids only last year. Now you are out of the prison and will not be satisfied with your home or with one woman. My heart tells me that this marriage will not be successful.'

'If you have nothing personally against Safinaz, this means you approve. The whole country wants me to marry.'

'That is because they want to have another celebration. I say you should not marry for at least another five years, and I know that Safinaz would also be willing to wait if I talked to her.'

'I won't wait five minutes,' Farouk snapped. 'Everyone wants me to marry, except you and Hassanain.'

'Yes, Hassanain has told me he advised you not to be in such a hurry. He also said your outlook on women would change and would not become fixed until you were thirty.'

'Hassanain is foolish. I have made up my mind and will not go back on my wish.'

The following day, the government announced the marriage date. Henceforth, Safinaz would take the name Farida (the Flawless One) in accordance with the family tradition, and superstition. It was a love name, Farouk told her. The Mohamed Ali family expressed its misgivings about the marriage; the king might have chosen his queen from among them, instead of people without royal blood. The country rejoiced, however. It approved Farouk's choice when the newspapers published pictures of the attractive girl who would be queen.

For Farida, the days that followed her engagement were her happiest. Farouk still acted the part of Prince Charming, escorting her to soirées and dances; even his restless, fickle nature pleased her. Half-way to a party, on an impulse, he would turn about and make for the desert. Hassanain had inspired a love for the desert in him and he delighted in driving flat out for hours. He was intelligent, witty, and generous. But that was in those early days. Long before the wedding, he began to change; she detected a hardening of his nature, sometimes even a cruel streak. And he appeared to interest himself more in the programme and the ceremony of the wedding than in his fiancée. Sometimes, he seemed to prefer the company of his Italian servants to her's.

From the servants, Farouk was learning how he should treat his bride. Only the weak, they said, listen to their wives, or discuss things with them; the strong man commands and the wife has to obey. One said he had beaten his wife on their wedding night for no reason; after that she had given him no trouble. The impressionable Farouk took this advice and, before long, his wish to dominate Farida led to quarrels. His behaviour, too, caused Farida to doubt if she had made the right decision. One night, driving together in Alexandria, the headlights of their car picked out a cat's eyes on the road; he might have slowed down or avoided the animal, instead he accelerated and drove straight over it, leaving it dead on the road. Farida then felt she was marrying a callous man.

Farida and her family tried to make the king at home. With such a capricious character this proved impossible. Madam Zulficar would arrange a meal for him, he would dash in for two or three minutes then say, 'Keep something hot for me. I'm just going off with Pulli and will be back in an hour.' They would see nothing of him until the next day. He appeared fidgety, always on the move, forever indulging some new collecting mania or experimenting with new gadgets which he ordered from Europe and America. Even at that time, Farida began to sense that he was abusing her love for him; she had the impression that his servants and confidants had convinced him he had raised her from a lower rank to the status of a queen and this was the price she had to pay. They had their lovers' tiffs which culminated in a row on the eve of their marriage. Describing this, later, to the Egyptian editor and publisher, Mustapha Amin, Farida said she told Farouk bluntly she would never become his slave. 'I do not know Farouk, the king, but I know Farouk, the man,' she said. 'People admire the man for his way of behaving, not for the crown he wears.' Farouk scarcely paid attention; he stalked out, leaving her crying.

'I stayed in my room, weeping, alone,' Farida told Amin. 'People were dancing in the streets. Every street had a party, and the whole of Cairo was lighted. Everything was lighted except my heart. I felt that all the world envied me because I would be a queen the next day. I didn't know what to do. I made up my mind to call him and tell him I had decided not to marry him, but I was afraid he would revenge himself on my family. I did not sleep at all that night, and lay awake feeling I was going through hell for the sake of my family. I had read *Joan of Arc* and had the same feeling that she had the night before they burned her. I knew that queens were not happy, but my pain was more than a human being could bear.'

Farouk and his four sisters on their arrival in England for the coronation of King George VI and Queen Elizabeth 1937

Farouk at Saint Moritz

Farouk wearing the summer
uniform of Field Marshal

It was too late; Farida's family convinced her that she must go through with the marriage.

The next day, millions turned out to see Farida, in a Paris wedding dress of white, silvered lace with a train more than fifteen feet long, passing in her carriage to Kubbah Palace where the ceremony would take place. Her veil had been worn by the Empress Eugénie and given as a gift to one of Ismail's daughters at the opening of the Suez Canal. She wore a diamond tiara and a necklace which had cost Farouk a fortune. Farida was conducted to a room adjoining the marriage salon where she broke Moslem tradition by watching the ceremony. The king would not, in fact, see his bride until after the wedding, since a woman has no place at a Mohamedan marriage. Farouk, in the black and gold uniform of an Egyptian Field Marshal, waited for the contract to be sworn; with him were his witnesses, Ali Maher and Saad Zulficar, the Grand Chamberlain.

First, the bride's father received an envelope containing half the royal dowry. Then Farouk and Judge Zulficar shook hands, pressing their right thumbs against each other; Sheikh el-Maraghi, representing the Church, threw a green silk cloth over their joined hands.

'I betroth you to my daughter, Farida,' Judge Zulficar said.

'I accept her betrothal to myself from thee, and take her under my care and bind myself to offer her my protection, and ye who are present bear witness.' Three times the king spoke the words. Nothing then remained but the signing of the marriage contract. The king and his queen, now united, descended the long staircase; a white flag was run up to the palace masthead, and the guns of Abbassiah began firing a hundred and one times to salute the new queen.

Gifts had showered on them from all over the world. Hitler presented them with a Mercedes sports car; King George sent tennis and squash rackets and a set of golf clubs. ('Why golf clubs when they know I can't play the game?'). The British royal family also sent jewellery for the queen, and Sir Miles Lampson gave Farouk a pair of Purdie shotguns which he did prize. From

Italy he had a bust of Diocletian; from Arabia a stable of the finest horses. His presents filled a drawing-room at Abdin; the gold and jewelled ornaments were estimated to be worth more than a million pounds.

The whole of Egypt celebrated. The peasants had a rare feast of meat from sacrificial bullocks; in Cairo huge marquees stayed open day and night to feed more than a hundred thousand poor people at Farouk's behest; fireworks punched trails of light through the cold blue evening above the Nile; the king's handsome profile was traced by thousands of coloured bulbs across the façade of the Rio Cinema; the post office quickly sold out of stamps commemorating the marriage. Beneath the palace balcony the crowd fought a battle of flowers and yelled their delight when the king and queen made an appearance together, something of a revolution in strict Moslem circles. Farida wore only the scantiest veil, another break with tradition. For three days the celebrations went on; crowds packed open-air theatres to hear the great cabaret artiste, Badia; at nights they slept in the parks or the squares of the city.

Farouk seemed aptly named. In those days he could do no wrong. Every house flaunted his portrait, sometimes a handsome full-faced youth with a small moustache, wearing morning dress and a red tarbush, at others a striking figure in full military regalia. He also appeared to everyone to be carrying out the pledges he had made on his accession. Workers on his royal estates now had good housing in model villages; he gave away hundreds of acres of his own land to the peasants; new Farouk schools and hospitals sprang up in cities and villages; he moved among them at Friday prayers, something his father had never done. On one occasion, he handed his new prayer rug to a poor man in exchange for his own and astonished him by saying, 'In the eyes of God all men are equal.' He spoke their own tongue, not like a sheikh or a scholar, in high-flown language, but so that they could understand it.

Stories about him spread throughout the country; in a few months the Egyptians, renowned myth-makers, had created several legends around their king. The piastres he tossed to the poor in Cairo as he drove past gained interest with each telling; and had he not given millions of pairs of shoes to the peasants? He had, indeed, distributed seven thousand pounds to buy shoes, but no one among his courtiers told him how few of his barefooted subjects would benefit. When several people were killed and injured in the crush watching him reviewing troops in Cairo, he visited the patients in hospital and sent personal cheques to the next-of-kin of the dead. Behind him, inspiring most of these actions, was Hassanain. None the less, the people worshipped him, giving him the title of Farouk the Beloved.

He had to unveil a statue to his father in Alexandria and had not seen the sculptor's work, so the day before, he went to look. As he made to lift the cloth veiling the statue a guard stopped him. 'You have no right to touch that,' he said.

'And why not?'

'Because my king is unveiling it tomorrow.'

'Don't you think I look like the king?'

'Nothing like him.'

'Not even a vague resemblance.'

'Never.'

'If I told you I was the king, would you believe it?'

'No. It's a hot afternoon and the king is snoring in his palace.' Farouk gave him a slap on the back. 'Well, I am the king and I'm not snoring and you will see the proof tomorrow.'

He had another title: Farouk the Pious. The miniature Koran he carried in his pocket was reputed to have saved him in the summer of 1938 when a Syrian student shot at him as he was leaving a swimming pool in Alexandria. Another time he was visiting the home of a former tutor in Alexandria when a lorry crashed into his parked car. 'You were lucky,' the tutor remarked. 'Oh, nothing would have happened to me. I had my Koran in my breast pocket.' Who could guess then that Farouk was putting on yet another disguise, striking another public attitude?

Only his intimates began to discern in his daily routine the genesis of the dual personality which became marked later on. He appeared to desire to turn his life inside-out, sleeping all morning

99

and wandering the city at night. A few hours at his desk and he would itch to summon Pulli and other Italian servants and drive to some restaurant or night-club. Often, he did not return to his palace until dawn when he would ring for a valet to prepare a snack before he went to bed. He might eat caviar, chicken or a thick steak, several ice-creams, and drink half a gallon of sweet fruit juice at this hour. Rarely did his bell ring again until midday when Pulli would answer it. Pulli was fast becoming the king's *homme à tout faire*. He would have done the rounds with Farouk the previous evening but would have risen early in case of a royal summons. He never proffered advice, never questioned an order, never failed when the king wanted something. He was the perfect servant. He would bring breakfast, a tray of thirty boiled eggs, toast and sweet tea. The king would eat perhaps four eggs by which time the others would be cold; Pulli would bring another tray with as many eggs again, and this ritual continued until Farouk wished to tackle his second and subsequent courses – lobster, steak, lamb chop, chicken, quail, pigeons – the breakfast became a morning banquet. Yet, within a few hours the king would feel the pangs of hunger again. No one who had a late lunch, or dinner, with Farouk ever forgot the virtuosity with which he put away food. And drinks. In a day he would get through more than thirty bottles of sweet, fizzy lemonade or orangeade, often grabbing the bottle and pumping it up and down until the pressure rose and it spilled over. Then he would down the bottle at a gulp. He seemed unhappy when not eating and would carry a bag of toffees which he would munch. He might have used these, however, as a substitute for the cigarettes he did not allow himself to smoke in public.

This obsessive eating had its effect. It did not, as appeared to some people, suddenly transform Farouk from the handsome, willowy youth into a jowly, puffy Gargantua; it gradually laid down fat on his chest and stomach. One of those who noticed his growing corpulence was a certain Major Mohamed Neguib who, in 1938, had taken over the Military Museum in Cairo. Of their first meeting he wrote, 'Farouk, whose acquisitive instincts were even stronger than his father's, had decided to start a private collection of his own. I was ordered to drive down to Alexandria where he was spending the summer to present him with two truckloads of exhibits. Farouk was eighteen at the time and I was thirty-seven. It was a very hot day, and the king was taking a bath when my men and I arrived at Montazah palace. We were told to unload our trucks and await His Majesty in the palace garden. Although we were in full uniform, in spite of the heat, Farouk chose to appear before us naked from the waist up, wearing nothing but a sun helmet, slacks and sandals without socks.

'Among the contents of the trucks were two small guns. One was a brass cannon dating from the reign of Ismail, Farouk's grandfather; the other was a whale gun of about the same period. My soldiers were so nervous in the king's presence that I held the guns in my own hands for fear they might drop them.'

' "Oh, Major, you're so strong," Farouk said. "What do you eat? Beans?" '

'He then held the guns in his own hands to show that he was just as strong as I was. As he did so, I was struck by the flabbiness of his muscles and the rolls of fat on his chest. I was twice his age, but my body was in far better condition.'

Why did Farouk stuff himself with food and soft drinks? Undoubtedly he inherited part of this trait. All his family were great trenchermen and his father had been a stubby, stout man. Did he feel, like many of his subjects, that a fat king was a great king and his prestige would increase with his girth? Hardly likely, since his reputation in those days needed no boost. Was it the compulsive gourmandising of the neurotic who feels insecure, unloved or frustrated? Here we come closer to the reason for Farouk's perpetual hunger; we can catch the echoes of his childhood when, deprived of food and water, he escaped into the harem and raided his mother's refrigerator.

The problem had, however, deeper psychological roots. Farouk the king, who must embody perfection, realised soon after his marriage that nature had dealt shabbily with him. His classical good looks, his handsome figure, his powerful physique, his restless desire to live – all these seemed to mock him for his lack of sexual development, his lack of virility. Effeminate was the euphemism Fuad used to describe the boy Farouk to his nephew, Prince Abbas Halim. It worried the king so much that he invited several doctors to treat Farouk for his lack of manhood. They shrugged. Perhaps they might try virilising hormones. But these had only been used experimentally and who could say if they would help. Would they not also produce side-effects? Fuad dropped the idea.

For the average man it would have been a blow; for a king, a tragedy; for a king in an oriental country where masculinity and virility are vaunted, and lack of them ridiculed, it was unbearable. It bred in Farouk a sense of inferiority and with this the fixation that no one must know; the frustrations drove him to seek other forms of pleasure and finally perverted his judgement. Those who saw him change in his early twenties argued that he had glandular trouble; as we shall see, there are grounds for deducing that Farouk did suffer from a hormone disorder which affected his behaviour and caused obesity.

For the moment, however, he could ignore, if not forget his disability. The people revered him; he loved his queen who was expecting his child. But even that occasion was marred when the queen went into labour and they had to hunt for the king to tell him. Of course he had disappeared with Pulli, this time pursuing his current passion of salvaging old cannons; it took them a day and part of the night to trace him. He was lying asleep on the beach, the other side of Alexandria from Montazah, exhausted by the effort of recovering an old Napoleonic howitzer and dragging it up from the foreshore. He got back in time for the birth, on the seventeenth of November. It was a baby daughter, not the heir he had hoped for. He stood, a bleak figure, outside the operating room as the guns boomed twenty-one salvos; for a son it would have been a hundred and one. In Cairo they heard the salute stop at the twenty-first salvo, then a few minutes later a battery began to fire again. 'It's a boy,' the crowd shouted. No, the artillery commander at Abbassiah had heard the news later than the other gunnery officers and had fired after the appointed time.

Farouk hid his disappointment. 'It will be loved just the same,' he muttered. He called the baby Ferial, after his paternal grand-mother. Every child born that day in Egypt received one pound from the king; the poor had free food and clothing, the children sweets.

CHAPTER EIGHT

For, of a truth, mighty was Pharaoh in the land, and one who committed excesses. (X: 84)

ONE afternoon, early in March 1939, the Minister of the Interior, Mahmud Fahmy el-Nokrashi pasha, sought an interview with his prime minister at which he handed him a secret report from the police. The premier, Mohamed Mahmud pasha, ran an eye over it, picked up the phone and requested an immediate appointment with the king. The report stated that Farouk had several times visited cheap night-clubs with his Italian servants; if he persisted in frequenting such places, the Ministry of the Interior could no longer vouch for his safety. The premier had to act; the king's conduct and his associations with the Italian clique perturbed not only his government; at the British Embassy, Sir Miles Lampson was muttering darkly about their influence, their backstairs politics and their links with fascist Italy. Nevertheless, Mohamed Mahmud did not relish warning the king against his confidants.

A few days later, when he entered the panelled study at Abdin, he opened his interview with another point. As prime minister, he did not care for the speech the king had made to mark the beginning of the Arabic new year. Nor did the people. 'It was a mistake to deliver a speech which was not seen by the prime minister,' he remarked. Then, thinking one of the palace staff had prepared the address, he added, 'The man who wrote it for you doesn't deserve to be a letter writer in the bazaar.'

At this, Farouk bridled. 'I wrote it myself,' he cried.

'Since when does the king write his own speeches?'

'There is nothing against you in the speech. It was against Ali Maher.'

'Do you think it is right for the king to quarrel with his government?'

Farouk shrugged. All right, he would let Mahmud see his speeches before giving them in future. Was this the urgent problem that had brought the prime minister to see him?

'No,' said the premier. 'There is a more serious problem. The government wishes to get Verrucci out of the palace.'

'Why?' Farouk sounded incredulous.

'Because he has a bad reputation, and as prime minister I cannot approve of men with bad reputations associating with the king.'

'What do you mean – bad reputation?' Farouk asked.

'There are stories about his dealings with women, about procuring women for people.'

'Is he supposed to bring women to someone in the palace?'

'Frankly, I don't know.'

'Well, he does not bring them to me,' said Farouk.

Mahmud warned Farouk that people were beginning to speak openly about him, and this might damage his prestige in the public eye. He went on, 'There is another thing: the king must not visit night-clubs.'

'But I am a democratic king.'

'Going to night-clubs is not democracy.'

Farouk looked at him. 'Don't you ever get tired of your home and want a change?'

'I don't sit in night-clubs. Anyway, the queen does not approve. Every woman likes her husband to keep his dignity.'

'Where do I go?' Farouk asked. 'Everyone goes to night-clubs, why not me? The Duke of Windsor used to visit night-clubs.'

'Perhaps that's one of the reasons they forced him to abdicate,' Mahmud retorted. He stressed that his government could not hold itself responsible for the king's security if he continued his night-club visits.

'Does anyone want to kill me?' said Farouk.

'No, but suppose some drunk comes and strikes you, what can the police do with such a man? He will say, "I couldn't imagine that you were a king, because kings don't normally go to night-clubs". If I were the judge hearing the case, I should have to acquit him.'

'Thanks be to Allah that you are not the judge.'

Farouk's quip broke the tension. Mahmud, the elder statesman even in his father's day, talked frankly and less formally to him. 'These Italians will do you no good,' he said. 'People will wonder why you cannot find Egyptians to act as companions, so why do this in front of your people. They will assume these people are bringing women to you.'

'Is that what the queen says?'

'If the queen says it, the people will soon say the same. If you had chosen respectable people, no one would have mentioned it.'

Farouk lit a cigarette without, as he normally did, offering one to Mahmud. He puffed nervously. 'I shall tell you something I have not told anyone before. I regretted my marriage the very next day. I felt that it had not been a success, that I had failed.'

The premier murmured that such reaction and sentiments were normal; they would vanish as he settled down to married life.

'Unfortunately, the differences between us are increasing every day,' said Farouk. 'What did you do when you were bored at home?'

Mahmud replied that he sought the company of men like Saad Zaghlul and his associates, and advised the king to make the same sort of friends. Farouk ended the audience by promising to dismiss the servants gradually; to do it too quickly would lead people to assume that the government had forced his hand. Some weeks later, the palace announced that Ernesto Verrucci had resigned his post as architect to the royal palaces of his own accord. However, Pulli and Caro and Pietro and Cafazzi stayed.

Even in Mahmud's version of the interview, the king had struck a stubborn attitude to advice from a politician he had inherited from Fuad and whom he accepted as a friend. Nevertheless, his cabinet advisers noted a change in his habits; he kept more to the palace and stopped his excursions to nightclubs; he even took Farida on a Joy Day cruise in the Mahroussa. When they returned to Cairo, he complained of feeling tired and his doctors discovered he had caught chickenpox. Despite warnings that she might catch the illness, Farida nursed him at his bedside and, a day or two later, fell ill herself. When Farouk had recovered, he remarked to Mohamed Mahmud, 'You don't really appreciate your wife until you are ill.' As he had done in the first days of his engagement, he began to take Farida with him: to an English Opera Group performance in Cairo, to the tennis championships at Gezira, to parties in the noble palaces of Gezira, Garden City and Zamalek.

One evening, he went with the queen to Kubra Palace, a magnificent piece of arabesque architecture in pink brick which lay in the Kubbah quarter. The palace, with its mixture of French, Turkish and Persian furnishings, its medieval ceilings enchanted the queen. 'I shall make you a present of it,' Farouk said, grandly. He forced his cousin, Prince Mohamed Tahir, to strike a ridiculous bargain and the palace changed hands for forty thousand pounds. Before the sale, the king sent his surveyors to make a report on the building. When they had departed the prince noticed that silver articles worth about fifteen hundred pounds had vanished. Who could call the king or his men thieves? He said nothing. Farouk named the palace El-Tahra and placed it in Farida's name. Was it a gift, or a bribe? Some contended he offered it so that she might overlook his associations with the Italian servants. He could not see that a bribe would fail with a proud woman like Farida, who still reproached him for spending too much time with the Italians, when he had promised to get rid of them. Enmity between her and the servant clique grew more bitter and helped to poison the relations between her and Farouk.

Before long, Mohamed Mahmud was reminding the king of his vow to kick the Italians out, and taking him to task over still another piece of strange behaviour. The prime minister had been sitting on the government bench listening to a debate when he spotted a figure entering the visitors' gallery in the Chamber of Deputies. He nudged Ahmed Maher pasha, one of his ministers, and pointed to the balcony on which the man was leaning. Both ministers could hardly believe their eyes; it was Farouk. The prime minister had to speak to the parliamentary motion; as soon as he had finished his secretary told him the king was waiting for him in his room.

Farouk was grinning. 'Did you see me during the debate?' he asked innocently.

'Yes, I did,' Mahmud replied. 'You had no right to be there.'

'Why not? Surely the king has the same rights as anyone else?'

Mahmud shook his head. 'You can only attend parliament during the opening and to hear the speech from the throne. It was very dangerous. And you came wearing informal clothes.'

'I was incognito,' Farouk replied. 'No one could recognise me.'

'The members will. They will see you and think you are interested in certain speeches, and it might influence the way they vote.'

The prime minister threatened to resign unless the king understood the role of a constitutional monarch and respected it. Farouk nodded his head. Already, he had determined that Mahmud would have to go. He had even chosen the man to replace him: Ali Maher.

Ali Maher and the king thought with one mind at this time. The chief of the royal cabinet had sketched his vision of Arab unity to Farouk, who had seized on it. From this concept sprang the young king's desire to unify Egypt with other Arab states through a series of marriages. Fawzia, his quiet, obedient sister, was the first. At the beginning of 1939, the heir to the Persian throne, Prince Mohamed Reza Pahlevi, visited Egypt at Farouk's invitation. The king filled the prince's day with official receptions and informal engagements, his evening with banquets and entertainments. Fawzia accompanied the party everywhere, and Farouk did not conceal his wish for the young couple to get to know each other. He was overjoyed when his sister came to say that the prince had asked her to marry him.

Nazli resisted the idea. She scoffed at the thought of Farouk as the Caliph of the Moslems, declaring that a marriage arranged by politicians could only lead to unhappiness. Farouk settled the argument by sending for Fawzia and putting the question to her. The girl, then seventeen, answered that she would obey the king's wish. The ceremony took place at Abdin Palace on the fifteenth of March, Egyptian Independence Day and the then Shah's birthday. Before the marriage, Sheikh el-Maraghi made a plea for

108

unity between the two Moslem sects of Egypt and Persia. Farouk, in tails, pinstripe grey trousers and tarbush, represented his sister and signed the contract on her behalf.

He and Ali Maher envisaged this as the first of their series of marriages which would make the Middle East look for its leadership to Cairo and to them. Faiza, they thought, would marry a son of King Abdullah of Jordan; they would find other political partners for the other two sisters; even Ferial, his infant daughter, Farouk considered would make a bride for Faisal of Iraq when they both came of age.

Religious unity must march hand in hand with political ties, according to the second part of Ali Maher's grand design. Sheikh el-Maraghi never tired of repeating to the faithful how devout, how zealous, how reverential was the King of Egypt. So the sheikhs began to whisper that Farouk might assume the title of Caliph of Islam, protector of the faith, spiritual head of the Moslem world of three hundred million souls. The office had lapsed since the deposition of the Turkish Sultan, though Fuad had convened a conference in 1926 to discuss its restoration, hoping to gain the office himself. Farouk, too, saw the caliphate as a way of extending his empire. In January 1939 he led prayers as Imam, the caliph's designate, at al-Qusun mosque in Cairo. He had gathered the Emirs of the Yemen and Saudi Arabia as well as Egyptian political and religious leaders. Spontaneously – or so it appeared – the congregation rose and proclaimed Farouk their Caliph. Though this demonstration carried no significance, Farouk dropped at once into his new role; he began to grow a beard and wear a long cloak and assume the pious expression of a spiritual leader.

Farouk and Ali Maher could sit back and congratulate themselves. Mohamed Mahmud had resigned for health reasons and Maher had become premier; in two years, the king had smothered *Wafd* aspirations and now ruled the country as he willed; ultimately, he could see himself head of the Arab world. Of course, he still had to contend with the British, though he and Ali Maher foresaw an end to that problem. They could leave Germany and Italy to take care of the occupation forces. Ali

Maher took the view that Munich had only bought time for the Western democracies who would soon find themselves embroiled in a war against the fascist dictatorships. Of that war there could only be one outcome, according to the prime minister; a British defeat. Farouk accepted this reading of international politics which tinged every one of his actions during the first years of the war. They could rely on the Germans and Italians to cope with Britain. And had not Mussolini described Italy and Egypt as 'Two peoples united by the same sea?' The palace and the government of Ali Maher could afford to condone, if not encourage, the massive propaganda build-up by Italy and Germany in the months before the war. They promoted exchanges between the three countries. To Egypt came Marshal Balbo of Italy and Dr Joseph Goebbels of Germany; throughout the country, anti-British demonstrations took place, whipped up by el-Banna's Moslem Brethren and supported even by *Wafd* newspapers. Everyone looked the other way when reports reached Cairo that the Italians had massed a hundred thousand men on the Western desert frontier and were even landing aircraft in Egypt to reconnoitre airfields.

When Germany invaded Poland and Britain declared war, Sir Miles Lampson called on Ali Maher to take the necessary steps to implement Article Eight of the 1936 Treaty which stated that Egypt would aid Britain in the event of war. A state of siege was declared and the country split into military districts. German nationals were arrested and their property confiscated. Ali Maher delivered a typical tongue-in-cheek speech to the Egyptian parliament which opened six weeks later. 'At the start of this new session, while the war is raging around us, it is a pleasure for me to repeat to you that collaboration with our ally will be in the future as it has always been in the past, our best guide in the accomplishment of our task. Our ally will therefore receive from us every possible assistance.'

No one in government circles doubted where Ali Maher's real loyalty lay. Or Farouk's.

CHAPTER NINE

*It needs not that I swear by the Lord of the East and of
the West that we have power.*
*To replace them with better than themselves: neither are
we to be hindered.*　　　　　　　　　　　　(LXX: 40 and 41)

IF Farouk imagined the war would present him with the
opportunity to settle scores with Britain he had miscalculated
badly. So long as the country remained reasonably stable, con-
fining its quarrels to the square mile of Cairo encompassing
Abdin Palace and the Chamber of Deputies, the British meddled
very little. They cast a tolerant eye on the king's misdemeanours
in private and his bid for absolute rule. Between the
palace and the *Wafd* what was there to choose? They contented
themselves with gentle suggestions about political corruption
and improving the lot of the fellahin. But a possible threat to the
Canal Base! That they could not ignore. The mere hint that
German and Italian divisions might move into Suez and shut the
gate between Britain and the Far East brought troops from every
part of the Commonwealth into the Delta and the Western Desert.
During the period of the 'phoney war' Britain's front line lay as
much astride the barbed wire separating Egypt from Libya as
along the Channel coast. Far from helping to solve Farouk's
problems, the war heightened them; it pointed him on a crash
course with Britain and forced him into direct conflict with the
formidable personality of Sir Miles Wedderburn Lampson, British
Ambassador and last of the pro-consuls.

Lampson had not long arrived from China to act as High
Commissioner when Farouk encountered him for the first time
at an air force display outside Cairo. It was 1934; Farouk was
fourteen and Lampson just forty years older. The young prince
appeared to take an instant dislike to the towering figure who
stood about seven feet tall, measured from his spatted shoes to his

111

sleek black topper. The High Commissioner's laboured small-talk about the British part in the display sounded to the prince like a history tutorial at Kubbah. When he returned to the palace, his sick father asked him whom he had met and how he liked the display. Obliquely, the boy answered, 'I liked the German and the Swedish ambassadors best.' Fuad rasped at him, 'It's not your place to like anyone better than another. It is up to you to get on with everyone.' His father's advice went unheeded. At no time did Farouk ever try to conquer his antipathy towards Lampson, not even when the ambassador introduced him to duck-shooting. As High Commissioner he had personified those unreadable tomes about British Army regiments or flags which the young prince received, bound in calfskin and monogrammed in gold, every birthday; as Ambassador, he represented duty and authority against which the young king rebelled; he embodied the power which the would-be autocrat resented. To a young king in quest of adventure or fun Lampson symbolised something more subtle – the voice of conscience. 'He still treats me like a schoolboy,' Farouk lamented. And later, with a flash of wit, he remarked, 'What that man does not realise is that I am the power behind the throne.' Lampson would take the edge off this witticism.

Ironically, the Ambassador was the sort of Briton Farouk really admired, the type he might have wished to be himself. Lampson stood out in any company, whether holding the floor with some anecdote at a diplomatic cocktail party, trying his hand in the baccarat room of the Royal Automobile Club, or duck-shooting with the best guns in Egypt. He based his diplomacy on unswerving integrity coupled with shrewdness and persistence. A crisis immediately evoked the best in him and he could toil round the clock yet turn out fresh and immaculate the next day. His high-point came in 1936 when he pushed through the treaty of independence after many others had tried and failed. It abolished his own post of High Commissioner and the Residency, converting him to an ambassador. It is easy to say now that Lampson should have disappeared with the residency. Egypt had a new deal and a new king; it should have

112

had a new man, untainted with the old ways. But so impressed were Egyptian politicians with Lampson that they asked Britain to appoint him the new ambassador. If he still carried the imprint of the High Commissioner he could justify this by pointing to the ten thousand troops and RAF squadrons on the Canal Zone, and the pitifully inadequate Egyptian defence forces.

To a young king, accustomed to bowing and scraping ministers and officials, Lampson might have seemed high-handed. For his part, the ambassador refused to truckle to the king's whims. 'Leave the boy to me,' he would say to the Foreign Office if pressed for some action involving Farouk. The king, however, often appeared to delight in tantalising the ambassador. Lampson once wished to make an urgent appointment and telephoned the venerable Said Zulficar pasha, who had served five Egyptian rulers. The king could not possibly see his excellency for at least a week, the chamberlain said, echoing Farouk's order. 'I will not take this sort of treatment from that boy,' Lampson shouted. A few minutes later, Farouk stepped into the chamberlain's office. 'So I'm "that boy",' he muttered; he had overheard the conversation on the extension.

Before the war, relations between the embassy and the palace had become strained to the point where the king and Lampson hated each other so much that it poisoned Anglo-Egyptian diplomacy. With increasing contempt and some concern, Lampson watched the king frittering away his mornings in bed, his nights going the rounds with his seedy crowd of servants, like some low-life Harun el-Rashid. In Lampson's view, the king was an irresponsible playboy who might jeopardise his own throne; he certainly would not threaten British interest if he could help it.

The feud between the two men had spiteful overtones. Farouk spotted the first of the new British battledresses and, with his schoolboy craze to try anything novel, he sent an ADC to the embassy to fetch one. 'What does he want with a battledress?' Sir Miles said, dispatching the man empty-handed. What indeed? In those days when Cairo streets resounded with anti-British slogans and demonstrations, the king would hardly have dared drive one of his British cars out of the palace grounds. Then, he wanted one of the new twenty-five-pounder field guns to add to his collection. Request again refused. Farouk brooded over these incidents. One week-end he was shooting alongside the ambassador and had brought down several duck; he patted the stock of his gun and shouted to Lampson in the next butt, 'You see – German gun.'

Farouk caused talk with his collecting which, up to now, had stopped short of actual thieving. When German houses were sequestrated and marked with a red cross, the sight proved too much for Farouk. After dusk, he and his servants would procure the keys, open the doors and loot whatever they fancied. He tried to trick Russell pasha, the Chief of Police and a man who had devoted most of his life to Egypt; during the first crisis in the Delta, the British Embassy appealed for weapons and ammunition for the home guard. The king telephoned Russell pasha, requesting a look at the collection. As soon as the police-man's back had turned, a lorry arrived and carted the best guns off to the palace. Knowing the king's acquistive habits, Russell sent a polite note demanding the return of the weapons. They were recovered, though a mountain of confiscated material did find its way to the vaults of Abdin and Kubbah to be catalogued and stored by the assiduous Pulli. Russell pasha saw so much of this form of appropriation that he, too, lost respect for the king. 'I refuse to parade before that thief,' he muttered once when the king was reviewing the police. And he stayed away.

The British Ambassador might overlook the king's private peccadilloes; he could not afford to condone the use of his palace as a clearing-house for military intelligence to the enemy. Through the secret service, the embassy and military headquarters knew that neither the palace nor the Ali Maher government could be trusted. They had proof that Maher was passing information through one of his ministers who made a weekly trip to Ankara. Since Fuad's day, few people doubted that the prime minister had sold his services to the Italians. Nor was he alone. Ismail Sidki pasha also received a handsome retainer from Rome; and Aziz el-Masri, chief of the Egyptian general staff, always carried a wallet bulging with lira. When Italy entered the war at the beginning of June 1940, the prime minister dragged his feet instead of expelling Italian diplomats and interning their nationals. Count Mazzolini, the Italian Minister, hung on for the best part of a month while Maher temporised, waiting for the invasion. After all, he was a king's man, and Farouk's father had lodged a considerable fortune in Italian banks.

Finally, the British Government had to act. In a note to Farouk it demanded the dismissal of Ali Maher for his failure to collaborate under the terms of the treaty. On the twenty-second of June 1940 he resigned because 'for reasons outside our will and that of the Egyptian people, we see it is impossible to remain in power. This is why I have to tender my resignation to Your August Majesty, with the firm hope that, under the aegis of Your Majesty, the country will emerge from this crisis with its head high.' Still convinced that the Axis would triumph, Maher delivered an anti-British speech to the Senate which effectively ended his political career while the British influenced Egyptian politics. Farouk called on Hasan Sabry pasha, an old associate of Nahas and the *Wafd*, though now an independent. His coalition came to some understanding with Britain, but he lasted only four months. While reading the king's speech, within five yards of Farouk, Hasan Sabry collapsed and died. The speech, the shortest ever made, promised co-operation with Britain 'both in letter and spirit'. The succeeding government, under Husain Sirry pasha, also conciliated the British.

In those days, though, Cairo and Alexandria took their temperatures from the fighting front. An allied reverse and politicians grew restive. With customary brashness, Nahas had already demanded a promise that Britain would clear out of Egypt after the war; the Foreign Office gave this piece of blackmail short shrift. In September 1940 when Marshal Rodolfo Graziani punched through the frontier to Sidi Barani, students fêted the Italian victory in the streets and several more politicians defected from the British camp. Things grew quieter when General Sir Richard O'Connor made a brilliant counter-stroke, capturing thirty-eight thousand Italians, four hundred guns and fifty tanks for a few hundred killed and wounded, and when Field Marshal

Sir Archibald Wavell thrust into Cyrenaica and destroyed the Italian army. The arrival of General Erwin Rommel in the spring of 1941 swung the situation back in the favour of the Axis, and again Egyptians began to gamble on a British defeat. After Rommel had taken Tobruk and was pursuing the Eighth Army towards Sidi Barani, Hitler suddenly ordered his armies into Russia. For the Allies in the Middle East, this began the blackest period of the war. To informed Egyptian opinion, it looked as though King Farouk and Ali Maher had reasoned correctly after all. Even the British in the Canal Zone seemed resigned. Cairo started to speculate about the consequences of an Anglo-Russian debacle; it troubled them little, for most people viewed Germany as the least of the evils.

The capital had become a cosmopolis of spies. They were everywhere: in the embassies, in the palace, in military head-quarters. Anthony Eden, the Foreign Secretary, who arrived in Cairo to discuss switching troops to help Greece, received a cable from Churchill which said, '... While you are on the spot you should deal faithfully with Egyptian Prime Minister, Farouk, and anyone else about our security requirements. It is intolerable that the Rumanian Legation should become a nest of Hun spies, or that the Canal Zone should be infested by enemy agents. I am relying on you to put a stop to all this ill-usage we are receiving at the hands of those we have saved.'

One Egyptian leader who fervently hoped the days of the British were over was General Azziz el-Masri, the king's former military tutor. Even as chief of the Egyptian general staff, he scarcely concealed his pro-Axis sympathies and contacted every anti-British faction, from the Moslem Brethren to saboteurs like Lieutenant Anwar el-Sadat. Masri also kept in touch with the Italians and the Germans in Libya. Proof that he worked for the other side came when British troops captured the head-quarters of Italian General Maletto at Sidi Barani. There, they unearthed a top-secret letter, sent to el-Masri by Sir Henry Maitland (Jumbo) Wilson, the C-in-C British Troops in Egypt. The Egyptian commander was dismissed his post, though he still remained a focus for action to oust the British.

In March 1941 a Wehrmacht agent contacted him at his home. The Germans would help him escape and make use of his military services, he said. By now, el-Masri had another collaborator, the fanatically anti-British el-Sadat, who had graduated with Gamal Abdel Nasser in 1938. Something of the cloak-and-dagger atmosphere of Cairo comes through in el-Sadat's account of how and where they met. El-Sadat, convinced that violence alone would wrest Egypt from Britain, had established secret contact with Hasan el-Banna; the Supreme Guide, quick-stepping from one mysterious rendezvous to another, muffled in his red cloak, had also decided that force would lend point to his religious message, that he would become a political as well as a moral leader. Now his oath was administered with Koran and revolver, his armed phalanxes numbered several hundred. They whispered that palace money had bought some of the German and Italian arms, a rumour which the Egyptian government confirmed a year later when premier Husain Sirry arrested el-Banna and had to release him on Farouk's orders.

Sadat wanted to meet the disgraced el-Masri; el-Banna told him how. He would present himself as a patient at the dental clinic in Saida Zeinab Square of one Dr Ibrahim Hassan, vice-president of the Brethren. When Sadat arrived he found another patient, a tiny rugged figure with striking grey eyes: el-Masri. He told Sadat of the German offer, and the young officer leapt at the opportunity of fomenting a rebellion. They began to scheme the escape. The Germans, said el-Masri, would pick him up by plane from the airstrip near Gabel Rozza on the Siwa Road. The first time they arrived too late; the Germans had landed and departed. The second time their car broke down on the way. The third time they arranged with Squadron-leader Husain Zulficar to steal an Egyptian military plane and fly him out; on take-off, the plane slewed across the runway, hit a post and crashed. El-Masri lay some time in a military hospital on his way to jail for conspiring against the state.

Sadat summed up the plot by saying, 'I still think that, if ill-luck had not so dogged our enterprise, we might have struck a quick blow at the British, joining forces with the Axis and changed the course of events.' For Sadat, however, the end of one abortive conspiracy merely marked the beginning of another. He helped two German spies who set up a transmitter and receiver on a Nile boat and, when they were arrested, he was captured, cashiered and sent into detention.

With the co-operation of Allied intelligence, the Egyptian government rounded up and detained many of the spies and subversive individuals; it sent Ali Maher to rusticate on his country estate and found el-Banna a teaching job in Upper Egypt. From there, however, he still directed the movement.

Still the security leaks continued; still the Italian radio at Bari played back the type of information which could only have emanated from the palace or the government. Rome seemed to know what was happening in the palace and the Chamber of Deputies quicker than British GHQ or the Embassy ten minutes' walk away. How did they pierce the blanket censorship? There was one obvious answer: the palace. At Inchass, the model palace thirty-five miles outside Cairo, the king had, as well as his private zoo, model farm and stables, the most powerful radio equipment in the Middle East. British intelligence soon proved this to be the gap in their security fence; they added a nought to the number of divisions deployed in the Delta, dropped a hint to the palace and waited for Italian reaction. The bewildered re-deployment of troops made certainty out of British suspicion.

Who in the palace? Not unnaturally, the finger pointed to the seventeen Italians working for Farouk. Particularly Pulli, Pietro della Valle and Eduardo Cafazzi, the royal kennelman. When other Italians had quit Egypt or lay in detention, Farouk thought of a stratagem to spite Lampson and the British on behalf of his servants. He conferred Egyptian nationality on all of them. To cap this, he gave his man-of-all-work, Antonio Pulli, the title of bey. He then showed he had lost none of his knack of giving the schoolboy prank an oriental twist by making them pay for their new nationality. Summoning them, he said, 'You know that Moslems are circumcised and Christians are not. I have therefore given the surgeon orders to carry out this operation for you.' He waved aside their protests. 'It is a royal decree,' he said.

118

Pulli, Pietro, Caro and others reluctantly consented, but the kennel-master refused. His first cold drink knocked him out, and he woke up beside the others in a bed in the palace hospital. Farouk was standing in the middle of the ward chortling while his assistant barber was rolling on the floor helpless with laughter. Later the king threw a party, handing out song sheets to the Italians and leading the singing himself.

The king's scheme did not deter the British Ambassador from urging the palace to sack the Italians. Farouk paid no attention to the requests from Husain Sirry or Hassanain and finally Lampson made a personal approach, asking when they would go. The king pointed out they were Egyptian citizens and not Italians. 'I'll get rid of my Italians when he gets rid of his,' he muttered, though after Lampson had departed. The Ambassador had married Jacqueline Aldine Leslie, daughter of the Italian Professor, Count Castellani, in 1934 after the death of his first wife. Lampson was furious when someone repeated the king's insult. It was tit-for-tat, because the Ambassador was not above making undiplomatic remarks or recounting the latest story about Farouk in a voice which carried throughout the roof restaurant of the Semiramis Hotel. To Egyptians he often quoted the Turkish proverb, 'A fish stinks from the head.' When Sheikh el-Maraghi ran, horrified, to complain to a senior British official, Lampson laughed it off. 'I mean the people who are surrounding the king,' he said. He delighted in one story which revealed Farouk's anti-British attitude, and his fear. The king had a recurrent nightmare in which two lions were pursuing him. The dream so troubled him that he went to Ali Maher to ask for an interpretation. Never at a loss to exploit the situation, Ali Maher reminded Farouk which country had a lion as its emblem. The king then sought el-Maraghi's counsel, and the old sheikh told him he could exorcise his dream by shooting several lions. Immediately, Farouk went to the Cairo Zoo and shot every lion there. Did he realise that among them was Jackie, the cub presented to him by the RAF and one of his favourite childhood pets? But the dream continued to haunt him and disturb his sleep; he began to act like someone with a phobia about British troops, studying

119

their dispositions in Egypt as though they might imperil his throne.

He sought distractions. Night after night he would make his way to one of the tables reserved for him in half a dozen night-clubs; his figure was filling out, his face fattening, his hair thinning. He never danced but sat, his eyes roving the length and breadth of the club, sipping orangeade or guava juice. Invariably, he would call for a bowl of pith balls which he would flick at the dancers or cabaret stars, or people at the next table. He had a good eye, and when he scored a hit his guffaw would drown music and talk. The laughter, like the antics, was sad, alas. The behaviour of a man trying to make up for his lost adolescence.

At half a dozen clubs his table stayed empty, by the cabaret floor, until he entered; he would often arrive in one of his many uniforms, in the tawny service dress of an Egyptian Field Marshal, in the blue of an Admiral or the grey-blue of his air force. A deferential pace behind him would come the *fantoche* form of Pulli, in every way his antithesis. The slight, unremarkable figure shrank into Farouk's shadow; the long face smiled when the master boomed with laughter; it nodded at the king's whim; it gestured at waiters to keep the royal glass of orange juice filled; he paid from a choked wallet. Pulli it was who would flit to this or that table to whisper that the king would like the lady to join him, who would ensure she appeared at the place of assignation, who would take her home when the king had finished with her, who would pay her off if necessary. As the king's servant and confidant, Antonio Pulli bey had become one of the most important men in Egypt. Ministers and pashas ran to him when they wanted a favour from Farouk. To his credit it must be said that Pulli did not abuse his position, or Farouk's trust, as much as others.

Some of the king's cronies acted with less scruple. Such was Karim Thabet, perhaps the most evil of all Farouk's clique. Thabet's family came from the Lebanon; his father, a highly respected journalist, had founded the newspaper, *Al Mokkatam*, and trained the son as a newspaperman. If young

Thabet had a talent for writing he had a genius for smooth-talking his way into the right company. Integrity, he soon discovered, was a poor paymaster; the right people wanted to hear the right things about themselves. So Thabet wrote for the British, the Germans, the Italians, the French, for whomever might leave an envelope at their embassy to fatten his wages packet. To him the young king was natural bait. When Farouk was touring Upper Egypt Thabet approached him. The people would like to read a popular life of their boy malik which he would write. Farouk listened, flattered. Hassanain, who knew Thabet's background and distrusted him, scotched the notion.

Thabet had another characteristic: brazen tenacity. Aware that Farouk liked to glean what was happening in the British Embassy and elsewhere, he took to carrying tit-bits of gossip to the palace. During the day Hassanain blocked the door to the king's study; at night, however, Thabet wormed into the royal circle at the Auberge des Pyramides and the other night-clubs. The stunted figure with hunched shoulders, the foxy, knife-blade face could be seen with the king. Farouk would throw his head back and bellow with laughter at Thabet's risqué stories or his corrosive comments about ministers and diplomats. That was power and influence in Egypt. At first it did nothing more than increase the Lebanese's fringe benefits from the embassies, his ransom from contacts who believed he was more than a royal jester; later, his hold on the king became more sinister. That, however, had to wait for changes at the palace.

Why did Farouk choose such company when he realised that a few minutes in his presence conferred power and influence on them, when he turned down embassy parties, when the best families in Cairo were throwing their houses open to him? His prime minister, Husain Sirry, wondered about the question the day in 1941 that his Minister of the Interior brought yet another report about the king's activities. When he tackled Farouk, the king's first reaction was, 'What's the matter? Is it a political crisis?' Sirry produced the report which the king read; he began to laugh. The premier did not share his amusement. 'This is a report that you and Pulli were with two artistes, two foreign girls, at a house in Emad ed-Din Street. You were also with Pulli and two Egyptian dancers in another street in Cairo. Are these incidents true?'

'What if they are?' Farouk said. There the interview ended. Farouk had changed from the diffident boy who had yielded to Mohamed Mahmud two years before; he showed no embarrassment or remorse. It was as if he wanted people to know about his women.

Adding to the apocrypha of stories about Farouk became a favourite game in wartime Cairo. Some of these tales emanated from the servants' quarters of the palace, though the inbred diplomatic community would contribute its share. Embassy officials could dine all round the town on their latest bit of scandal from the royal household. The rococo interior of Shepheard's Hotel buzzed with Farouk stories.

Have you heard? The king has pinched another couple of brass cannons. From the Alexandria Yacht Club. Yes ... he sent a truck and whipped them. Just like that.

D'you know he had Ahmed Sadik, the sequestrator, send him a safe full of gold from an Italian bank. It took six servants to carry it down to the basement at Abdin where the king was waiting to congratulate them and gave them backsheesh. What d'you think he did? Took a handful of gold coins and threw them into a bucket and shouted, 'Fish for those.' They all made a dive and came up screaming and clawing at their hands. HE HAD FILLED THE BUCKET WITH ACID. So-and-So saw their hands.

He's had trouble with Nazli again. She got furious when he didn't turn up to meet her at the station. Threatened to jump from the car which was taking her to Abdin instead of Kubbah. Do you know what she did when he greeted her? Slapped his face and ordered him out. In front of everybody, and him the king. Old Mohamed Ali had to abandon his water colours and his banyan grove and play the peacemaker. It was the chamberlain who ended the row by telling the mother her son was barmy and the son that his mother was capricious. Very Egyptian, don't you think?

You won't believe this one. He's shaved a man with a blow-lamp. One of his barbers. It seems the only thing wrong with the man was that his chest had more hair than the king's. So they stripped him, stretched him out and Farouk shaved him with this blow-lamp. They say the man laughed when he got out of hospital.

Would you guess? He broke his rule last night and had a glass of champagne to celebrate the sinking of the Ark Royal.

You know he has a signed picture of Hitler which he keeps in a drawer. And he's now taken to wearing a German helmet – in the palace, of course. They tell him when Lampson's on the way over to see him, and he puts it on.

Some of the stories went as far back as the British Empire, applying to any country where WOG stood for wily oriental gentleman. Farouk had run into a British army lorry and the driver was giving his evidence. 'Sir,' he said, 'I was proceeding along the Ismailia Road when this car came at me with two wogs in it . . .' The chairman adjourned the court of inquiry to give a sergeant the chance to brief the man properly. He recommenced, 'Sir, I was proceeding along the Ismailia Road when this car came at me with His Majesty King Farouk and another wog in it . . .'

Farouk could have done nothing to stop the gossip about himself. He made no attempt. On the contrary, he seemed amused on hearing some of the anecdotes. One night, three RAF officers were going to a night-club along the Pyramids road when their taxi broke down. A car drew up and a jovial character told them to jump in, he was going their way. What did they think of Egypt? In straight, servicemen's jargon they answered his question, finishing by singing a snatch or two of the most popular street songs of the moment – about Egypt's king. Everyone was chanting it, from the Canal base to the front line, to the tune of the Egyptian national anthem.

> King Farouk, King Farouk,
> He's a dirty old crook
> As he walks down the street,
> In his fifty-shilling suit.
> Queen Farida's very gay
> Cos she's in the family way . . .

Thanking their chauffeur, the RAF men found a table in the club. Hardly had they sat down than a Sudanese waiter placed a magnum of iced champagne before them. 'With the compliments of His Majesty,' he said, pointing towards a table in front of the dance-floor where, beaming across at them, sat their driver, Farouk.

Others failed to see the ridiculous side of Farouk; he was still popular with the people while the sixty thousand Allied troops in Cairo bought their popularity with their pay. Neguib wrote of the British at this period, 'They expected Egyptians to behave as loyal allies while being treated as conquered subjects. Their troops marched through the streets of Cairo singing obscene songs about our king, a man whom few of us admired, but who, nevertheless, was as much a national symbol as our flag. Farouk was never so popular as when he was being insulted in public by British troops, for we knew, as they knew, that by insulting our unfortunate king they were insulting the Egyptian people as a whole.'

The gossip reached into the palace as well. In April 1940 Farida gave birth to another daughter whom Farouk named Fawzia, after his favourite sister. For several days afterwards, Farouk hardly appeared in the palace; even Pulli dared not utter a word in the king's presence. So, the whisper circulated that he and Farida were quarrelling; about his broken promise to rid himself of his Italian hangers-on; about his long absences and the erratic, reversed pattern of his existence; about his night-clubbing and the scandals it inspired. Farida's mother, Madam Zeinab Zulficar, watched the growing estrangement between Farouk and her daughter. 'It was tragic to see him. He seemed never at rest for a moment. My daughter had to beg him to spend a few minutes with the children. Queen Nazli used to complain about Fuad, but he at least passed the evening with her. My daughter never saw the king during the day. She never had a lunch or dinner with him. And his evenings he spent with the servants, like Pulli.'

Later that year, she was sitting in the garden at Kubbah with Farida who was studying Arabic when the king suddenly joined them.

'I have had a consultation with the doctors,' he announced.

'What for?' they both asked.

'I should have an operation.'

They looked at him incredulously. Was this another of his practical jokes? No, he appeared thoughtful, earnest.

'What operation?' Madam Zulficar asked.

'An operation on my glands. So that I shall be more of a man.'

He took the subject no further. Nor did he pursue the idea of the operation. 'It might have been better for everyone had he received treatment,' Madam Zulficar said later, 'for I am certain he was a sick man.'

Farouk did give the impression in those days of a man who had become bored with life. Kingship he put on like a mask during the day; he moved through the formalities of interviewing and instructing his ministers, of signing his pile of documents, of appearing at ceremonies. But he brought to them an air of polite pretence, as though he had one eye on the ormolu clock on his study desk. Hassanain really ran the palace in that obtuse manner of his, by suggesting that the ideas came from the king then putting them into effect. Farouk seemed to consider himself a cypher and his hours in his study no more than intervals between rounds of pleasure. He acted as though believing, unconsciously, that his real existence began when he drove through the gates of Abdin or Kubbah bound for some night spot.

His life was becoming a series of evasions, not only from duty but from reality. Government ministers he had appointed, or his own palace cabinet officials would approach him with some problem or project. 'Yes, yes, I've already thought of it and dismissed it,' he would tell them. Or they would bring him information only to hear him comment, 'Why tell me this? I know it already.' Yet, could he have heard everything, even from his valet Mohamed Hassan, who was gaining influence, or from Thabet? As well as shutting his mind to the intrusions of his ministers, he began to shun them, except when state obligations forced him to meet them: at Friday prayers, during cabinet meetings or at formal dinners. Did the society of his equals frighten him? It seemed that way. Perhaps they might peer too closely at the masquerade of infallibility, of omniscience, of perfection; they might perceive him as a fraud or a failure.

At the beginning of 1942, Hassanain persuaded the king to take his first real holiday, away from the war in Upper Egypt. For the moment Cairo had grown quiet, except for a few sporadic shouts by nationalists; the government of Husain Sirry could handle things without the palace for a few weeks. The British had levered the Afrika Korps back to Derna. There was one small dust-storm; Sir Miles Lampson still demanded the eviction of his Italians and was urging the suspension of diplomatic relations with the Vichy French and the closing of its legation which the Ambassador contended the Germans were using as a spy centre. It hardly seemed enough to detain the king and leading members of his court in the capital, so they took a steamer to Aswan.

At the end of January he returned to a changed situation. Rommel had counter-attacked, forcing the British back to Tobruk and el-Gazala where they looked like giving more ground. Mobs

126

were parading the streets of Cairo and Alexandria, shouting, 'Down with England'. Students were marching with them, singing, 'We are Rommel's soldiers'. The voice of Ali Maher and several other politicians could also be heard through this uproar. The Allied reverses and the demonstrations did not bother Farouk; he raged, however, when his cabinet officials informed him that Lampson had triumphed over the Vichy affair. Husain Sirry had taken action at the Ambassador's insistence without referring to the king. On top of this, Farouk faced renewed pressure to sack his Italians. It was too much! To one of Sirry's cabinet ministers, Salib Sami bey, the king stormed, 'Sir Miles thinks he has won the first round, but I shall knock him down in the second.' As though at some secret sign, students from Al Azhar began a riot inside the university and holding street parades; the government discovered that Sheikh el-Maraghi, no friend of the British, was stirring up the discontent, that Ali Maher was again flitting between the palace and his old cabinet ministers. When Husain Sirry went to demand Farouk's support in suppressing the student troubles, the king merely shrugged his shoulders. That gesture meant Sirry was out. Who next, but Ali Maher?

On Sunday, the first of February, Lampson had gone to the embassy shoot at Fayum with Julian Amery; an urgent message in the afternoon from Terence Shone recalled him when it seemed certain that Husain Sirry would have to hand his resignation to the king. Ali Maher's shadow was lengthening. That, and the fact that Rommel had re-taken Western Cyrenaica and was advancing on Egypt, forced Sir Miles to scrap his moonlight duck shoot and hurry back to Cairo. That night he dragged Sirry out of a dinner party at his home to explain the situation. Farouk, the premier said, was determined to appoint another palace government; if not Ali Maher, a coalition of those who had served him since he dismissed Nahas and the *Wafd*. Even Sirry agreed that there was only one way to settle political unrest and palace intrigues: bring back Nahas.

Both men had no doubts about how the king would react to such a suggestion. To Farouk, the *Wafd* and Nahas constituted

127

an even greater menace than Lampson and the British. Collaboration between his two enemies he would resist as far as he could. The Ambassador saw this; so did Sirry, the king's relation through marriage. No one would give ground. The clash when it came set the three-legged stool of Egyptian politics rocking for the rest of Farouk's reign.

Farouk and his first queen, Farida

Farouk driving his sports car

Duck shooting at Mansouria,
near Cairo

CHAPTER TEN

*When we are gracious to man, he withdraweth and turneth
him aside: but when evil toucheth him, he is a man of long
prayers.* (XLI : 51)

By the next morning the crisis had blown up. Premier Husain
Sirry phoned to tell Lampson that the king was demanding his
resignation by noon. Ali Maher would probably receive his
summons to the palace that afternoon and the king's mandate
to form a new government. The Ambassador well knew what
that news would convey to the students and the sheikhs, to the
German and Italian troops probing their way through the
Eighth Army positions. Unless he acted quickly the British situation in Egypt might be undermined and the Canal base itself
threatened. Putting down one phone he picked up another to
speak to Hassanain at Abdin. As usual, the chief of the royal
cabinet prevaricated, temporised, but Lampson insisted on seeing
the king at one o'clock that day.

Not only Lampson suffered misgivings about the security of
the base. Oliver Lyttleton, sent out by Churchill several months
earlier as Minister of State with ultimate responsibility for the
country's defence, had interrupted his tour of Syria, another
trouble-spot, to fly back to the crisis in Cairo. Hardly had he
got over landing in a dust-storm than he summoned the Defence
Committee which included the service chiefs, General Sir Claude
Auchinleck, Admiral Sir Andrew Cunningham and Air Marshal
Sir Arthur Tedder. Lampson, Shone and Sir Walter Smart joined
them. To this group Lampson outlined the situation, making it
clear they might have to force the king to bring back the *Wafd* by
delivering an ultimatum. To this, the military chiefs dissented,
and it fell to Lyttleton to resolve the dispute. In his memoirs,
he wrote, 'The ambassador favoured strong action. It was clear

E 129

that words would be futile and that a show of force would be necessary if we were to get our way. The C-in-C and the military demurred, but I asked that at least the necessary measures should be concerted so that if an ultimatum from us became necessary, we could enforce its terms. The abdication and removal of the king might be involved. They reluctantly consented to make a plan, but at the same time pointed out that we should probably have tumult in Cairo and a sit-down strike of all the civilian labour upon which we relied. I retorted that the disturbances which would follow the flouting of the popular party were likely to be much more severe because backed, and rightly, by the mass of the people.'

Just after one o'clock, the burly figure of Sir Miles confronted Farouk in his study at Abdin. To his amazement, the king could not have treated him more affably. He listened as the ambassador presented the points the Defence Committee had agreed that morning. Lampson dwelt at length on Article Five of the 1936 Treaty which stipulated that neither Britain nor Egypt should adopt an attitude to foreign countries inconsistent with the treaty provisions. This meant, Sir Miles went on, that the king must call on a government which would remain loyal to the treaty and which would command support in the country. It followed from this that the king must send for Mustapha el-Nahas pasha. He had twenty-four hours to act on this advice, said Sir Miles. Farouk agreed that the treaty must be respected, that a strong government should be appointed. But Nahas, his old enemy! At this he began to argue, to waver. However, the ambassador left both the king and Hassanain in no doubt that Nahas, and no other, could fulfil the treaty obligations.

Oliver Lyttleton backed the stand the ambassador had taken at the palace. Now, even the army had quashed its misgivings and had evolved a complex and ingenious plan to abduct Farouk if the Minister of State and the ambassador decided they must depose him. Where would they take him? No one had thought of the question until it was posed by General R.G.W.S. Stone, Commanding British Troops in Egypt. Admiral Cunningham supplied the answer. 'I have a cruiser lying at Suez. We can take him down there and cruise around in the Red Sea until the politicians decide what to do with him.' Auchinleck's staff officers offered their plan with some pride: cars would leave Abdin main gate, making for Alexandria and Port Said to decoy any royalist groups which might cause trouble; the vehicle carrying the king would drive out the rear gate and take several detours before joining the Suez Road. A battalion of picked men would surround the palace if the ambassador had to deliver an ultimatum. Four tanks would move into the square outside the main gate to support the troops in case of riots. A platoon of officer cadets would accompany the ambassador to deal with the palace guards or the staff it they resisted. By midnight on Monday, the second of February, Farouk realised that perhaps he had blundered, that the British meant to enforce their demands.

However, the king still decided to bluff things out. He might yet persuade Nahas to enter a coalition government which would include some of his old palace group of ministers. Little did he appreciate that already the *Wafd* leader had given assurances to the British that on no account would he agree to serve in anything but a purely *Wafd* government. So, when Farouk sent for Nahas the next afternoon and proposed the coalition, the old statesman rejected it out of hand. He would, nevertheless, help the king out of the critical situation his ministers had created. This, with indelicate irony.

Lampson had kept London informed of the developing crisis, intimating that if the *Wafd* did not receive the king's mandate to form a government he might have to force Farouk to abdicate. The Foreign Office concurred in his action, agreeing that the king must be prevented from nominating another palace government. Security of the base came first. Accordingly, Lampson summoned Hassanain late on the evening of the third of February and instructed him to tell the king that he must send for Nahas by six o'clock the following evening. 'Unless I hear that the king has sent for the *Wafd*, he must accept the consequences,' the ambassador repeated. Once again, the chamberlain attempted to compromise. Could they not form an interim government which

131

would then be replaced by the *Wafd*? No, said Lampson. There is no alternative.

The next day Al Azhar and Fuad universities flared up, despite the fact that Farouk had personally passed a message to the heads to keep their students quiet. They marched in and around the universities crying, 'Long live Rommel' – 'Down with the British' – 'Long live the king'. At Zagazig, mobs broke shop windows and doors then attacked people suspected of pro-British sympathies. In the middle of all this, word leaked from Abdin Palace that Farouk had packed several trunks and was preparing to make a dash for freedom. To where no one knew. Just in case, an alert went to British troops and military police to watch all airports in the country and every road out of the capital. The embassy took the view that the king would only lose face if he tried to escape.

Sir Miles Lampson had on his hands the sort of operation at which he excelled; he seemed to revel in mulling over the detailed plans for the deposition of the king in the event that he failed to comply; his massive frame had, it appeared, expanded to fill the crisis; he and his embassy were the dead eye of the hurricane, sitting inert while everything spun madly around them. It was like the old days of Cromer and Kitchener, Allenby and Lloyd. He had prepared the event. Down to the last man and tank, the personal escort for himself and General Stone; down to his peroration before delivering the abdication document; down to the hourly checks on the will-o'-the-wisp movements of Nahas who must be on call; down to the phone message which would bring Mohamed Ali, the old pretender, into Abdin Palace and Farouk's vacant seat; down to the air-raid sirens which would clear the streets and the way for the dispossessed monarch. He left nothing to chance.

There was the abdication document to draft. By an ironical twist, Sir Walter Monckton, who had drawn up the abdication form for King Edward the Eighth, was attached to the embassy. Who better? Oddly enough, it took Monckton longer to find a suitable piece of paper on which to ask a king to surrender his throne than the form of words. In wartime Cairo such paper hardly existed, and who could expect the King of Egypt to abdicate on British Embassy foolscap! The best efforts of the embassy still only produced a folio which was noticeably grubby and dog-eared.

While Lampson was rehearsing the dethronement of Farouk, things were happening in Abdin Palace. The king had summoned all the former presidents of the Chamber of Deputies, including Nahas, who sat impassive, savouring the moment as much as Lampson. Across the table was his old adversary, Ali Maher, believing his moment had returned. In the study at Abdin, the king had enough prime ministers and party leaders to fill every cabinet post in the coalition which he saw as the solution to the crisis. He made a short speech, calling for unity and an end to personal differences to bring the country out of its hours of danger. He spoke firmly, even eloquently. 'I am asking all of you to help form a coalition government. I think that if each of you will sacrifice something, the nation will gain much. I am hopeful that you will accept my advice. In these grave hours, we must forget self and remember only the country. When the British Ambassador was here today, I told him that I had already decided to give Nahas pasha the post of Prime Minister.

'When yesterday's consultations were ended, the British Ambassador met my chamberlain who informed him that Nahas pasha refused to form a coalition government, and he asked that I be informed that it was his desire that Nahas pasha be given full freedom to select his own cabinet. My chamberlain communicated to him that the question was being considered by Nahas pasha and the party leaders, and that they are in the midst of forming a new government. The king has faith in the patriotic sentiments of the leaders and feels that they will surmount all difficulties to his satisfaction. I leave you now to discuss the matter freely, counting upon your patriotism to study the question and to refer the opinion of all to me. In this matter I wish you to know only one thing... that I am not afraid of anything, that I am ready to sacrifice everything in the interest of my country.'

It was mid-afternoon; over the pyramids to the south-west the sun was slanting; the afternoon siesta had thinned out people

133

and traffic in the streets; nothing seemed amiss. Except that, at Kasr el-Nil barracks in the middle of Cairo, the pass-word had gone to those troops who would oust the king. Further down the Nile, the embassy staff sipped their tea, having set everything in motion. It was three hours from Lampson's deadline.

Exactly at six o'clock, the phone rang on Lampson's desk. A court chamberlain, Ismail Teymour bey, informed the ambassador that Hassanain had just quit the palace with the king's reply to the ultimatum. In ten minutes, the cabinet chief arrived, his long, sad face grey with anxiety; he read Lampson a communiqué from the palace saying the king had gathered his ministers together to decide their course of action. 'In their opinion,' ran the communiqué, 'the British ultimatum is a gross infringement of the 1936 Treaty and of the country's independence. For these reasons, and acting on their advice, His Majesty cannot consent to an action resulting in an infringement of the Anglo-Egyptian Treaty and of the country.'

Lampson concealed his surprise as Hassanain read the document over to him; he considered it a piece of cool cheek, to accuse Britain of breaking the treaty. But the document had also shocked him, for he noted that among its signatories was the name, Nahas. The man he was backing, relying upon, seemed to have sided with the others. How had Farouk won over Nahas? Or was the *Wafd* leader convinced the Axis would triumph and unwilling to sacrifice himself and the party by siding with the British? It meant that he, Lampson, was staging a *coup de palais* which might inflame the masses and could have no point without the one man who could control the mobs. Lampson, who never lacked courage, turned to Hassanain. In blunt language, he warned the chamberlain of the gravity of the situation. The king, he said, could expect him at the palace at nine o'clock that night. He omitted to mention that he would come with an armed escort.

Did Farouk have an inkling that the British would try to topple him by force? They said he had once posed the question to his chiefs of staff: 'How long could Cairo hold out against the British?' They replied, 'Two hours, Sire.' Then he asked: 'How long would they take to capture all of us?' The reply: 'Two and a half hours. Sire.' The joke had too sharp a point to escape Farouk who was gambling that Lampson, Lyttleton and the army would go so far and then compromise; he would then appear to have gained victory over them. However, he startled his mother and her ladies-in-waiting by bursting melodramatically into the haremlek at six o'clock that evening and announcing, 'There's going to be bloodshed tonight.' He amplified this by saying that if the British troops started fighting in the streets, the people would rise against them. But, significantly, he had alerted neither the army nor the palace guard. He did not expect trouble.

The British, for their part, betrayed no hint of crisis. Phlegm seemed to be the password. The embassy staff were told to dine out normally, but listen for the air-raid sirens which would warn them to return; the Duff Coopers, on their way from the Far East to London, left their room at the embassy to keep a dinner engagement with Alexander Kirk, the American minister. Only the fact that Oliver Lyttleton and his wife had arrived from their villa near the Pyramids just before eight o'clock might have signified something. Before dinner, Lampson, General Stone and senior embassy staff conferred. Their conclusion: the king had rejected the ultimatum and must go. Then, over the coffee and brandy, the ambassador suddenly remarked to Lyttleton, 'What do we do if the king agrees to our terms?' The ultimatum had expired, but could they push Farouk off his throne for acceding to their demands only three hours after the deadline? Lyttelton felt uneasy about unseating the king on such a technicality. How would they justify it to the House of Commons let alone world opinion? Not only might it cause friction between Britain and Egypt; it could set the Arab world alight. As they rose, the states-man and the diplomat decided that if Farouk climbed down they could not compel him to sign the abdication.

Just before nine o'clock, Lampson and General Stone drove out of the embassy. With them went twenty picked men. As their small convoy moved towards the palace they passed lorries laden with troops lumbering in the same direction; tanks and armoured cars groped through the indigo night, their lights blinkered, to deploy round the palace; already steel-helmeted

135

soldiers, armed with rifles and Sten guns, were taking up positions in Abdin Square. The palace gate lay open and the two men passed into the courtyard. Flanked by their armed ADCs, the ambassador and the general marched up the stairs to the king's study; before them, the whole court seemed to scatter; Egyptian ADCs were running from the palace windows towards the king's rooms with the news they were under siege; whispered conferences took place while the ambassador paced the ante-room impatiently. Finally, a court official entered to tell Lampson that the king would see him.

As both men reached the door, Hassanain stepped forward. Seeing the general and the soldiers, he barred the ambassador's path crying, 'Not this way, Sir Miles ... not with soldiers.' Lampson brushed him aside and strode into the king's study.

The ambassador was suffering from a painful sty in his right eye, which did nothing to soften his expression. From this and the general attitude, Farouk realised this was no ordinary audience. 'May I keep my chamberlain with me?' he asked, and Lampson nodded assent. He dispensed with formalities, going straight to the point. The king had received the ultimatum to which he had replied, through Hassanain, in terms which could only mean he did not accept it.

'We did not reject the terms. We offered an alternative suggestion,' the king shot back.

Lampson waved this aside, flourished his prepared text and read it to Farouk. The king, he said, had broken Article Five of the Anglo-Egyptian Treaty by following the advice of politicians who were working against Britain and for the enemy. Furthermore, the king had acted irresponsibly in creating a crisis over the Vichy French question which was embraced by the letter of the treaty. Thirdly, he had flouted democratic ideals by refusing to appoint a government which had popular support and could therefore ensure that the treaty terms were observed. By these actions, the king had jeopardised the security of Egypt and was therefore unfit to rule, Sir Miles concluded.

The wording of the document and the stentorian delivery had so shaken Farouk that he kept glancing at Hassanain, as though

136

back in his schoolroom waiting for a tutor to supply the right answer. But worse was to come. Lampson drew the abdication document from his pocket and threw it in front of the king, remarking that he had better sign it if he did not want further trouble.

Farouk picked up the abdication form. 'Isn't it rather a dirty piece of paper?' he asked, in that inconsequential manner which mystified so many people. The three men watched his eyes wander over the text, slowly, as though he wondered what to make of it. Monckton had worded the document thus:

'We, King Farouk of Egypt, mindful as ever of the interests of our country, hereby renounce and abandon for ourselves and the heirs of our body the Throne of the Kingdom of Egypt and of all sovereign rights, privileges and powers in and over the said Kingdom and the subjects thereof, and we release our said subjects from their allegiance to our person.

'Given at our Palace of Abdin this Fourth of February 1942.'

Farouk took hold of a pen from his desk and bent over the paper to sign away his throne. Another few seconds and he would have ceased to be King of Egypt. But, as his hand moved, so did Hassanain; quickly he advanced towards the king, shouting something in Arabic which neither of the Britons understood. Farouk paused, glanced up at Lampson and said, almost tearfully, 'Won't you give me another chance, Sir Miles?' Now it was Lampson's turn to hesitate. He had counted on the king to sign the document, on being rid of the boy he hated so much. But he had given his word to Lyttleton, he had therefore to agree. However, he stressed that the king must send for Nahas at once.

'I shall send for him now, in your presence, Sir Miles, and ask him to form a government,' Farouk said.

'Of his own choosing?' General Stone put in, and the king nodded.

They decided Nahas should be summoned as soon as the ambassador left. The tension broken, the king produced cigarettes and all four men sat chatting about anything but politics and the

137

war. It was then that Farouk surprised Lampson by thanking him for his assistance in the past.

The king's own fanciful account of those moments describes how he had a hand on his revolver, ready to shoot the ambassador in the stomach; his Albanian guards, posted behind the curtain, would have shot the general and the ADCs. He would abdicate, he declared, at his own pleasure and in his own language, and would appoint Nahas only to prevent blood from flowing in the streets of Cairo. As for Lampson, he warned him he would regret the deed for ever.

In this the king was right, though his reasoning was wrong. The rest of his days in Egypt Lampson regretted not having kicked out the king there and then. Back in the embassy, Sir Walter Smart asked how the operation had gone. When Lampson explained, Smart muttered, 'You've scotched the snake, you haven't killed it.' The ambassador could only concur; he did not see eye to eye with those who fancied Farouk had learned his lesson; in his view, Farouk's hatred would grow. He was a scoundrel who really did not deserve the throne.

The crisis had its element of farce. Minutes after Lampson had quit the palace, the troops still guarding the gate stopped a man who drove up and demanded admittance. In vain he pleaded that he was Nahas pasha, that the king had sent for him to form a new government. To the officer on the gate he looked more like a carpet pedlar than a prime minister, so he refused to let him through the cordon. Nahas had, therefore, to return to the British Embassy to receive a *laisser-passer* before he could answer the king's summons. Half an hour later, he was back, this time at Farouk's behest, to discuss with Lampson and Lyttleton the best way out of the political crisis.

The embassy was crowded with diplomats, their wives and several officers, all discussing the night's events. To the Duff Coopers, coming back after dinner, it looked like a theatre foyer with first-nighters arguing whether the drama had been a success or failure. No one doubted that Lampson and Lyttleton had done the right thing by bringing back Nahas. Except Axis propagandists who, for once, failed to penetrate the flimsy Egyptian security.

138

The *Wafd* leader had stirred up the masses against the British, they said. So this represented a diplomatic reverse for the Allies. They overlooked the fact that Nahas, unlike many other politicians, had never truckled to the Axis. Nonetheless he had everything to lose by backing the British war effort. In the stifling July days when Auchinleck was battling at Alamein to set up Montgomery's victory by halting Rommel, when refugees were clogging every road east out of Alexandria, when the Navy had pulled out, when smoke and charred paper floated over Cairo from top-secret documents burning at service headquarters, Nahas and the *Wafd* stood by their promises. The cities of the Delta stayed quiet; on the whole, so did the base.

February the Fourth ranks as one of the quietest *coups de palais* in history. It made no headlines. Censorship fixed that. The people had the *Wafd* which pleased them, and by the time the insult to Farouk filtered through to them they had other worries. For the first, and last time in his Egyptian career, Lampson's great bulk was borne shoulder-high by an Egyptian crowd when he appeared with Nahas outside parliament four days after the siege of Abdin. Reaction to the coup was muted. Only the British took the field at a polo match between the Royal Artillery and a team of Egyptian diplomats and pashas who knew the situation. Farida invited the wife of a British official to the haremlik and wept to her, saying, 'Why does your husband treat mine like this?'

By a strange twist, the king gained some popularity and public sympathy from the incident. Much of this he owed to Hassanain, who lost no chance to condemn Lampson and praise the king for resisting British tanks and guns to the last moment. Something of this shows in General Sir 'Jumbo' Wilson's comment in his memoirs. 'I was in Syria when the news of the events in Cairo on the Fourth of February reached me, describing how the King of Egypt had been forced by our ambassador to change his government under threat of removal from his throne, with his palace surrounded by British troops and tanks in the courtyard. I was astounded and horrified at this news, as one felt that all one's efforts at getting the goodwill and co-operation of the Egyptians in the early days of the war had been thrown away; the reaction of the Egyptian army to such a proceeding might well have had a serious effect on our war effort and it was enrirely due to the careful handling of the situation by (Ibrahim) Atallah pasha, its Chief of Staff, that incidents were prevented. On one of my subsequent visits to Cairo, I met Hassanain pasha, who spoke very bitterly about it and said the coercion of the king was unnecessary ... I returned to Syria with the impression that the personal equation had had a good deal to do with it.'

The coup had little effect on the army. One officer, Colonel Mohamed Neguib, did feel the slight so deeply that he wrote to Farouk, 'Since the army was given no opportunity to defend Your Majesty, I am ashamed to wear my uniform. I hereby request permission to resign from the Egyptian Army.' The king rejected his request on the grounds that he had forbidden his own Royal Guard to resist. A few of the young officers smarted at the high-handed British action. But not until a decade later did it look to their leaders, officers like Nasser and el-Sadat, like some watershed in Egyptian history, the nub and focus of the revolution. From February the Fourth they created a new Egyptian legend, a new myth about Farouk.

How does el-Sadat put it? 'Up to now,' he wrote long afterwards, 'the King had been synonymous with the patriotic ideal, and the violation of the Royal Palace was regarded by all patriotic Egyptians as an outrage against Egypt itself. But from now on, Farouk changed utterly, and Egypt began to despair of him. He had suffered a severe shock, which was followed by chronic nervous depression. Unstable and anxious by temperament, Farouk became the prey of psychological inhibitions. He suffered from persecution mania. He was irascible and violent. It became gradually obvious that he was a paranoiac. He underwent a physical change at the same time. He became fat and prematurely aged.'

How did Gamal Abdel Nasser see it? 'The seeds of the revolution were present in me long before the episode of February Fourth, 1942, a day after which I wrote to a friend, saying, "What is to be done now that the die was cast and we accepted what

happened on our knees in surrender?" As a matter of fact, I believe the imperialist was playing us with only one card in his hand,
with the object of threatening us. But once the imperialist realises
that some Egyptians are ready to shed their own blood and meet
force with force, he will beat a hasty retreat.'

These views, written after the revolution, have the high colour-
ing of hindsight. Imperialism was not a word which Nahas, in
his wilder moments, el-Banna, or the militant lawyer, Ahmed
Fuad, would have used at that time. Nor did Farouk mope in
his palace. Seven days after the siege he was waving to thousands
who acclaimed him in Abdin Square on his twenty-second birthday. He greeted them later with this message: 'My dear people
– how my heart has rejoiced to see these manifestations of joy
and gladness on the part of all of you...' Not long afterwards
he was sitting at his favourite table in the Auberge des Pyramides
night-club when a British major approached him, saluted and
said, 'Would Your Majesty do us the honour of having dinner
in our mess?'

'Of course, old boy,' Farouk beamed. He had always remained
on good terms with the services. 'Which regiment are you?'

'The Royal Armoured Corps, Majesty.'

'Oh no,' Farouk said, shaking his head. 'No. Not the tanks.
How do I know I should ever get back?'

A royal quip? Perhaps, but the scar had burned deep. From
that day, until the moment Lampson left for a holiday in South
Africa towards the end of the war, Farouk closed the palace
gates to members of the British Embassy, except official callers.
Then, the king hit on an oriental way of pointing the snub. The
precise moment the ambassador's plane took off from Cairo, his
court chamberlain delivered an invitation to embassy staff to
dine at the palace. After February the Fourth he feared as well
as hated Lampson; in his mind, he now bracketed him with
Nahas and the *Wafd*. And those he could never forgive. He resented, especially, the impudence of Nahas when he replied to his
letter inviting him to form the government. The *Wafd* leader had
reminded the king that he and his ministers had brought the
country to such a perilous situation.

141

Instead of profiting from the crisis, Farouk emerged as an embittered man with a grudge which he meant to settle. He failed to appreciate the delicate construction of Egypt's political pyramid, that a weakness in one facet might cause the whole structure to crumble. The perfect youth could or would not grasp that his were the fatal flaws which threatened to demolish the pyramid.

CHAPTER ELEVEN

For when the birth of a daughter is announced to any one
of them, dark shadows settle on his face, and he is sad:
He hideth him from the people because of the ill tidings;
shall he keep it with disgrace or bury it in the dust? Are not
their judgements wrong? (XVI: 60, 61)

For nearly forty years Princess Shevikiar had kept aloof from
Egyptian society. When Fuad, the man who had spurned her, was
ruling the country she spent most of her time in Turkey, returning occasionally to open her baroque palace in Cairo and
winter in the more benign climate. She remained still a royal
princess who had her own fortune and was richer now by the three
million pounds her ill-starred brother, Prince Ahmed Seif ed-Din,
had bequeathed her. He had died in 1937, and since Fuad had
also gone and most other people had forgotten their drama, the
princess saw no reason why she and her fifth husband, el-Hamy
Husain, should not settle in Cairo. Now a fragile figure of sixty,
Shevikiar had, nevertheless, lost none of her passion for living
or ensuring that the society around her did the same. Soon her
lavish soirées became the talk of Cairo, attracting the best names
in the country. She felt only one thing was missing: King Farouk.

Of course, Shevikiar had heard her quota of stories about the
king's differences with Farida, his preference for servants and
night-clubs to his palace advisers and upper-class homes, his
mother's loss of influence over him. He was a young man in
search of amusement, distraction, so she invited him to several of
her parties where the food was good, the girls the prettiest she
could find. He would wander round restlessly for half an hour
and take his leave. How to keep him? She and her friends hit on
the idea of teaching him to play cards. Soon, the youth who had
swept playing cards off the table and damned it as a Koranic sin,
was playing bridge for a few piastres, poker for larger sums, and

143

finally baccarat. He now listed Shevikiar's pink-and-grey palace on Kasr el-Aini street with his night-club haunts and the Royal Automobile Club. Shevikiar probed for his other weaknesses. It was easy to arrange for him to meet a pretty girl he fancied. Shevikiar and her friend, Helene Mosseri, wife of a Jewish banker, began to ensure that the king never went short of female company and always had a place of assignation. With two such hostesses arranging his night life Farouk was on the road to depravity.

Why did Shevikiar play such a part in the king's corruption? Was she merely making sure that a footloose young monarch was enjoying himself, or bent on her own self-promotion? Or, as some maintain, was she determined to revenge herself on Fuad through his son? She made no secret of the fact that she detested Nazli, her first husband's second choice. And several women friends heard her mutter from time to time, 'J'ai juré de ruiner cette famille.' Brigadier Ahmed Kemal, head of the palace police, told the revolutionary tribunal, that Shevikiar had pledged herself to deprave Farouk. According to others of her coterie, the princess had a sincere affection for the young king, treating him like a son. She just had a bizarre way of behaving, they said. Whatever the motive, Shevikiar exerted just as baleful an influence on Farouk as on his father. He, himself, acknowledged this in his memoirs, referring to the sinister influence her family had exercised over his. But too late.

While the fighting went on in the Western Desert, Shevikiar's palace was burning a bright hole in the Cairo black-out. Rarely fewer than fifteen hundred people jammed into the ramshackle structure and the revels continued long after the *muezzins* had intoned the call to dawn prayers. Most of her vast fortune the princess threw into those entertainments, outdoing the king, the queen mother and every other grand family in Egypt. Any German aircraft dropping a stick of bombs on the fairy lights in her garden would have obliterated half the Egyptian ruling class and with it the British Embassy, a few hundred yards away. Why did Farouk, knowing the history of his father and Shevikiar, her hatred of his mother, dally at these parties? There was feasting, dancing, gambling. There was also Princess Fatma Tussun. For Shevikiar had also discovered that the king had become infatuated with the wife of one of his relations, so she invariably invited her.

Farouk had met her the week after his confrontation with Lampson. He had gone to spend an hour at a dinner and dance given by Alahadin Mukhtar pasha, at Marg, on the outskirts of Cairo. There, he saw Fatma, and stayed until dawn. Even among Turkish and Egyptian beauties, Princess Fatma stood out; she was a Shereen, of fair-skinned, blonde Circassian stock. Farouk knew her but had never spoken to her. That night he felt he was looking at her for the first time. Naturally, Fatma had been officially introduced to the king. Like many other girls of her age and status, she admired his handsome bearing; she might even have been remotely attracted to him.

But she was married, too. Two years earlier she had married Prince Hassan Tussun, a man twenty-two years older. Their marriage had been arranged between their families, according to Islamic custom. Her husband's father, Prince Omar Tussun, was a Turk of the old school who lived and breathed by the tenets of Islam; his forty-one-year-old son he treated like a schoolboy permitting him neither to smoke nor drink, nor even cross his legs while he sat. Hassan grew up with two passions: horses and whisky. This was the atmosphere in which Fatma lived. In the Tussun household, she lived in the harem, dressed as a good Moslem lady should be, covering her arms and shoulders and abjuring Western customs. Prince Omar Tussun's strictures on the men and women in his home made Fuad's seem enlightened.

So, that evening at Marg, when Farouk approached and began to talk to her, Fatma was embarrassed and fled from him at the first opportunity. Several times he tried to strike up a conversation with her, but on each occasion she eluded him, not realising that she could not have adopted a more effective way of increasing the king's interest. For him the hunt was always more exciting than the kill. Fatma he found a strange, mysterious girl. Soon the idea of her infatuated him. He took to driving, alone, to her house hoping for a glimpse of her; he would scan the party lists and if her name appeared he would attend. But somehow, when he saw her close at hand, his courage failed him and he would abandon the attempt to get to know her. He then had a brainwave. To give a party at Abdin and invite her to watch a private showing of a film.

For this occasion he chose a cloying, American screen romance instead of the Westerns which he watched by the dozen. He sat between Fatma and Farida. Suddenly he turned to the princess and asked, 'What is that perfume you are wearing?' Without giving it a thought, she answered, 'Chanel Number Five'. The party ended, the guests departed. It was three o'clock when Farouk rang for Pulli. He must fetch the king the biggest bottle of Chanel Number Five Cairo could produce. Never mind that it was three o'clock. Phone the shops, waken the owners, but bring it back. Unmoved, Pulli obeyed, returning with the bottle; then, on the king's instructions, he took it to Fatma's house, leaving it with a servant. There was no card; Farouk relied on her intuition.

A few days later an invitation arrived bearing Shevikiar's monogram. Farouk scanned the list, noting that Prince Hassan Tussun and his wife would attend the party at Kasr el-Aini. He cancelled a state function at Alexandria and went to the party. Seeking out Fatma, he asked if she had received the gift. She said yes, though she could not guess who had sent it. 'I didn't like to imagine you had sent it since you are the head of the family and would not make such an approach to me or anyone of my family.'

Farouk invited her to dine with him the next night at nine o'clock at Coin Farouk, his private house at Helwan on a bend of the Nile twelve miles south of Cairo. She accepted. The whole of the next day he spent at Helwan supervising the arrangements for the rendezvous. At nine o'clock the princess arrived and he went to greet her. To his astonishment and chagrin, Prince Tussun appeared at her side. Farouk concealed his anger, but the incident merely increased his determination to win her. Even if it meant divorcing his queen. In fact, at this time he first mooted the idea of divorce with Hassanain who countered with a hundred excuses and quashed the idea. The more he saw of Fatma the more his infatuation mounted, and the more frequently his hints of divorce recurred. Hassanain had to enlist the support of the country's religious leaders, such as el-Maraghi, to dissuade the king.

But the rift between him and Farida was deepening. The queen was also invited to Shevikiar's parties, many felt for the same reason as her husband. There she would sit, humiliated, when Farouk deserted her to go off with Fatma or some other woman, or even with Pulli. She warned him that if he persisted in these friendships, she, too, would seek other companionship. The people to whom she turned were Wahid Yussri, the son of Shevikiar, and his wife, Princess Samiha, daughter of Sultan Husain Kemal. That irony was not lost on Shevikiar.

Wahid was the brother of Hassanain's first wife and, at one time, the chamberlain had tried to bring him and the king together. 'I have attempted to have him educated with people of his own age, but I find him escaping from this to the young Italians,' Hassanain explained to Yussri. 'You must try to isolate him from this atmosphere which attracts him, for he imitates people.' Yussri promised to do his best. About twenty years older than Farouk, he had the stamp of the man of the world. Baccalaureat in Paris, a term at Sandhurst and West Point, service in the Egyptian Embassy in Washington, an expert rider, polo player and gun, a raconteur in half a dozen languages. When his first marriage failed and he married Princess Samiha, a tranquil woman twenty years older, Cairo gossip predicted a short romance. They were wrong, for both were happy.

Farouk and Yussri had diametric temperaments; the moment they met, the king challenged his cousin. 'Your father, Sefullah Yussri, was my father's enemy.' This Yussri denied. When they discussed the government of Egypt, Farouk gained the impression that his relation outdid Nahas in revolutionary ideals, simply because he argued for the return of a constitutional monarchy. Farouk cut him short by declaring that he was constitution, government and people all in one. Their encounter left Farouk with the conviction that this man really wanted to make himself

147

the president of an Egyptian republic. But, before they quarrelled in earnest, Farouk ran into Yussri at a party at Shevikiar's. 'I want you to meet my wife, Farida,' he said and introduced them.

Now the king had something with which to reproach Yussri. Farida would disappear from the palace, driving her own car, to spend her evenings with Wahid and Princess Samiha; many of her week-ends she also passed with them, in the country or the desert. Gossips made the most of this relationship and took every opportunity to whisper the worst to the king. He went to his cousin, Princess Samiha, and said, 'I wish you to stop Farida from coming to your house.'

'And why should I forbid the queen and my friend from visiting me in my home?'

'Because she comes to see your husband.'

Princess Samiha politely rebuked him, dismissing the idea that there was anything between Farida and her husband. The king then tried to persuade Farida from calling so often at the house in Zamalek, but this he never succeeded in doing. He had not, after all, given up seeing Fatma.

From this point, the king did not content himself with meeting women at Shevikiar's palace or at night-clubs; he flaunted them openly in front of Farida as though determined to humble her. Why do this, why talk of divorce when everyone in the palace knew he loved his queen more than anyone else? It was a game, a savage game inspired by his perverse character and his complex about manhood. He wanted to teach Farida a lesson, or perhaps arouse her jealousy. He had failed to understand her proud and stubborn nature. So, with little pretence of concealment, the girls he had picked up, the dancers and singers from night-clubs, would scamper up the back stairs and make merry with the king until sunrise. Whereas he had once attempted to suppress stories of his night life he now injected them into the general gossip by recounting them to intimates. Here is one example:

A certain Englishwoman, wife of a high official, had taken his eye and, of course, agreed to meet him at her house in a suburb of Cairo. They were just beginning to make love when her husband returned, unexpectedly, from his trip to Alexandria. They heard him open the front door and the king only had time to grab his clothes and step out on to the balcony. That night it rained hard, and he stood, shivering, on the balcony, waiting until the woman got her husband out of the bedroom and he could slip out the front door.

A Freudian analyst might have made much of that anecdote in terms of Farouk's sex complex and his anti-British attitude. His friends, however, noticed one thing: none of his mistresses stayed long. He was no Don Juan though, since they were not exclusively his, that would hardly have mattered; he was still King of Egypt. What they found impossible to bear was his meanness. He was *naashif* (mean), like his father, they complained, and several of them added a few well-chosen insults about his love-making. One prominent Egyptian cabaret artiste slapped his face because of her poor reward. One lady, who had grown fond of him, went to a doctor whom she knew had treated Farouk several times. Ostensibly, she consulted him about herself, though he wondered why she was making a fuss about a non-existent complaint. The equivocation broke down; she confessed she had really come about her boy friend. Could anything be done about his lack of sexual development? The doctor shook his head. Then his lack of desire? Perhaps, the doctor said. If it were mental it might be difficult, if hormonal it would be easier. She was the king's mistress and he knew it. He could have told her that Farouk had secretly consulted an eminent Jewish hormone expert who had advised him there was no treatment.

His close friends realised the king was constructing the myth of his sexual prowess too successfully; it had damaged him with Lampson, it could lose him prestige elsewhere; the legend of the young debauché might injure his reputation in the Moslem community just as deeply as gossip about his impotence. His confidants tried to reason with him. One put it as tactfully as he could. 'Majesty, some people are better endowed by nature than others and they live with it. In your case you have intelligence where others have none. You should see that your deficiency does not matter. Women won't love you for your sex alone. Why not admit the weakness to yourself?'

Farouk looked at him. 'That is a mad thing to say to a descendant of Mohamed Ali,' he replied.

Whatever time his wild parties finished, however late he rose the next day, Farouk still made some pretence of governing. He had to keep an even more wary eye on the British, for he was bent on winning the third round against Lampson; he was determined to oust the *Wafd*. He still looked to Rommel to accomplish this with no help from him. The Germans, at that time, had taken Tobruk and now nothing lay between them and Alexandria. Churchill summed up the situation in his telegram to R. G. Casey, who had taken over from Oliver Lyttelton. It was dated the thirtieth of June 1942, and said; 'Everyone in uniform must fight exactly as they would if Kent or Sussex were invaded ... No general evacuation, no playing for safety. Egypt must be held at all costs.' Five weeks behind the cable, Churchill arrived himself to tour the battlefields and appoint Montgomery. Farouk decided he would put his complaints in person to the British prime minister and invited him to dinner at the Mena House Hotel, close by the Pyramids. Churchill accepted unwillingly; he was flying out to Gibraltar and home that night; he had little time for Farouk whom he knew to be playing a double game. He felt, also, that the king was losing the respect of his people by his conduct.

At that time Farouk's current mania was picking pockets. He boasted of having released a criminal from Turah prison to teach him the art by practising with a suit into which tiny bells had been sewn. The king grew so adept that he could pick the criminal's pocket without ringing any of the bells. His latest play became notorious in Cairo, for he could never resist pinching watches, cigarette lighters and powder compacts which he collected by the hundred. It was a royal joke, though often the articles disappeared forever into the palace collection.

As they sat down to dinner, Churchill decided to emphasise how short a time he had. He fished in his waistcoat pocket for his gold hunter to place it on the table. A look of horror crossed his face. He knew Farouk's reputation for practical jokes, his light-fingered habits and mania for hoarding watches. The king, he was certain, had stolen his watch. 'Your Majesty,' he said, 'the famous watch that was given to my ancestor, the Duke of Marlborough, by Queen Anne after he had won the Battle of Blenheim, has completely disappeared. I would like it back as quickly as it can be arranged.' Churchill threatened, in fact, to put off his departure until the watch was recovered.

Farouk denied taking the watch. 'When did you last see it?'

'A little less than hour ago.'

'Who were you with after that?'

'I was at a meeting with your hereditary cabinet.'

'Then the pasha has it,' Farouk cried. He was referring to one of his palace officials who had a penchant for petty thieving. Farouk left the table and within ten minutes was back with the watch dangling from his hand.

'And what did the pasha say when you asked him for it?' Churchill said, astonished.

'He doesn't even know I've got it yet,' Farouk giggled. The premier accepted the king's version of the story. But would someone other than Churchill have seen his watch again?

The British prime minister left Farouk with no illusions about the ultimate Allied victory, though the king remained sceptical. He still played both sides against each other, though he did this with some flair. Those who met him during the critical years of the war found him impressive; he still had the old trick of camouflaging his ignorance. General Smuts thought him, 'a surprisingly intelligent person'. Oliver Lyttleton and his wife saw him one sultry evening, garbed in thick Scotch tweed, while they were dining on a Nile boat; he conversed freely and easily about his days at The Shop, consumed gallons of orangeade and left an impression of ability and charm. Senator Richard B. Russell, then with the American forces, summed him up as an 'attractive, clear-eyed young man at that time... He seemed to be very much on the job. I was under the impression that he was well above the ordinary run of rulers in that area at that time, but apparently

151

later he did a great many things he should not have done.'
Winthrop Aldrich, the American financier and diplomat, concluded, after a chat with the king, that he understood the international gold market better than anyone he had met outside big-business circles.

Astutely, he refused to back either Britain or the Axis openly. He would mutter, 'The British say I'm pro-German, the Germans say I'm pro-British. The truth is that I'm neither. I'm pro-Egyptian.' What else could he do? Had he sided with the British he would have lost face with his own nationalists and compromised himself with the Germans, who could still win; had he revealed himself too violently nationalist, Lampson would have made good his threat to kick him out? So, like the horse in the fable, he was ready to gallop off in all directions at once. The British had wounded his vanity and he showed his resentment by cultivating the Americans; they gave him his jeep, his DUKW, a private plane and other playthings while the British still treated him meanly.

Soon, however, he had no alternative but to choose the British. Alamein, the miracle which no one really hoped for, had happened; Rommel was losing the last desert battle; the king and Egypt now realised where their security lay, if not their loyalties. Lampson was not so sure. When some of Farouk's friends among British generals and air force chiefs put a request through the embassy that Farouk should be appointed an honorary colonel of one of their regiments back came the reply from the embassy: a curt No. Privately, the ambassador scoffed at the suggestion. 'What has he done to deserve it?' he asked. In vain, the military leaders argued that it would solder the Anglo-Egyptian alliance for the rest of the war.

Farouk now turned to his other old enemy: Nahas. The *Wafd* leader had just arrested Ali Maher for breaking his parole and the king decided that, British or no British, he would finish him for good. Though never as brilliant as his father's, the king's private intelligence service functioned well. In the last months of 1942, Hassanain brought him information which Farouk felt would ruin Nahas. The *Wafd* was splitting from top to bottom. At the centre

152

of the row sat the Christian Copt, Makram Ebeid pasha, thin-lipped and sharp-minded and with a passion for rooting out cor-ruption. As Nahas's right-hand man and chancellor he began to protest that the *Wafd* was handing out too many plum jobs to pashas and its own supporters, that contracts invariably went to a few families in the Delta. The Press started picking up Makram's hints and dropping several of their own about the profits in land and cotton made by a certain, unnamed Cairo lady. A transparent veil through which everyone could see the face of Madam Nahas, Zeinab el Wakil. The promotions, the contracts, the cotton rigging were a web of her spinning. Makram's meddling had angered her so much that she intrigued against him; soon, the Copt and Nahas were quarrelling so bitterly that it ended their twenty-year friendship and led to Makram's dismissal from the cabinet.

Two months later, his Black Book appeared. In it Makram had enumerated every piece of graft that he had challenged dur-ing his short term of office – one hundred and eight charges. Nahas, he claimed, had closed a school in Garden City at a day's notice, taken over the site and built his own residence at the country's expense; he had ordered the London embassy to buy six silver fox furs for Zeinab; his cousin had conveniently acquired four hundred acres of arid Delta land just before the government had decided to instal irrigation, thus increasing its value a thousand-fold. Just as damning were Makram's allegations about Zeinab. He catalogued her black market deals, her speculation in land and cotton, her spoils in furs and jewels. Makram could hardly publish the Black Book overtly, but copies were selling in every Egyptian city at three and four times their price; thousands more circulated clandestinely in the Lebanon, Syria and Jordan.

The king could not act while the publication remained un-official, but Hassanain solved that problem by persuading Makram to send a copy to the palace with a petition to the king requesting action. Farouk then ordered Hassanain to deliver the petition to Nahas with a note demanding an inquiry. Nahas was staggered; he rounded on Hassanain, accusing him of treachery by putting an official seal on the document. Makram rubbed more dirt into the injury by defying Nahas openly to bring libel charges against

153

him. The *Wafd* leader cleverly ducked this by retorting that parliament only could judge the issue. All this time, Farouk was beside himself with delight at the public slanging match between the *Wafd* leaders. When he considered the moment had arrived, he made a move to dismiss the *Wafd* government and restore palace rule. He had, unfortunately, mistimed the blow, which Lampson had anticipated; the ambassador had obtained approval from London to sustain Nahas's government with force if necessary. Once more, Farouk had to concede. His only hope lay in the defeat of Nahas when he answered the charges in the Chamber of Deputies. The Wafd leader, however, carried parliament with him, though more by a blend of demagoguery and legal hair-splitting than a complete rebuttal of Makram's accusations. If the members did not doubt his personal honesty, they suspected he had allowed himself to be duped by his wife and her associates in his cabinet. In the country, the scandal did the *Wafd* permanent damage, and the public would no doubt have applauded Farouk for sacking the government. Nahas celebrated his narrow escape by locking up Makram for having fomented unrest. Something else supervened to reprieve Nahas from the cat-and-mouse game which Farouk and Hassanain were playing.

CHAPTER TWELVE

And they have treated the prophets as impostors, and followed their own lusts; but everything is unalterably fixed.
(LIV: 3)

On an impulse, Farouk decided in the afternoon of the fifteenth of November 1943 to spend a few days at Inchass Palace. He climbed behind the wheel of his red Cadillac, with Pulli sitting beside him, his barber and bodyguard in the back and made out along the Ismailia road. Anyone who had ever sat in a car with the king wondered how he had survived, he drove so madly; many of his close friends had met death or injury on the roads; he trusted his skill, and his *baraka*. That afternoon both failed him. He was travelling at eighty miles an hour near the bridge at Kassasin village when he pulled out to pass a British army lorry; at the apex of the long bend in the road he had breasted the vehicle when he suddenly saw another car dead ahead; he spun to the right to avoid it and glanced off the lorry. His car skidded, slewed broadside-on across the road and hit a tree. When they reached Farouk, the soldiers found him lying groaning over the steering wheel which had struck him in the ribs; they freed him and summoned help from the British base close by. An ambulance took him and Pulli to the field hospital in Kassasin base.

At no time did Farouk lose consciousness. Nor had he hit his head. Nor did he suffer from shock, as his pulse and blood pressure proved. Professor Mohamed Kemal Husain, the orthopaedic specialist who examined him within an hour of the accident, found him in pain though talking normally and recounting the details of the crash. When they scanned the X-rays they discovered he had cracked two ribs and a pubic bone in his pelvis. To Sir Ralph Marnham, Acting Consultant Surgeon to the Middle East Forces, and Dr Andrew Lowdon, who treated

155

the king, he presented a straight-forward case. Only his weight made nursing a problem. They could have moved him within a week to one of his palaces in Cairo or Alexandria where they had better facilities for treatment and nursing. The king, however, surprised them by rejecting this suggestion from his own doctors and insisting on remaining in an ordinary army bed in the Nissen-hut ward. 'I prefer an army hut to Abdin,' he grunted as his reason. He could hardly confess he had more confidence in British medicine, and doctors, than in his own staff. He grumbled a little at one British nurse who had to massage him; she merely rolled his big frame over and set to on his back. Within several days he was chaffing the hospital staff, sending them food which his kitchen at Abdin had cooked for him; in a week he was hoisting himself up on the Balkan Beam they had rigged over his bed to allow him to do exercises. Kemal Husain and the other doctors thought it an impressive performance from a man weighing nearly seventeen and a half stone.

He apologised for upsetting the field hospital routine. They had to erect a special marquee for members of his family and other dignitaries who paraded through the Nissen hut. 'When will Your Majesty be fit to return?' Hassanain asked him. 'When I feel in tip-top form,' he replied. Apart from minor peaks in his temperature chart and a few restless nights he was well enough to leave ten days after the crash. And his bad days often had nothing to do with his injuries. 'I always knew why, when they told me about his slight relapses. They invariably followed visits by Princess Fatma Tussun,' said Professor Kemal Husain. The British and Egyptian doctors began to hint he was strong enough to leave; members of the government complimented him on his quick recovery. He ignored them, showing a curious reluctance to discharge himself, though giving no motive. He seemed to enjoy his stay in the army hut and his escape from the problems of Cairo; he rambled on nostalgically about his hard days at The Shop, cracked schoolboy jokes with the nurses and requested everyone to treat him like any wounded soldier. He waved away the bedside conferences with ministers and had not even bothered to order his barber to come and shave him. On getting up he saw the beard he had sprouted, liked it and decided to keep it.

Finally, after three weeks, an exasperated Nahas started to mutter that government business was stacking on the king's desk; someone had to persuade him to return. Not, however, Nahas to whom the king would never listen. The premier approached General Stone who agreed to mention it to Farouk. He began, 'I'm glad to hear that Your Majesty is quite well...'

'Then,' said the king, interrupting with a twinkle in his eyes, 'I suppose I ought to get back, oughtn't I? I'll tell you what I'll do. I'll go back the day after tomorrow if you'll let me take the corporal who has been looking after me.'

On the seventh of December they helped him into a car. His ribs were still strapped and they cautioned him against putting too much weight on his cracked pelvic bone. Certain members of the court knew of his return; so did Nahas, but the *Wafd* leader and the government newspapers kept silent about it. No official notice was given. The premier wanted Farouk to drive inconspicuously through Cairo. But in Egypt he could not keep a secret like that. As the royal car approached villages, fellahin turned out to wave flags; when it reached Cairo it had to slow to walking speed to avoid knocking people down, such were the crowds waiting to greet the king; the city streets, the squares seethed with people shouting, 'Yahia Farouk'. Farouk levered himself up and stood for the best part of an hour in the open car, acknowledging the crowds. 'It was a jolly good piece of bluff to convince them I was one hundred per cent fit,' he told Kemal Husain.

In the Farouk legend, the Kassasin Incident has a prominent place. According to popular belief, Farouk emerged from it a changed man. But had the accident done any permanent damage? The three doctors mainly concerned in his treatment deny absolutely that it left any permanent impairment. The physical injuries were painful but not grave; they ruled out concussion, shock and any other factor which might have affected his nervous or hormonal system. But what are three doctors compared with the Egyptian genius for invention? A pubic bone? Isn't that another way of saying his sex had gone? Why keep him three weeks for a minor fracture? Story was overlaid on story until the Garden City and the Groppie set was certain that the accident had left the king with as much virility as one of his eunuchs. Why, they had even let him drop from a stretcher on his private parts, then they found they could not operate to repair the wrong they had done! What can you expect from the British when they were going to kick him out only eighteen months ago?

Farouk himself gave credence to these rumours by dropping hints that the accident had destroyed him sexually. One day he was gambling at the Royal Automobile Club with his boon companion, Faizi Dellawar, a garrulous man, when he threw an impulsive arm round his shoulder and said, despairingly, 'You know, Kassasin... that finished me as a man. I'm no good any more and you've no idea what it is to live with that thought.' And, as though to corroborate public and private gossip, he appeared to change suddenly; even his gross appetite seemed to increase and his figure become bloated. Yet he was sensitive about his corpulence and spent vain hours on patent weight-reducing machines. His queue of women grew longer, if anything, and he had dropped all secrecy about his gambling which had now developed into a mania. His preceptor, Hassanain, and experienced officials of his palace staff, like Hassan Yussef, the assistant head of his Cabinet, really began to believe that the accident had left permanent scars which were transforming him mentally and physically; others sought simpler explanations for his gluttony. He had always admired his grandfather, Ismail the Magnificent, and eating was one field at least in which he could emulate him. For his card-playing they had no motive, though they dreaded it more than his affairs with women. They could see an end to his love life one day, but reasoned that a king who would stake a small fortune on a card might be driven to risk his crown in the same way.

But the gluttony, the gambling, the women – all these added up to a not uncommon syndrome. Farouk was a voluptuary, and a frustrated one. Professor Kemal Husain, who observed the king closely, said, 'There is no doubt he was sexually incompetent and this tortured him. I believe his eating mania was due to

158

several factors. From it he could get pleasure and it therefore became a sex substitute. His obesity did him no harm in the public eye. In Egypt it is no sin to be fat, if anything it is a sign of virility and a good disguise for an unvirile king. Food would also quieten his nerves, for he was nervous, and make him feel better. As for his gambling, this was another proof that he was a man among men, a part of the exhibitionism that he showed with women. He often reminded me, by his behaviour, of the Freudian picture of the old man who asked why he went to the opera every night with a new mistress. "At my age, the only thing you can do with them is show them off".'

But does Farouk's mental attitude account for such a rapid change in behaviour and temperament? As a boy, Farouk had appeared effeminate to his father; this, and his sexual under-development, caused Fuad to seek the advice of hormone specialists. At this period, his photographs reveal him to have a girlish face; other evidence proves he had delicate, sensitive skin and no hair on his body. In his late teens he had epicene good looks, a sensual face and slim figure. Yet, in the course of five years all that had vanished; Farouk had suffered some strange metamorphosis. He had a thick, jowly face with a plethoric complexion; fat and muscle had obliterated the youthful shape, giving him a massive chest and stomach; hairs sprouted all over his body, even to the phalanxes of his fingers. Obesity had something to do with the gluttony caused by his sexual frustration. But the changes in appearance and behaviour also point to a condition which has been described for thirty years by endocrine specialists. Since 1950 it has been known as adipose gynandrism. Some cases are obvious; the highly-strung, fat boy with badly-developed genitals; other cases take longer to mature and may not be so apparent. Farouk is thought to have belonged to the latter category.

The condition is caused by over-activity of the pituitary, the master gland located in the mid-brain, and the adrenals at the apex of the kidneys. These glands secrete overdoses of cortisone which is associated with the full-faced fatness which Farouk had. The glands also produce androgen, the sex hormone, in large quantities and this causes the hairiness which may be associated, falsely, with virility. These hormone disorders create personality changes, too. The clinical picture of people with heightened pituitary and adrenal activity reveals them to have a tendency to be romantic, even sentimental; in spite of their girth they can be light on their feet; they often have artistic flair and are good companions; temperamentally, they have periods of elation alternating with depression.

Such is the portrait of Farouk at the beginning of 1944, as he appeared to his palace staff. Baffled by his ballooning figure and personality change, they attributed the transformation to his accident. Perhaps they had some justification, since the shock might easily have affected the pituitary gland and accelerated his hormone disorder; it might also have produced subtle changes in the hypothalamus, the part of the brain regulating primal physical and emotional behaviour. This might have accounted for his uncontrolled appetite, for it did appear that Farouk, never a man to pick at food, had developed an eating mania.

However, those outward signs betrayed only part of Farouk's personal despair. He had already hinted – to Farida and her mother, to Faizi Dellawar and others – that there was a deeper tragedy. Impotence. His courtiers, servants and women who knew him well would trace his impotence to the beginning of 1943, before the birth of his third daughter, Fadia; but it had probably manifested itself before then, around the time he mentioned treatment to Madam Zulficar. It was not that any one woman failed to stimulate him, but almost every woman. The condition was undoubtedly psychological; nevertheless there were a few occasions when his sense of inadequacy or inferiority fell away or some woman succeeded in piercing his mental barrier.

Nobody need look hard for parallels in his ancestry. A walk down the gallery of flattering portraits in Manial Palace proves that the whole Mohamed Ali dynasty had much the same shape; they ran readily to corpulence, their cummerbunds strain to contain their paunches, and the artist has done his best with their jowls and dewlaps. If no one can impute impotence to any mem-

Farouk, his second queen, Narriman and their infant son, Ahmed Fuad

Farouk at the opera in Monte Carlo in April 1956

ber of the dynasty, except perhaps the loathsome Abbas, there is none the less no record of the sexual supererogation which Farouk pretended to practise. Mohamed Ali scorned the harem. To him, sex and human accomplishment were mutual exclusives and he spent more time breaking in his brood of Arab stallions than with his women. Ibrahim and Said, too, were out-door men, and even Farouk's model, Ismail, gives the impression that his harem of three thousand Turkish and Circassian women was an exercise in self-promotion rather than self-gratification. Tewfik and Abbas Hilmi lacked the character of great lovers or men of action.

If Farouk's ancestry moulded his character, his early environment might well have sown the seeds of his impotence. The Freudian archetype of the neurotic child with a remote, authoritarian father and a doting, protective mother might well have been based on Farouk's boyhood. Only in the few short months in England might he have had the chance to show himself a man. Then, when he became king, the hand-kissing servility of elder statesmen only served to sharpen the irony of his inferiority, his inadequate personality and inexperience. Soon he realised how impotent he was as a king; soon, he ceased to care about his duties. These factors overlying his complex about his sexual under-development had much to do with his failure as a lover. We can imagine some of the subconscious signposts in the progression of his impotence; the shock and humiliation a sensitive boy must have suffered on finding out about his mother and Hassanain; the sense of defeat in his marital relations which he confessed to his prime minister not long after his marriage; the blow which Lampson dealt him by flourishing the abdication paper in his face. Little wonder that he needed encouragement from his servants and the women they procured for him. Even there, however, he met shame and affront. One dancer stalked out of his bedroom in Abdin Palace spitting insults to his Italian staff about wasting her seductive talent on a boy with no spunk, king or no king. Another found herself lured, only too willingly, to Coin Farouk at Helwan where the king had prepared an elaborate feast lead-ing up to the final scene in his bedroom; the mystified girl had to sleep alone, undisturbed. She went back to her cabaret with a purse full of money, the king's mistress in name only.

Though this psychological impotence had no direct connection with adipose gynandrism, the hormone disorder contributed in another way. The fatter he grew, the more lethargic he became and the more incapable of sexual stimulation. His corpulence itself made the act of love embarrassing. But there seemed nothing he could do either about his obesity or his impotence.

His ministers and courtiers wondered about the frenzied parade around Cairo night-clubs, the gluttony, the topsy-turvy existence. But his Don Juan pose fooled them. They did appreciate one thing: no longer were they dealing with the intelligent, progressive ruler who put Egypt above everything else; this transformed being was developing into a selfish autocrat. An autocrat who had a soft, sentimental streak and who might be too nervous to pick up a telephone and give his own orders. But an autocrat just the same. It made some of them yearn for Fuad's days when at least there was a certain logic to despotism and corruption, not mere whim.

Perhaps Nahas spotted the metamorphosis of Farouk before anyone else. The feud between him and the king was growing more bitter every day. At Hassanain's suggestion, Farouk decided to make a gesture to the villagers of Upper Egypt who were dying that winter in their thousands during an epidemic of malaria. The king and his cabinet chief went together on a tour of the areas of Kena and Aswan on his twenty-fourth birthday, speaking to the villagers and headmen, and handing out ten thousand pounds from the privy purse to buy medicine. The two-man expedition made headlines in Cairo which were not lost on the *Wafd*. Almost before the king had quit the scene, Nahas and a small army of *Wafd* leaders were trumpeting through villages along the Nile, convening gatherings and collecting money from pashas to pay for relief. He capped the royal effort by founding the Nahas Institute at a cost of one hundred thousand pounds. He took the opportunity, too, for a dig at the king's beard which had been grown, he claimed, to confer the look of a caliph on Farouk.

162

It was still another reason for getting rid of Nahas, though since the war had receded from Egypt, the king had itched to sack the *Wafd*. Hassanain would plead with Lampson for the dismissal of Nahas and a fresh election. 'No change,' the Ambassador would say. In the spring of 1944, Farouk heard that Nahas was touring Alexandria to address factory workers; it meant yet another snub. He called Hassanain. 'Either that man goes, or I go.' The chamberlain could see he meant it; he proposed a plan which appealed to Farouk and would end Nahas's term of office.

Hassanain fancied he could gauge Lampson's reaction to the sacking of Nahas, if he went through the motions of forming a new government and relied on British Intelligence to inform the Ambassador. On the seventeenth of April, he convened a cabinet of ministers in his office; within minutes, the rumour of a change was circulating in Government House. But there was no call from Lampson. Did he know it was a ruse? They would have to go a step further, Hassanain thought. Farouk therefore emerged from his study at Abdin in the presence of dozens of witnesses and called for the cabinet documents to sign. Now Lampson acted, making an urgent appointment with the king. Would he repeat the tactics of February the Fourth? Farouk feared so; he instructed Hassanain to watch from the guards' barracks to ensure that the Ambassador had not brought an armed escort. 'If he has troops I shall not wait to receive him,' Farouk added.

Hiding behind a curtain, he observed Lampson arrive in a car with his first secretary. No sign of soldiers. The Ambassador entered, came to the point. The king, he had learned, wanted a change of government under Hassanain pasha.

'It is quite true, Sir Miles,' Farouk replied. 'I have the support of the people and I cannot put up with Nahas and the *Wafd* any longer.'

Lampson retorted that he could not agree to the change and would resist it if the king proceeded.

'But the documents are signed,' Farouk pleaded.

'Then I would advise you to sleep on it,' Lampson said, and stalked out.

For the third time, Farouk had failed to dislodge Nahas. However, the British Ambassador did prevent the *Wafd* leader from stirring up trouble in Alexandria, thus postponing for a few months the showdown between him and the palace. In the autumn of 1944, the formation of the Arab League renewed the tussle. Farouk viewed himself as titular head of the organisation while Nahas insisted on making it a pact between political leaders. The idea of the League grew out of a speech by Anthony Eden, the British Foreign Secretary, at the Mansion House in 1941. Middle East countries should construct stronger political and economic ties, encouraged by Britain, Eden said. Such a bloc, in Britain's view, might resist communist pressure after the war. From the spring of 1942, Britain had been counselling Nahas to take the initiative in bringing the Middle East countries together; it had given similar advice to Nuri es-Said, the pro-British premier of Iraq. Nahas worked hard on the project, succeeding in calling a conference in Alexandria during the first week of October 1944 at which the Protocol of the Arab League was signed.

The *Wafd* leader was congratulating himself when, the following day, the head of Arabic affairs in the king's cabinet, called on him and handed him a note from Farouk. It read: 'My dear Mustapha el-Nahas pasha, Being anxious to see our country governed by a democratic ministry working for the Fatherland, applying the spirit and letter of the Constitution, establishing equality of rights and duties between all Egyptians, and finally assuring food and clothing to everyone, We have decided to dismiss you from office.'

That, and a few ritual words of thanks, ended Nahas's administration. Could anyone really reproach Farouk? If the *Wafd* had preserved order for two and a half years, it had a poor domestic record and, as ever, the odour of corruption floated around its leaders. For once Lampson could not intervene; he was enjoying his first holiday since the war out of Egypt. This had allowed Farouk to square the account with Nahas and, at the same time, assume leadership of the new Arab League.

With Nahas out of the way, Farouk felt he could now govern

164

through the palace. He made his intention clear to Abdel Salam Fahmi Gomah pasha who was replying to the king's speech at the opening of parliament a month later and referred to the will of the people. 'My good pasha,' Farouk said. 'Don't you know the will of the people emanates from my will?' The young reformer, the young idealist had gone.

If only he could resolve the problems of his private life...

Farida now kept to her own suite of rooms in the various palaces, and the king to his. Cunningly, he had placed Pulli in charge of Farida's household so that the queen had to seek approval for all her expenditure from one of the men she accused of degrading her husband and for whom she had a personal dislike. In his turn, Pulli did not care for the queen which made things even more difficult for Farida. Farouk himself lost no opportunity to deflate her, boasting about his conquests in front of her. One evening she found a dancer blundering about in her apartment, searching for the king's room in Abdin Palace and this created a scandal. He humiliated her. Once, when she lit a cigarette, after a meal with Queen Frederika of Greece, he ordered her to put it out. When she protested, he invoked the old justification. 'It is a royal decree.' Every palace now resounded with the king's cronies and his women companions who treated Abdin or Kubbah like an extension of some night-club. And there was always the infatuation for Princess Fatma Tussun.

Late in 1944, he called Hassanain into his study. 'I wish to divorce Farida and marry Fatma,' he said.

'But Your Majesty knows that Princess Fatma is a married woman,' Hassanain replied, blandly.

'I know that better than you,' Farouk growled.

'Then how does Your Majesty propose to marry someone who is already married?'

'It is up to you to search for a way. Ask her husband to divorce her, or get the Royal Court Council to divorce them.'

Hassanain went over all the arguments. Divorce was impossible for Fatma unless her husband had deserted her, had been declared insane or was ill-treating her. And, as the king well

165

realised, none of those conditions applied. The wrangle continued. 'If you want to make it easy you can find a way,' Farouk pleaded.

'I want to help, but this is a complicated problem,' Hassanain said, then adding, 'Remember you will be the first Egyptian king to divorce his wife.'

'Why? Abbas divorced his wife.'

'The circumstances were different.'

'So everyone can divorce except me. Even you divorced your wife.'

'I can assure you it was the biggest mistake I ever made.'

'Well, I want a divorce,' the king insisted.

'Then I am afraid this decision will cause a crisis,' Hassanain remarked. 'Farida is very popular with the people and this may create trouble for you.'

Farouk's anger erupted. 'I have wanted a divorce since 1942 and you said "No" because the position between us and the British was bad. Then I tried in 1943 and you said there was a misunderstanding with the *Wafd* and Nahas might use the divorce to cause trouble. Then when the *Wafd* went you said the new government might resign if I divorced. When can I divorce?'

'At the right time, when you are popular and the people will forgive you the divorce. It is in your hands.'

'Nonsense,' Farouk shouted.

'Suppose,' Hassanain argued, 'you have your divorce and the husband refuses to give Princess Fatma a divorce. You would be creating trouble for yourself without cause. If you did have a new queen it would be no advantage to you if the people did not like her. Remember that King Edward the Eighth had to give up his throne because he married a divorced woman, and I do not want that to happen to you.'

'I don't want any more philosophy. I want a divorce immediately.'

'This is not philosophy but common-sense. Is Princess Fatma prepared to be divorced from her husband?'

'Would any girl refuse to be the Queen of Egypt?'

'First ask her.'

Princess Fatma abruptly rejected the idea of divorcing her

166

husband to marry Farouk. However, the king would not leave the matter there. He summoned several of his courtiers. 'I have something important to tell you,' he announced. 'Fadia is not my child.' He had heard this, he said, from Princess Shevikiar.

Hassanain reasoned with him. 'I advised against your marriage because you were very young, but I tell you, frankly, your wife is innocent.'

Farouk wanted proof. He had doctors perform a blood test on his third and youngest daughter and himself and this confirmed Hassanain's assertion; both blood groups matched. Nevertheless, Farouk remained sceptical, so the chamberlain thought of another way of convincing him. To his friend, Mustapha Amin, publisher of *Al Akhbar,* he produced two pictures, one of Fuad and the other of Fadia. Would Amin print these pictures side by side? Of course, the publisher said, but why?

'The king says that Fadia is not his daughter. By printing these pictures which show a similarity between his father and his daughter he will see that he has no reason for his doubts.'

The photographs appeared, with a commentary by Mustapha Amin. They merely inflamed the king's suspicions. Hassanain found himself confronted by an irate monarch waving the magazine which had run the pictures, and shouting he now had proof of his wife's infidelity.

'It would seem to me to prove the contrary,' Hassanain murmured.

'Why should the queen want to print such pictures if she weren't trying to cover her guilt?'

Hassanain then had to confess it was he who had requested Amin to publish the photographs; the publisher corroborated this, explaining that he and others had observed the similarity between the grandchild and the grandfather; he had therefore asked for sanction to comment on this. It placated Farouk for the moment, though it did not entirely quash his doubts. His accusation had merely given him another pretext for seeking a divorce. This time he took the problem to Ahmed Maher pasha, who had just formed a government to replace the outgoing *Wafd*ists and was preparing for elections at the beginning of 1945. When the king mentioned his proposal to the premier, that portly little man forgot the royal presence and collapsed into a chair. 'This is the end of my government on its first day,' he gasped. 'The people will say you brought me in to arrange your divorce and will throw me out at the elections.' But Maher produced more powerful arguments than Hassanain. 'The deputies will ask why the queen does not love you and may even discuss your private life in parliament.'

'So they mean to insult me,' Farouk muttered.

'The constitution gives them privilege to discuss such matters.'

'We shall leave it till later,' the king said.

Other questions caused him to postpone the idea of divorce. A telegram arrived from the British and American delegations to the Yalta Conference saying that Winston Churchill and President Roosevelt were visiting Egypt to discuss the political situation with King Farouk and other Middle East heads of state. Could the king contemplate divorce at this time? Even Farouk admitted he could not.

CHAPTER THIRTEEN

The desire of increasing riches occupieth you,
Till ye come to the grave.   (CII: 1 and 2)

His private life apart, everything that Farouk touched he seemed
to transmute into success. Huffed at the treatment of Nahas, the
Wafd boycotted the January elections which returned Ahmed
Maher and the *Saad*ists; once again the palace had become the
real source of power in Egypt. Farouk gave his attention to
the Arab League which he envisaged as a pact between the real
Middle East rulers, the kings and emirs rather than the politicians.
So, he set out on his yacht, Fakr el-Behar, to pay his respects
to Ibn-Saud and his vast family, to make the pilgrimage to the
Holy Places of Islam and scatter largess – in moderate amounts –
among the Meccan poor, On his return, Cairo and Alexandria
tried to outdo each other celebrating his 25th birthday; a relay
of athletes carried a flaming torch from Alexandria to light a
flame at the foot of a pharaonic statue in Abdin Square; for hours
the army paraded past the palace and crowds massed to shout
their greetings to the king on the balcony.

Cairo had also developed into a centre for international politics.
A few days after Farouk's birthday, the Arab leaders were meet-
ing in one palace to thrash out a pact uniting their countries,
while Churchill and Eden, with the American Secretary of State,
Edward Stettinius, were holding talks with the Emperor of
Ethiopia, King Saud and Farouk. Donning a different uniform
for each meeting, Farouk assumed each role like an actor.
Churchill was wearing R.A.F. uniform, so Farouk turned up as
an air marshal, puffing on a cigar that little bit bigger than the
British premier's. Roosevelt, already a dying man, received
Farouk (now an admiral) on board a United States destroyer
anchored in the Bitter Lakes.

The Western Desert had been quiet for two years; neither

Germany nor Japan could survive long. Eden pointed out to Ahmed Maher that if Egypt declared war on the Axis before the first of March she would have a seat at the San Francisco peace conference. Farouk agreed; it was no time to quibble about principles. The two chambers were convened in secret session to hear Ahmed Maher expound the arguments for the declaration of war. While the lower chamber wrangled over academic points, the premier decided to put the case before the senators and walked through the pharaonic hall to make his speech. From a table where he had been sitting with two companions, a young man rose and fired four shots at Ahmed Maher. He was a member of the pro-Axis Young Egypt movement and a son of the under-secretary at the Ministry of Communications. He stood trial, but escaped to Syria before being sentenced.

Violence seemed to be in the air. Not long before, two members of the Stern Gang, which was conducting a campaign to drive the British out of Palestine and make a home for the Jews, had shot Lord Moyne, Britain's Minister of State in Cairo. Now Ahmed Maher. Who next? The fact that the king and his government scarcely seemed perturbed by these assassinations must have encouraged other organisations to consider political murder a legitimate weapon. Young Egypt had its commandos, the Moslem Brethren its terrorist arm. These extremists drew up a black list. Next on it was General Ibrahim Atallah pasha, who had co-operated with the British during the war. They shot him. Then, at the beginning of December, someone planted a bomb in Nahas's car; it exploded prematurely, showering steel splinters and shrapnel over Garden City though leaving the *Wafd* leader unhurt. Later that evening, at Shevikiar's palace two or three hundred yards away, someone asked about the bang. Farouk, who was there, roared, 'Oh, somebody threw a bomb at Nahas, but the silly ass missed.' The next month they succeeded in killing Amin Osman pasha, principal intermediary for the *Wafd* and the British. One of those jailed was Anwar el-Sadat, who denied having any part in the crime.

Farouk might erupt with juvenile *bonhomie* about these tragedies; in those days, he appeared smug and sure of his impregnable popularity. Hadn't his late call of war on the Axis assured Egypt world status? Hadn't Churchill and Roosevelt come to him? Hadn't the Arab states chosen Cairo to sign their pact of unity? Hadn't the crowds acclaimed him, the army shown its allegiance? Egypt had, after all, emerged almost untouched from the war; indeed it had flourished while other countries bled. Now it had four hundred millionaires instead of fifty; its industries, compelled to expand to make good the lack of imports, had doubled their profits; a new bourgeoisie was infiltrating the smarter districts of Cairo and Alexandria; and Britain owed the country more than three hundred million pounds. Why shouldn't Farouk congratulate himself and consider the future secure?

What he and every other person in authority failed to detect were the undercurrents. While the rich had waxed richer, the peasants had to toil harder to keep alive. Already they were muttering about their poverty. The new élite expected something more enlightened after the war than the crude horse-trading of the *Wafd* and the cynical autocracy of the palace. In their homes, the disbanded Green Shirts met to talk about Marxism as a possible catalyst for Egypt; in the mosques, and their meeting places, the Moslem Brethren were bidding to capture the souls of the poor and had already enrolled half a million members. Many of these found their way into the militant arm of the Brethren. If they answered el-Banna's summons, a guide would lead them, blind-folded, through a labyrinth of dark streets to the Saliba district of Cairo. In a room, an inquisition of leaders of the secret arm confronted them. On the table before them lay the Koran and a revolver. With one hand on the Moslem bible, the other on the gun, the recruit would swear loyalty, obedience and secrecy in the cause. The cause was Hasan el-Banna who felt the time had come to make his political entrance. Did el-Banna see himself as king of Egypt? Perhaps not, but certainly as the president of a theocratic state. Who could guess what went on behind the Supreme Guide's black-bearded face, except that now he was willing to use terror and assassination to fulfil his dreams.

Even Captain Gamal Abdel Nasser, now an instructor at the

171

Military Academy, and his restive companions, were considering terrorism. Of this period, Nasser wrote later, 'The Second World War and the short period before it, fired the spirit of our youth, and moved our whole generation towards violence. I confess – and I trust the Public Prosecutor will not take me to task – that to my excited imagination at that time, political assassination appeared to be the positive action we had to adopt if we were to rescue the future of our country. I considered the assassination of many individuals, having decided they were the main obstacles which lay between our beloved country and its destined greatness. I began to study their crimes and to take it upon myself to judge the harmfulness of their actions.'

But Nasser and the others would have to bide their time. Farouk still remained the public idol; his picture still graced almost every home and if it were losing its resemblance to the thickening face and figure of the original it did not matter. A fat king was a great king. In the bazaar, the stories about his love life demonstrated that he came from the right stock, and excited envy, if anything. And if he stole it was only from the rich. And what wealthy man resented making a gift to his king?

Farouk's collecting mania was receiving more attention from the gossips than his romances. When Pulli preceded Farouk to reconnoitre the house of the party he was visiting, the host would discreetly hide or lock up anything the king might fancy. The more perceptive discovered, too, that to express pride of possession in anything increased the king's desire to appropriate it. In this fashion, he picked up a priceless silver teaset from Shevikiar. He politely asked the Emir of the Yemen to remove his jewelled dagger so that he could eat in greater comfort. It was never found again. He fastened on stamp albums, books, jewels, watches. Not that he took pleasure in these objects; he consigned them to his museums or his strong-boxes at Kubbah and promptly ignored them. If he felt generous he would send the deprived owner something in return. His friend, Elias Andraos, received a case of Coca-Cola for the valuable clock the king had lifted the night before, and was supposed to laugh at his good fortune and the royal sense of humour.

The king's greatest coup, however, was the theft of the Persian treasure. He had never cared much for his brother-in-law, Shah Mohamed Reza Pahlevi who, he thought, should defer to the ruler of Egypt. The Shah's father, deposed by the British at the beginning of the war for his Axis sympathies, had died in South Africa in July 1944; his body had to pass through Cairo on the way to state burial in Teheran. When it arrived there, horrified officials reported to the Shah that his father's ceremonial sword, his belt and medals had gone. They had been with the body on the plane before it arrived in Cairo. The Shah ordered them to recover the valuables at any cost. One of the officials then remembered that the King of Egypt had asked to see the items, so the investigation began in Cairo.

Farouk was politeness itself to the Persian ambassador. He regretted the disappearance of the sword, belt and medals; they must have been mislaid between Johannesburg and Cairo. At this point, the ambassador produced a document signed by a lieutenant of the Abdin Palace guard for temporary possession of the missing objects. The king undertook to look into the matter.

The ambassador next had a call from the king's ADC, Omar Fathi. Unfortunately a theft had occurred at Abdin Museum, and among the objects stolen were the Shah's treasures. The ambassador's own inquiries revealed, however, that no theft had taken place in the museum, that no other item had been lost. Again, he saw the king, stressing that the Shah insisted on the return of his father's possessions. The Persian emperor would even pledge himself to replace their value with other jewels, but these had a special significance for him as his father's heir and successor. Farouk now promised he would personally conduct a search and retrieve the jewels. This time the ambassador had to listen to another story: a fire had broken out in the museum and destroyed the Shah's regalia, among other things. The ambassador soon refuted that fable. The police confirmed that no fire had occurred at Abdin for more than ten years.

Impatient now with his brother-in-law, the Shah now threatened that, if the king did not return the sword, belt and medals, he would brand him a thief throughout the world by telling the

173

story. How could the King of Egypt, an Islamic ruler, treat the dead with so little respect! Like the master whose servant had stolen from him, he would give Farouk the chance to redeem himself by finding and returning the missing valuables. If not, he would close his embassy in Cairo. Unmoved by the pleas and threats, Farouk persisted with the story that the Shah's possessions had either been lost, stolen or burned. No one could really disprove these theories, so the Shah, still indignant, was compelled to drop the matter. However, when Farouk was dethroned, the articles came to light in Abdin Museum and were returned, with suitable apologies, to the Shah.

The row, which had dragged through 1944 into the next year, led to friction between the Egyptian and Persian rulers, who had always considered themselves rivals. Their next quarrel centred round Fawzia, the Shahira and favourite sister of Farouk. The king, who gave an ear to any and every gossip, heard she was unhappy in Teheran, that the Shah was ill-treating her. The last rumour contained no truth, but it suited Farouk to believe it. In fact, Fawzia had suffered a severe attack of malaria and had taken a long time to recover. Farouk seized the chance to get back at the Shah and invited his sister to Egypt for a visit; he had no intention of allowing her to return, though the Shah was unaware of this when she left.

The king had his story ready. Calling some of his staff together, he told them, 'Fawzia is going mad. I want you to come to the airport with me in case she attacks me.' Indeed, Farouk might have accepted his own fantasy, though again it had no relation to the facts. Fawzia had never been mentally ill. When she stepped from the aircraft she looked pale and drawn from her illness, but she behaved normally. No one understood why Farouk had tried to convince himself she was mad. Nor why he said so adamantly, 'Fawzia will not go back to Iran.' Perhaps only Hassanain had an inkling of what Farouk was plotting. The king had remembered the phrase his cabinet chief had flung at him when he wanted to divorce Farida ('You will be the first Egyptian king to divorce his wife'). Now, it seemed he was planning to separate the Shah from his queen. So Fawzia remained, though the Shah was writing to her, pleading for her return. Farouk hid some of the letters, sent a new ambassador to Persia and began the long process of persuading the mystified Shah to divorce his wife. Fawzia, who had obediently married at her king's wish, would now divorce when her brother decreed it. Did she or her emotions have any say in the matter? It seemed not. Between Farouk and his eldest sister there had been, since their isolated childhood, a much stronger bond than the normal love between brother and sister. Where Farouk was concerned, Fawzia appeared to have no mind of her own.

Farouk now sent Suleiman Kassain of his palace staff to Teheran to fetch Fawzia's belongings. When the two hundred trunks arrived he locked himself in a room at Abdin and took the pick of her dresses, filling eleven suitcases with the spoils. Of course the story leaked out and the Groppi and Shepheard's set capped it by saying that Farouk had instructed Pulli: 'Bull-bull, go and find me a girl this size' (indicating Fawzia's shape). 'I have some shoes and dresses for her.' Nobody thought it beyond him, for his reputation for meanness was growing in proportion to his paunch.

Once more, though, his divorce plans had to wait. The old cry of Independence and the Unity of the Nile Valley was echoing through Cairo streets; the *Wafd* was proclaiming new demands and threatening to turn to the Soviet Union if Britain remained deaf; Hasan el-Banna was openly preaching revolution unless the foreign invaders quit Egypt. His invocation, recited after prayers, went thus: *O God, these British usurpers have occupied our lands, denied us our rights, tyrannised our country and increased the corruption therein. Therefore, O God, drive from us their tyranny, confound them, disperse and punish them along with those who aid them, help them and temporise with them; punish and afflict them by Your might and power, O God, turn against them, visit them with injury, humiliate their state, and drive their authority from Your land. Let them have no means against any of the believers.*

Farouk identified himself with this movement when he opened

parliament in November of that year. He said: 'Today, Egypt is more resolved than ever to see an end to all restrictions to independence by the withdrawal of all foreign troops and to reaffirm the unity of the Nile Valley . . .'

The situation in Cairo recalled the dangerous days of February 1942. British troops still paraded through the capital; their officers and auxiliary personnel had installed themselves in the most comfortable billets with every sign of permanence. To Egyptian nationalists, it seemed that Britain had no intention of honouring the promise of the 1936 treaty and moving its occupation force to the Canal base. The moment had come to seek a review of the treaty, and accordingly Farouk ordered Mahmud Fahmy el-Nokrashi pasha, who had become premier on Ahmed Maher's death, to begin negotiations with London, but, as Ali Maher, Nahas and others had done before him, Nokrashi carried the argument into the streets, whipping up demonstrations against British occupation. Like his predecessors, he found it easier to unleash than to quell the mobs. The British Ambassador (now Lord Killearn) made it plain to Farouk that the British Government had no confidence in Nokrashi's ability to restore order; the king, therefore, demanded his resignation.

Farouk cast around for a strong man and a skilful diplomat. Nahas he would not have at any price, so he fell back on his father's favourite statesman, Ismail Sidki pasha, at seventy-one the doyen of Egyptian politicians. The new premier astutely gave the rioters their head for a few weeks to encourage the more reactionary members of the British cabinet to agree terms. So, Farouk's twenty-sixth birthday saw students shouting, 'Down with England and the criminal Bevin'. Outside Abdin Palace, a multitude roared for an end of the British occupation and a gang tried to burn the Victory Club with little hindrance from the police. In Alexandria, a mob fired a British military outpost and stoned two of its occupants. When he felt he had driven home the point, Sidki presented his demands to the Labour Government; the moment they had agreed to discussion he rounded on his old enemy, the *Wafd*, raided their offices and closed two of their newspapers; he arrested the leaders of the Young Egypt terrorist movement, banned Communist organisations and jailed prominent members of the Moslem Brethren.

That year, 1946 might still have become Farouk's *annus mirabilis*. In February he saw the departure of the man he hated and feared above all others. To ease negotiations and help win over Farouk, the British Government had posted Killearn to the Far East, replacing him with the more tactful Sir Ronald Campbell who had nothing of the pro-consular attitude. Ernest Bevin had even dispatched Lord Montgomery to speed up evacuation of the cities as a measure of British goodwill. Montgomery made some progress with Sidki, but he lost patience with Farouk. 'He didn't seem interested,' he said. 'He kept on saying that what Egypt was suffering from was forty years of British misrule.' On the ninth of August, British troops marched out of the Citadel, symbol of authority in Egypt. Farouk himself led the ceremony at which the Union Jack was lowered; he kissed the green Egyptian flag before it was run to the masthead. 'Cairo,' he told the delirious crowd, 'is the prelude to the complete evacuation of the occupying forces.' Soon, he added, only a small contingent of British troops would stay to guard the Canal. But did he have doubts even then? Not long afterwards, he could turn, cynically, to Nokrashi and murmur, 'Let the British go – but not too far away.' However, the surface looked placid. In a month or two the British would clear out of Kasr el-Nil barracks in Cairo and their headquarters in Alexandria. Who could tell what might not follow? An Arab bloc enriched by oil and commerce, with himself its head? The caliphate of three hundred million Moslems, a spiritual empire stretching from the west coast of Africa to Singapore. Everything seemed possible.

And yet, the portents of his decline had already cast their shadow. Not only in his own flawed character nor in the palace gang which was exploiting his weaknesses; not only in the break-up of his private life; nor even in the ominous signs of opposition from the Press, the Moslem Brethren and other extremist groups, nor the public. In the middle of February, the King lost the one man who might have redeemed him from his folly and weakness. who might have saved his throne.

On the nineteenth of February, the riots in Cairo had detained Ahmed Mohamed Hassanain at his office in Abdin Palace; he decided, at the last moment, to cancel a lunch engagement at Helwan and eat at his home in Dokki. The north wind had blown a rare shower over the city and the roads had turned slippery. As his car crossed the Kasr el-Nil Bridge, a British army lorry skidded and smashed into its side, crushing Hassanain. They carried him to the Anglo-American Hospital in Zamalek where he died five minutes after arrival.

Still in the palace, in pyjamas, Farouk heard the news. Dressing hurriedly, he went with Sidki to the hospital in time to hear of the cabinet chief's death. He surprised the premier by staying only to hear the details of the accident. Leaving the hospital, he drove himself to Hassanain's house in Dokki where the servant admitted him. For half an hour he rummaged through his dead cabinet leader's papers until he traced the document he was seeking. He shredded it into small pieces and thrust it in his pocket. It was the secret marriage contract between his mother and Hassanain. No one outside the family must know.

If his court looked for a reaction from the king to Hassanain's death they were disappointed. If he felt the loss – and he did – he disguised his emotions well. Hassanain he had respected and admired, though he treated him with less courtesy than he showed Pulli or his other servants. Whatever doubts he had about the chamberlain, he had followed his advice. What he now failed to appreciate was that the one real bridge between him and the British had fallen with Hassanain's death. Who, but the head of his cabinet, had the mental ambivalence or the diplomatic finesse to interpret between the east and west? Here, his mother showed more perception than the king. Several weeks after the accident he visited Nazli in her apartment and found her, dressed in deep mourning, reading lessons from the Koran with her ladies-in-waiting. 'This is nonsense,' he cried. 'Hassanain is dead and there is no point sitting sorrowing about it.'

'You don't know what Hassanain's death means,' the queen mother replied quietly. 'Hassanain has kept your throne for you, and now that he has gone you will lose your throne.'

178

Queen Nazli did not remain long in Egypt after Hassanain's death. For years she had suffered from a kidney complaint, and she persuaded Farouk to allow her to seek treatment in Switzerland. She left, taking her youngest daughters, Faika and Fathia, with her. She had other reasons for quitting the country: she sensed that Farouk was betraying the ideals which Fuad had established for the throne, that he was surrounding himself with advisers who could only destroy him; she objected to the life he was leading, the manner in which he was turning Abdin and Kubbah into night-clubs. When she left Europe to consult doctors in America, Farouk did his utmost to persuade her to return, but she would not heed either his coaxing or his threats.

CHAPTER FOURTEEN

Bad women for bad men, and bad men for bad women; but virtuous women for virtuous men, and virtuous men for virtuous women!
(XXIV: 26)

WITH Hassanain and Nazli gone, Farouk sought other company and consolation. While his chamberlain had lived, the companion of his night life, Karim Thabet, had never dared show himself inside the palace gates. Now a royal decree conferred the title of Press Councillor to the Palace on this malevolent, quick-witted Lebanese. At night he was the court jester, filling the king's ear with scandal or making him guffaw at the latest joke. 'Get down on your knees and bark like the dog that you are,' Farouk once ordered, and Thabet obeyed. During the day he became the royal mouthpiece on whom the Press and diplomatic circles relied for their interpretation of palace policy. Thabet soon had his hand in everything, and rarely without seeing money stick to it. A title or a concession, a good word in the royal ear – he handled everything. If Farouk spied a pretty girl, he would even assume the role of procurer royal. One of his first ventures in this field provoked an international incident which embarrassed Farouk and cost him a great deal of prestige.

Camelia, as she came to be known, started life in the poor quarter of Alexandria. In the summer of 1946, an Egyptian film producer spotted her in a cafe in the Mediterranean seaport, followed her to Ramilly Station where he accosted her and bought her a drink. He then offered her a film contract for one thousand pounds, which included playing the part of his mistress. To a penniless girl who had been born Lilianne Cohen it was a fortune which she accepted quickly. The producer changed her name. No one in Egypt would pay to see a Jewess called Lilianne Cohen, he said, and gave her the name of Camelia.

Not long after this meeting he made one mistake: he took

Camelia to the Auberge des Pyramides to flaunt her in front of the king whom he disliked. He chose a table near Farouk, who was sitting with Thabet and appeared to ignore the beautiful, dark-haired girl. But when the producer and Camelia left the club that night, Thabet had ordered someone to follow them home and wait until he could speak to Camelia alone. Would she like to be presented to the king at Abdin Palace? Camelia could hardly credit her luck; from a girl with a few piastres for pocket money to a meeting with the king, all in a week. She was sixteen.

Farouk was enchanted with her. She sang quaint yiddish songs, danced for him and could weep and laugh at the same time. Though a slip of a girl, she could pretend that he was teaching her the tricks of love while she, in fact, was making the running. Camelia was, in fact, one of the rare women who could temporarily obliterate his feelings of sexual inadequacy, who could overcome his impotence. Between the Egyptian king and this Jewish waif there developed an extraordinary affection. For his part, Farouk used the old approach, whispering that he found something strange and mysterious in her that he had met in no other woman. It turned Camelia's head. How could she know he had used the same, unoriginal gambit a hundred times? He would like to take his first trip out of Egypt since the war with her, he said. Did she have a romantic place she wanted to visit? Camelia mentioned that her family had a house in Cyprus, that the island was beautiful, and could they go there? The king promised they would.

In the autumn, he suddenly ordered Pulli to prepare the yacht Fakr el-Behar for a Mediterranean cruise; he chose half a dozen friends who knew of his relationship with Camelia. Nothing of the trip was mentioned to his own cabinet, nor to the prime minister, Ismail Sidki. They would have advised against it, for he had picked perhaps the most critical moment in post-war Egyptian history. The great wrangle over the treaty had lasted the best part of six months and Sidki, though showing his age and poor health, had patiently and cleverly managed to persuade Britain to make a tentative offer to withdraw its troops in stages. Even this success caused strife between Sidki's coalition and the

*Wafd*ists, who wanted complete evacuation immediately, while in London Clement Attlee's Labour Government was having just as much trouble with Churchill, Eden and the Tories. Egypt and the Canal still had the evocative aura of empire, though Bevin argued, logically, that when India had parted from the empire Egypt's strategic and commercial importance would diminish. Bases could be established in East Africa, Palestine or Cyprus. When Attlee announced the acceptance of the principle of complete evacuation, he drew the retort from Churchill in the House of Commons that 'things are built up with great labour and cast away with great shame and folly'. The Conservative leader pointed out that, in the event of war, Egypt might well revoke the right of British troops to occupy the Canal base. 'Can one imagine the British Government in such a situation, when the dread issue of peace or war in a renewed world struggle may be hanging in the balance, forcing the issue . . . ? It is a positive act, an act which will be widely regarded and denounced as an act of aggression, as an act destroying the last hopes of peace . . .'

In Cairo, the delegation led by Lord Stansgate was toiling to find some compromise for withdrawing troops without leaving a defence vacuum; at the same time, it was contesting any Egyptian claim to sovereignty over the Sudan. For his part, Sidki was trying to muster enough support in parliament to lobby the compromise through against vehement denunciation from Nahas who had joined forces with the Communists and other extremists against the government and the palace. The old statesman, Sidki, believed that a treaty offering speedy evacuation of Egyptian cities and total withdrawal from the Canal by 1949 would appeal to the more sane parliamentary factions and stifle *Wafd* demagoguery in the capital. To strengthen his hand he had made successful overtures to Nokrashi and his *Saad*ists.

It was at this moment that the king vanished on his *voyage d'amour* with Camelia. She had flown to Cyprus before him, to avoid detection. In every way the trip turned out to be a disaster.

Farouk ordered the captain to sail for Cyprus, thinking that no one there would identify him. He actually thought he could

182

travel incognito, that his bearded face partly hidden by sun glasses, his thinning hair and paunchy figure would pass unnoticed. He overlooked the publicity he had been given during the war. No sooner had the yacht anchored off Famagusta than a British admiral, attracted by the Islamic green of the yacht and the Egyptian flag, called on Farouk and invited him to dinner; the Moslems then sent a delegation requesting him to lead prayers in their mosque that Friday: invitations to dinner came from the governor of the island, Sir Charles Woolley, and soon people were vying for his presence at their parties.

Farouk also thought he could stage his introduction to Camelia so that no one would guess the real purpose of his trip. After dinner in a hotel in Nicosia she was presented to him, curtsied and described her work for the Nefertiti film company. The king enjoyed the joke, received her and spoke flatteringly about the Egyptian film industry and its graceful actress. Minutes after this ironic performance, Farouk and Camelia were speeding to an hotel and night-club in the hills, previously reconnoitred by Pulli. In his moments alone with the dancer, he promised to buy her a house on the island to which he would come once a year; he would also take her with him on the next trip to Europe. Again his plans went wrong.

A few days after his arrival, a news agency on the island filed a story telling how Miss Lilianne Cohen, the Egyptian actress, had been introduced to the king. A Cairo newspaper picked up the item and published it prominently. (Thabet was on holiday in the Lebanon.) The queen read the account of the meeting and said, angrily, 'This is Farouk's birthday present.'

In Cyprus Farouk received a wire from the palace saying that his meeting with Camelia was causing gossip, that the queen had learned of it. One after another, cables began to reach him: they told him that Sidki was reshuffling his cabinet in an attempt to push the new treaty through parliament and needed his signature to the appointments of new ministers. In fact Sidki had threatened to throw in his hand when he heard that the king had slipped off to Cyprus to meet some low-class dancer. No one at the palace could inform him when Farouk would return and for more than a week he had to fob off the Press with excuses about the cabinet changes.

When he read the telegrams Farouk became panic-stricken. He accused Camelia of chattering about their relationship and revealing their rendezvous. 'Why did you mention this to people?' he shouted at her.

'I mentioned it to no one, Your Majesty,' she replied. 'Not even my mother knew I was here.'

'Everything is finished,' Farouk cried. 'I wanted to raise you to the status of the king's mistress, but you are not suited to the post.'

Next morning a member of the hotel staff rang the bell in Camelia's apartment and handed her a note, typed with no signature. It said: 'I have been forced to leave.' Inside she found fifty pounds. This meagre recompense made her more furious than the king's abrupt departure; she had spent about one thousand pounds on new dresses, shoes and underwear. She rushed down to the port to learn that the Fakr el-Behar had sailed at dawn, long before the message had arrived.

In a clumsy move to cover his tracks, Farouk headed for the south coast of Turkey, anchoring in the port of Mersin. The sight of the Egyptian royal yacht again created a flurry. A Reuter message alerted the Turkish government. Bewildered officials flew from Ankara to greet Farouk, followed by the secretary of the Turkish foreign minister. In London, the Foreign Office wondered exactly what the King of Egypt was doing, and speculation there and in Washington went so far as to suggest some alliance between Egypt and Turkey. Diplomats sought enlightenment in Cairo but discovered that the king's staff and Sidki were just as perplexed. The government wired the king, requesting his return to Alexandria; he tore up the cables and stayed at Mersin.

One telegram he could not ignore, however. It came from Camelia, still in Cyprus, and said, 'Either you return or I kill myself'. Fearing that she might carry out the threat and provoke a fresh scandal, Farouk once again sailed for Cyprus to find Camelia raging at his treatment of her. 'I'm only worth fifty pounds in your eyes,' she said, bitterly. He placated her by calling this a reward to her for having found and returned a ring he had lost in her bathroom. As a consolation, he offered to buy her a house in Cyprus; they spent several days in the Troodos Mountains and chose a villa.

By now, Sidki had grown desperate. The Press, badgering him for the names of his new cabinet, refused to wait; the talks with the Stansgate delegation had reached crisis point. He cabled the king, declaring that if he did not come back, he would resign and leave the country without a government. Farouk, realising he had gone too far, replied that he would meet the prime minister on the island of Rhodes. So Sidki, accompanied by the acting chief of cabinet, Hassan Yussef pasha, arrived by plane in the middle of October; the king received them on board the yacht and signed the rescripts for the new government. Neither of the men noticed that the Fakr el-Behar had an extra passenger: Camelia, the dancer, who had created the international incident.

Although the truth of the escapade leaked into British and Egyptian Government files, the king might still have salvaged his prestige by backing Sidki and arriving at some compromise with the *Wafd* and Britain over the proposed treaty. Instead, he gave his premier a tepid pledge of support while his distrust of the *Wafd* and dislike for Britain did nothing to ease the negotiations. None the less, Sidki departed for London to meet the Foreign Secretary, Ernest Bevin; from the seventeenth to the twenty-fifth of October they had five talks at which they pencilled their signatures on a draft treaty. This conceded the evacuation of Cairo, Alexandria and the Delta by the thirty-first of March the following year and the complete withdrawal of British troops from Egypt by the first of September 1949. Both men seemed even to have agreed the Sudan question; Bevin acknowledged the existence of a symbolic dynastic union between the two African countries, but insisted that the 1899 Condominium and the 1936 Treaty still applied to the Sudan and there could be no change in its defence system. Sidki flew back to Cairo with the draft treaty in his pocket, confident that the king and parliament would ratify it.

Stepping from his plane, exhausted by the talks and the long flight, the ageing premier made a statement to an Egyptian journalist which appeared thus: 'I said last month that I should bring the Sudan to Egypt, and I say now that I have succeeded, that it has definitely been decided to achieve unity between Egypt and the Sudan under the Egyptian crown.'

That one sentence destroyed the proposed treaty; it was seized upon in Khartum by the anti-Egyptian Umma party which became involved in clashes with pro-Egyptian factions in the capital and Omdurman; the British Governor-General, Sir Hubert Huddleston, spoke out against union with Egypt, stressing that the Sudan was working towards self-government. In the House of Commons, the Prime Minister felt compelled to regret the Sidki quotation which appeared to him 'partial and misleading'. The whole idea of a new treaty disintegrated around Sidki who again faced hostile demonstrations by *Wafd*ists and criticism in the Press. Farouk attempted to save the situation; on the seventeenth of November he appeared at the opening of parliament with the queen and received an ovation from members who were well aware of how relations stood in the royal household. His speech emphasised that Egypt regarded the Sudan as a brother state and aimed at helping it towards democratic government.

Farouk had acted too late. Sidki went, pleading ill health, and Nokrashi returned for a second term with the declared object of arraigning Britain before the Security Council of the United Nations. But Egypt had let slip the opportunity to unload the British; the primeval fear that the Sudanese would turn their country into a desert unless they had political control had some relevance to the breakdown of the talks; but the warring cliques in Cairo did more to sabotage the treaty. The *Wafd* celebrated Sidki's downfall, as though they alone had the right to settle the questions of evacuation and the Sudan. Did they even want them resolved, knowing that the solution of the foreign problem might leave them a party without a platform, without mystique, and also focus attention on their weak, corrupt internal government? In its hostility to Sidki, the *Wafd* had stirred up the Young

186

Egypt movement, the Moslem Brethren and, for the first time, the Communists.

The failure of the Sidki-Bevin talks marked the great divide in post-war Egyptian politics. If the threat to Farouk in 1942 had rocked the three-legged stool which symbolised government, the rupture of the treaty negotiations left it perilously unstable. No longer did Britain and the *Wafd* trust each other; the king and Nahas were still carrying on the contest for personal or party supremacy regardless of the country's interests. But Farouk was the real loser. He might have proved his authority by bringing the parties to some compromise on the Sudan and persuading them to sign, as his father and Lampson had done ten years before. But his amorous exploit and his lukewarm support of Sidki had helped to lose him the trust of Britain which had relied on him to keep the country stable when the troops left the Canal. It is doubtful if the king himself realised the significance of this catastrophe. He might have forgotten his father's advice to put his faith in the British, but he could not ignore the alignment of revolutionary elements with the *Wafd*. He probably counted on the backing of the masses, though already his popularity was diminishing. And he was contemplating a series of moves which would make him even more unpopular.

CHAPTER FIFTEEN

I betake me for refuge to the Lord of the Daybreak
Against the mischiefs of his creation;
And against the mischief of the night when it overtaketh me;
And against the mischief of weird women;

(CXII: 1 to 4)

PRINCE HASSAN TUSSUN and his wife had spent the autumn in Europe and were preparing to return to Egypt. Princess Fatma wished to fly back, but her husband vetoed the suggestion. 'It is far too dangerous,' he said, insisting on driving to Marseilles and catching the boat. Five hundred miles by road did not appeal to Fatma, who persuaded her husband to allow her to stay another day in Paris to buy some dresses before joining him and his brother, Said, at the port. On the sixteenth of November 1946, the three-car convoy left Paris after lunch. Said led the way; Hassan sat in the back seat of the second car with his latest trophy, a wooden horse's head. The third car carried luggage.

About thirty miles from Paris, Hassan's car swerved and plunged off the road; the driver leapt clear and with him, the jockey in the front seat; the car glanced off a tree and overturned before Hassan could free himself. Even then he might have escaped, but for his horse's head. One of the sharp ears pierced his side and punctured a lung. They carried him to a house close at hand, but he died within half an hour.

The following day Farouk was lying in bed when his private phone rang. His acting cabinet chief came on the line. 'I have bad news for you,' he said. 'Prince Hassan Tussun has been killed in a car accident in France.'

'And Fatma? What has happened to her?'

'She was not involved and is safe.'

Farouk sighed. Then he said, 'Render unto Caesar the things that are Caesar's'.

He ordered the court to observe three days of mourning. On the day of Prince Hassan's funeral, he followed the procession at a distance in a car with curtained windows. His driver heard him mutter, 'One man entered the tomb today, another was released from it.'

He had waited four years for this day, but the moment it arrived he became curiously tentative. When he saw Fatma he offered his condolences, keeping away from any discussion of marriage. Whereas, before the prince's death, he had invoked the divorce issue every other week, he now seemed content to let it rest. When he raised it with Hassan Yussef, the palace adviser put forward what Farouk would once have scoffed at as a frail argument: he would lose the support of every woman in Egypt if he deserted his wife, and they constituted half the population. Now he listened. His court had noticed the trait in Farouk before. The hunt seemed to have greater lure than the prize. Did the fact that Princess Fatma had no husband cause him to lose interest? Or was he just afraid? Mention of divorce was made once a month, then gradually the king dropped it altogether.

Princess Fatma, too, had changed her attitude. Though she accompanied Farouk to parties, she went more and more un-willingly. She had observed the change in Farouk; his gross manners, his discourtesy to women, his brusque treatment of his palace advisers – all these offended her. The shy, handsome young man she had met at Marg four years before had somehow been transformed into a corpulent boor who leered at almost every woman or kept them sitting in the Royal Automobile Club while he gambled and joked with his oily friends, Karim Thabet and Elias Andraos. When she remarked that he was ruining himself with this sort of life, he laughed, believing her jealous of his other women companions. She objected to his clique of night-club hangers-on. 'I don't like this life,' she said. 'My dignity prevents me from sitting with these people.'

'Why? You will be queen of Egypt.'

'What is the good of being a queen without a king? It is Pulli and these people who are really the king, and you are their servant.'

Fatma was right. Farouk viewed the business of governing the country more and more as an interruption of his personal pleasure; he always had an itch to put his study behind him and make tracks for Princess Shevikiar's palace and this or that night-club; now he had his special chair, strutted to withstand his bulk, at the RAC gambling room. His cronies would gather round him while he played baccarat, cursing his losses and those foolish enough to win money from him. His court had grown accustomed to his capricious temperament, though now they began to think he was suffering from a form of schizophrenia. During the day he was Jekyll, affecting some interest in signing documents, in holding audiences, in discussing politics with his ministers. And he did it ably. At night, he became Hyde, pursuing women, staking fortunes on the turn of a card and making himself the centre of orgiastic parties. Women are bad enough, his staff thought. But a man who can lose fifty thousand pounds in one night at the Royal Automobile Club is capable of losing everything.

His idealism had long ago evaporated; he now ruled by whim. In the case of Hamed el-Alaly, a prospective minister in Nokrashi's government, it was enough that his name did not ring well in the king's ears to see himself rejected. One day, Farouk was casting an eye down a list of politicians in Thabet's presence when he remarked, 'I like that man'.

'And why, Sire?' Thabet queried.

'Because of his moustache.' Thereupon, the king had him appointed Minister of Justice.

When Nokrashi's new cabinet presented itself at Abdin Palace to lunch with Farouk, he showed his contempt for his ministers in a peculiar way. On Nokrashi's right sat the doyen of his team, Abdel Meguid Ibrahim Salah pasha, Minister of Public Works. Everyone else had placed his napkin on his knees; the old minister had tucked his into his neck. The royal photographer was about to take a picture of the new cabinet when Farouk beckoned to him to stop. Turning to the veteran minister and pointing to the napkin, he said, 'It seems that's an old habit of yours.'

190

'Yes, Sire, I've done it since I was a child,' the minister replied, innocently.

'We should keep our good habits and get rid of the bad ones,' Farouk said acidly. The minister still made no move to rearrange the napkin; the king then summoned the majordomo, whispered to him and the man went and removed the napkin, draping it across the politician's knees. However, as soon as the photographer had finished, the minister carefully and pointedly tucked the napkin into his collar again.

Fuad Serag-ed-Din pasha came in for similar treatment when Minister of the Interior. Farouk objected to his smoking a cigar when he presented himself at the palace. The king might smoke cigars on such occasions, not his ministers.

His mean streak extended to things other than money. The woman who slighted or rebuffed him often became the victim of one of his vicious plots. He convinced one Englishman that his wife, who had spurned him, was having an affair with another man. He, Farouk, knew of the rendezvous. Would the Englishman go with him, and would he divorce his wife if they found her with the other man? Farouk's elaborate scheme misfired when they went and discovered the rendezvous empty. Once, he threw a party on the Mahroussa to celebrate *Shem el-Nessim* (the spring festival), and invited a woman who had also rejected his advances. When this Turkish lady went to speak to the queen, Farouk dipped into her bag, produced a photograph and said to the husband, 'Look, you fool, what I have found in your wife's bag. This is the picture of her lover.' The woman raged at Farouk, shouting, 'Yes, I love this man and am going to marry him.'

'I only did it to make your divorce easier and allow you to marry the man you love,' the king said, airily.

For such an exhibitionist with women, Farouk revealed himself a prude about his own family circle. He burst into the house of one European, searched it from top to bottom and left in a temper when he found nothing. Someone had informed him that one of his court ladies had visited the house alone.

In the middle of 1947 an impulse caused him to phone Camelia whom he had not seen since the escapade of the previous year. She had suffered desperately when he left her at Alexandria with very little money. Since no one was interested in the king's mistress, she kept to her small apartment, living on bread and beans bought with money borrowed from her servant. How could she go out? The king's mistress could hardly travel on trams and she could not afford taxi fares. The night the phone rang she had gone to bed early because she felt hungry.

'It is Farouk,' the voice said. He invited her to Abdin Palace but she refused. However, her hunger got the better of her and finally she consented to go. When she arrived, the king was wearing a red arab cloak. He had finished eating, but the silver trays remained, laden with every kind of food. Farouk wanted to make love to her, and when she kept staring ravenously at the banquet before them, thought she was still sulking at his treatment of her in Cyprus. He would make it up, he declared. He would buy her new clothes and shoes. He quit the room to search for fashion magazines.

As soon as he had gone, she fell on the food and he caught her stuffing herself when he returned. 'Why didn't you say you had not eaten?' he asked. Then she told him her story, how she had no job and no money. He gave her a hundred pounds, the last gift of money she had from him. Camelia knew the trait well. He would order dresses and jewels for her, then fly into a temper when the bills arrived. He never liked parting with ready cash. Perhaps this girl from the poor quarter of Alexandria knew him better than his staff or his servants. She often remarked that he had the head of a child and the heart of a wild animal; when he felt sure of her, he ill-treated her; when she stayed away, he grew desperate for her. He was the incurable romantic and sentimentalist, even swallowing her story that he was her first love.

For several months they saw each other. Again they parted when he accused her of gossiping about their friendship, this time with some justice. The break seemed final, until the day Farouk discovered she was engaged to a photographer. Camelia returned from the Metro Cinema to find a palace Rolls-Royce outside her unpretentious apartment. The king had sent her a propitiatory offering with Pulli. A basket of oranges! Apart from beans, the cheapest food in Egypt! She refused to answer phone calls from him, but once more relented and met him.

'You are escaping from me,' he exclaimed. 'Who is the man? I want to know the name of the man who is stealing my fiancée.'

'It is the man I am going to marry.'

'You are stupid,' he shouted. 'Which is better – to be the king's mistress or the wife of a foolish man?'

'The wife of a foolish man!'

Nevertheless, Camelia continued to meet him, even if she took none too kindly to the competition with dozens of other women and the fact that he expected her to obey when he commanded. One day he called when she was rehearsing a film part at the Pyramids studios; she protested that it was impossible to leave until the scene was finished, and went back to the set. Half an hour later a friend came to her and whispered, 'There's a fat man outside, with a hat and dark glasses, asking for you. He sounds like a foreigner.' It was Farouk. Two days later a news-paper published a story about a well-known man, unnamed, who had been spotted kissing an actress in a car on the Pyramids Road. Farouk became more careful after that, furnishing Camelia with detailed instructions about their secret rendezvous and choosing one of his many rest-houses rather than the palaces. Circumstances compelled him to avoid any association of his name with Camelia's, for she was Jewish and already the first storm clouds were hanging over Palestine.

CHAPTER SIXTEEN

And Pharaoh send summoners through the cities:
'These Israelites,' said they, 'are a scanty band;
Yet they are enraged against us—
But we truly are numerous, wary.' (XXVI: 53 to 56)

ON the sixth of May 1947, the eleventh anniversary of Farouk's triumphant return as Egypt's boy king, the Metro Theatre was dynamited. A violent hint to the king that his popularity was waning, as well as a reminder of the growing power of the Moslem Brethren who had chosen the date and the cinema, an example of western iniquity. Farouk knew that the Brethren now counted more than a million members; at his behest, intelligence men prepared a weekly report on the organisation and Hasan el-Banna's movements, and especially the activities of his terrorist followers. The king realised, too, that factory workers were muttering about unemployment caused by the withdrawal of the war-time forces, that peasants had little except beans and oil to sustain them. In addition, cholera was wiping out whole villages in Upper Egypt (an over-zealous Meccan pilgrim had emptied a bottle of holy water into a drinking-well at Assiut). No longer could the king amuse and content the masses by dropping prize-winning ping-pong balls from his private plane, by slaughtering a few *gamoosa,* by joining in the Friday devotions at mosques. Not even Thabet's saccharin journalism convinced the literate that they had a perfect monarch. 'Give me half a million pounds and I shall make you popular again, Sire,' the foxy Thabet said. 'Where,' replied Farouk, wearily, 'where would I get half a million pounds?'

Ever insecure, ever suspicious, he had begun to fear for his throne. Earlier that year, Princess Shevikiar had thrown a party for his twenty-seventh birthday; he turned up, flanked by body-guards – now Albanians whom he preferred to the Egyptians he did not trust. He sought out Shevikiar, greeting the old lady with the remark, 'Your son wants to kill me.'

'That is impossible,' she countered. 'I know him and he would never do anything like this.'

'I have documents to prove it,' Farouk insisted, fishing a newspaper article from his pocket. It was nothing more than an article by Wahid Yussri which generalised about democracy and the right of the citizen. Yet Farouk talked of it as though Yussri had the secret intention of usurping him and appointing himself president of a new republic. Then, the king believed so many people were plotting to oust him and take over his throne: Prince Mohamed Ali, Prince Ismail Daoud, Prince Abbas Halim. Even so, his accusations upset Shevikiar so profoundly that she left the party and took to her bed where she died just over a week later. Though he was quarrelling with her son, Farouk gave Shevikiar a splendid state funeral and appeared as her chief mourner. For those who knew her influence on the king's private life and his career, it was the final irony.

With these threats, real or supposed, he needed some impressive coup to restore his pride as well as his prestige. Nokrashi brought him such a project: they should arraign Britain before the Security Council that summer, charging her with maintaining her hold on Egypt by force of arms and dividing the Nile Valley. Sidky publicly opposed the plan; other statesmen privately advised against it. None the less, Farouk seized on it, urging Nokrashi to make the trip to New York to present the case personally. One matter disturbed the premier more than the United Nations debate: the presence of Queen Nazli in the United States. He thought she might make some statement, or take some action which would embarrass the Egyptian delegation and prejudice their case.

'I have tried to persuade her to return to Cairo, and failed,' said Farouk. 'Perhaps you can bring her back with you.'

Nokrashi refused the task. 'It is my duty to get the British out of Egypt, not to get the Queen out of the United States,' he said.

He did neither. Queen Nazli was taken ill while he was in New York and Nokrashi had to give permission for her kidney operation in the Mayo Clinic. At no time did she create trouble for his delegation.

In the United Nations debate, the Egyptian premier found Britain sticking firmly to the legal point that the 1936 treaty could not be scrapped or revised without the consent of both parties. Every charge he could imagine Nokrashi hurled at Britain. They had occupied Egypt by force in 1882 and had used their power to subordinate the country for their own purposes; they had discredited Egypt in the Sudan and had split two countries which were linked racially; they had no right to consider that the 1936 treaty should hold valid after the war; they had brought about the dismissal of Egyptian cabinets in 1940, 1942 and 1945.

For Britain, Sir Alexander Cadogan pointed out that Egypt had failed to negotiate a revision of the treaty because it was not prepared to grant the Sudan the self-determination it was claiming for Arabs elsewhere. As for the unity of the Nile Valley, this was a myth since the Nile was fed from Ethiopia, Uganda and the Belgian Congo. He countered Nokrashi's charges of British interference with governments in 1940, 1942 and 1945 by offering to produce evidence supporting the actions. How could the Egyptian premier take him up? Those documents, he knew, would reveal officially the part played by Ali Maher and the king in backing the Axis powers during the war. The debate got nowhere, the Security Council finally shelving Egypt's resolution when it adjourned on the tenth of September.

This came as a blow to Farouk. But, in the autumn of 1947 he had other worries, as well as another possibility of regaining popularity. The Moslem Brethren was now overtly bidding for political power; its daily newspaper was attacking both Britain and the Jews with equal vehemence. It had even indicted Britain for spreading cholera throughout the country, and went to the length of forging documents to discredit British diplomacy. The other issue masking the king's sense of failure over the treaty resolution was Palestine.

The trouble began when Egypt learned that the United Nations were discussing a report by one of its committees recommending the partition of Palestine between Arabs and Jews. Again, the agitation was led by the Moslem Brethren which, with other extremists, saw the evil hand of Britain favouring the half million Palestine Jews who were out-numbered three to one by the Arabs.

Britain had, in fact, despaired of settling the Palestine issue on her own. From 1923 she had governed the small, arid strip along the Levantine coast under a League of Nations mandate. Now, with the war throwing fresh economic burdens on her which the home exchequer could not meet, she wished to relinquish the mandate. In the post-war years, Britain had been attacked by both sides. The Jews accused her of stifling immigration, the Arabs of favouring the Jews. Stern and Irgun terrorists had killed one hundred and twenty-seven soldiers and officials, and wounded three hundred and thirty-one. To complicate the matter, President Truman, with an eye on the powerful Jewish lobby in the U.S.A. and the coming presidential elections, would not listen to proposals for limiting immigration into Palestine. In desperation, Britain passed the problem to the United Nations. But, before that body could reach a decision, the British premier, Clement Attlee, decided to surrender the mandate and quit Palestine the following spring. 'It was one of those impossible situations for which there is no really good solution,' Attlee said. 'One just had to cut the knot.'

The Jews viewed this action as an open invitation to the Arabs to thrust them into the Mediterranean; the Arabs condemned it as yet another British plot to weaken them by provoking war with the Jews. Long before the mandate ended, guerrilla warfare had erupted and both Arabs and Jews were preparing for the inevitable conflict. Cairo became the centre of the Arab war effort, though the states belonging to the Arab League bickered among themselves about their course of action. Iraq proposed cutting economic relations with the West, which did not appeal to Ibn-Saud who saw his oil revenues cease; Transjordan advocated withdrawing from the United Nations and this was interpreted by Egypt as a move by King Abdullah to seize Palestine as his Mediterranean outlet. Political circles in Egypt shied away from open conflict with Israel; too well did Nokrashi know the weaknesses of the Egyptian army. But he had little say. Dominating Egyptian policy was the sinister figure of Haj Amin el-Husaini, the Grand Mufti of Jerusalem, who had backed Hitler during the war then fled from Europe to Cairo to continue his intrigues there. He screamed, 'No compromise with the Jews.' It was a holy war. Behind him, his equal in fanaticism, stood the Supreme Guide of the Moslem Brethren, Hasan el-Banna. The slums of Cairo were daubed with anti-Jewish slogans and white-on-green banners proclaiming a *jihad*, or holy war; el-Banna's oratory fired the faithful to burn and pillage Jewish shops and attack Jews in the streets; his terrorist arm, so long underground, could now prise open their secret arms caches and emerge. What could Nokrashi or the Arab League do but enlist this fanaticism? The League formed an irregular Arab Liberation Army from el-Banna's men, civilian volunteers and army officers. Politicians, too, caught the war fever, Saleh Harb, former defence minister under Ali Maher, brandished a Koran and a revolver in front of the guerrillas, crying, 'Brother, these are what speak now.'

And Farouk? He looked on confrontation with the Jews as a cheap way of redeeming his fading authority. His earnest conferences with the Grand Mufti and Abdel Rahman Azzam, secretary-general of the Arab League, indicated the attitude he was striking. If he needed prompting, Thabet was there to flit between the Moslem Brethren and other extremists and encourage the king to take the biggest gamble of his career. But Farouk had already decided on this throw himself, believing it would place him indisputably at the head of the Arab League and renew his candidature for the caliphate, once he had snuffed out the new Jewish state. Mohamed Husain Heykal, the liberal leader in parliament, hinted at other reasons: the desire to distract public attention from the internal chaos, and the necessity to contain Abdullah's ambitions.

Shrewdly, Farouk threw his weight behind the Moslem Brethren, reasoning that if they wanted to die for Allah what better place than the sands of Palestine! His army handed out rifles and grenades to el-Banna's terrorists and ordered them to begin marauding Israeli villages. Other Egyptian recruits had gone to Damascus for training with the five thousand men of the liberation army. When the United Nations voted for partition, these units pushed into Palestine and attacked *kibbutzim*. Against defenceless and disorganised Israelis they did well, especially brotherhood members who combined zeal with some experience. These early successes convinced Farouk that nothing in Palestine could resist his armies if they took the field.

Others had doubts. Nokrashi urged caution on the king who brushed him aside. Several days before the fifteenth of May, when the British mandate ran out, the cabinet met in secret and agreed that the Egyptian army was unprepared to tackle a big military operation. Yet, on the thirteenth of May, Nokrashi suddenly changed his mind. Farouk and his army chief-of-staff had voted for war.

To boost morale, Farouk reviewed his troops before they left for Sinai; he doled out batches of miniature Korans to officers and men. He did his bit elsewhere. Into the baccarat room of the automobile club he would pad, then bellow, 'Bring me my enemies the Zionists so that I can take their money.' Several members of banking, business families and shop-owners would answer the challenge – and invariably rise much richer at the king's expense. The war raised one little private problem: Camelia, alias Lilianne Cohen. She came to inform him they were going to arrest her as a Jewess, working for the enemy. Could he help her to get a beach chalet in Alexandria as a hide-away? He turned one of his government ministers out of his chalet and installed Camelia in his place. He could thus visit her in secret, from Montazah or Ras el-Tin during the fighting.

He busied himself with the grand strategy of the Arab armies, sitting with his generals and ministers, planning the campaign like some boy with so many lead soldiers. However, his tongue was worth a squadron of tanks to the Israelis, for no sooner had he conceived another tactical manoeuvre than the card room buzzed with it. He grappled with the minutiae, too. How big should the flag of each Arab ally be? How many rooms should his engineers build into the new palace at Gaza where he would hold the victory celebrations? So sure was he of victory that he ordered the construction of a great avenue from Heliopolis to Cairo for the triumphant armies on their return.

On the fifteenth of May, Farouk sent his armies into action. His order of the day stated he was waging war to re-establish peace and security; it cited Jewish atrocities, claiming that Arab women had been butchered, prisoners had been tortured and killed. 'The Egyptian Government cannot remain passive before such acts against Arabs so closely united to them in territory adjacent to Egypt. My government gives full assurances that this military action is not directed against the Jews of Palestine, but against the Zionist terrorist bands, and only to help establish security and tranquillity in Palestine.'

At first it looked as though the Egyptian army – two brigade groups of about ten thousand men armed with tanks and guns – would sweep through Palestine. They took Gaza easily while the air force, reputed to be the best in the Middle East, bombed Tel Aviv. One Egyptian brigade group aimed at capturing Tel Aviv while the other was striking through Beersheba and Hebron to link up with Arab Legion troops from Jordan and take Jerusalem. Meanwhile, the Syrians and Iraquis had punched through the frontier around the Sea of Galilee and were threatening Haifa. Altogether, the Arabs out-numbered the Israelis by eight to one, had more armour and better aircraft.

Beyond the partition line, however, the Israelis fought like tigers. At Yad Mordecai, a coastal kibbutz, several hundred men held up the first Egyptian brigade's advance and inflicted heavy casualties; every village on the road to Tel Aviv became a major battle-ground, and the first prong of the Egyptian attack was blunted twenty miles south of the Israeli capital. The other brigade reached Hebron to discover that the Arab Legion, under Sir John Bagot Glubb pasha, had already invested the town, and Bethlehem to the north. As though exhausted by their sparring, both sides acceded to a United Nations truce after twenty-seven days.

While each side promised not to re-arm, the truce developed into a race for fresh weapons. Israel went to the Czechs, buying up war surplus stores; Farouk's men scoured Italy for guns and bargained with Turks, Greeks and former Nazis to re-equip their shaken forces. The king chose the opportunity to visit the front lines; he strolled round gun positions and turned up in command posts, garbed in a tawny, patch-pocketed jacket, a black beret and his invariable rubber-soled shoes. General Ali el-Mawawi, the commander-in-chief, had a pistol which the dignitaries of Palestine had presented to him; the king expressed a wish to examine it, and Mawawi bey lost it for ever.

On the eighth of June, the day before the truce expired, the Egyptians mounted another assault. Saudi Arabia had now joined the other five states. But the Arabs found themselves confronting a transformed Israel. Swiftly, the Jews recaptured Lydda Airport between Tel Aviv and Jerusalem; they thrust the Syrians out of Nazareth, broke through to help their beleaguered troops in Jerusalem, then turned south to face the advancing Egyptians. In ten days, Israel had crushed the attempt to extinguish the new state; the Arabs hastily assented to another truce. But the United Nations granted the whole of the Negev to Israel during the talks – and fifteen thousand Egyptian troops still remained trapped between Beersheba and Gaza.

Farouk realised that it was defeat, now or later. How could he avoid personal humiliation? Had he been given the chance, he would have pulled his armies out of Palestine there and then. But Abdullah would then grab that part of Palestine. And how could he explain the catastrophe to his people? One man had made such admission almost impossible: Karim Thabet. The war had opened up boundless scope for his perverse talent. Nowhere did his version of the fighting correspond with reality; the capture of Gaza he portrayed as an epic victory; each kibbutz which had fallen on the road to Jerusalem evoked glowing prose and tributes which the Press and the radio broadcast. And who had master-minded every military triumph? His August Sovereign, King Farouk. With his perverted accounts of Egyptian victories and Farouk's part in them, Thabet overlooked one thing. The Egyptian army might be unable to read about its imaginary successes, but it could listen to them on the Egyptian

201

radio. Major-General Neguib, who had been wounded three times, squirmed at the lies emanating from Cairo Radio; so did Captain Gamal Abdel Nasser, who had witnessed the reverse of the first two campaigns on the way to Tel Aviv. Sharing Nasser's view of this false propaganda, and of the deficiencies in the army command were several of the officers who had passed out of the Military Academy with him. Thabet's lies merely deepened the disgrace and led many of them to imagine they were being betrayed. Thabet had even landed himself in a quandary. With a string of unbroken victories on his files how could he write the last story? How could he gloss over the fact that Egypt was suffering from defeat? And, having given the king much of the credit for these feats of arms, how could he blame anyone else for the disaster? Those fables of the Palestine War would rebound on Farouk one day.

The king was already suffering, privately and publicly. He felt the humiliation profoundly, especially when crowds jeered as he left the Metro Theatre one afternoon. Though newspapers flaunted his pictures in full military regalia, people were whispering about his visits to night-clubs, his gambling, his women. A senior member of his staff tried to persuade him to forego his night life while the war was on, but he waved him aside, angrily. Prompted by the same official, Nokrashi had a frank exchange with the king about his relations with Camelia and his gambling.

The premier went to the king and told him, 'I have some information that some of the women you go out with are spies. The Jews get information through these spies, and I know that you are having an affair with a Jewish girl.'

'Nonsense,' Farouk snapped. 'Don't believe that story. I did have relations with a Jewish girl, but I left her.'

'The Jews could use this girl to kill you.'

'My life is my own affair,' Farouk shrugged.

'No, your life is no longer your own affair,' Nokrashi replied. 'The Jews are our enemies and people notice that you gamble with the Jews at the Royal Automobile Club. They ask, "How can the king gamble with the country's enemies?" '

'I gamble to take their money. They lose and I win, and in this way I get their money.'

'If they lose, it is to make you feel they are friends of Egypt. Another thing, this is an Islamic country, and those who gamble are against Islam.'

'I don't gamble in the streets.'

'No, but there are many members in this club, many waiters and servants. They go home and tell their wives and friends that the king is gambling.'

For a moment, Nokrashi believed the king was going to strike him; his face flushed and he rounded on the premier. 'If everything I do is going to interfere with my private life, then I don't want the throne. I don't know why you come to me with street gossip.'

'Those streets make up the nation, and when you lose the people you have nothing left. I must be careful that people do not start to lose trust in you. If your prime minister cannot advise you, who will?'

'But everybody in the country gambles,' Farouk muttered. 'My father gambled.'

'Yes, but he gambled in the palace with men of his own rank. No one knew, and yet during the 1919 revolution people said the king was gambling, and a newspaper published the information.'

'And you printed that paper,' Farouk retorted. 'How did you know he was gambling?'

'One of the servants at Abdin Palace told his friend who was a parliamentary servant. It made people angry, for they dislike gambling. I don't think that kings should gamble. I'm afraid the time will come when you will gamble with everything.'

'I feel I'm not going to stay king for very long.'

'If the king feels that, the country will be unstable and you will do foolish things. The throne is a duty which you have inherited from your great-great-grandfather and you have to pass it on to whoever comes after you.'

'I don't mind who comes after me.'

'You must think of your country.'

'The people hate me,' Farouk said, petulantly.

'Then you must stop annoying the people if you know why they dislike you. They feel you have surrounded yourself with a gang of people who are not Egyptians and who don't like this country. If you had been surrounded by Egyptians they would have told you why the people did not like you.'

Grim news came from the front where, in October, the truce was again violated and the Israelis were hammering at Egyptian positions in Arab Palestine. Not even Thabet could manipulate the Press and radio to turn these defeats into triumphs. The Israeli assault had caught the bulk of Egypt's first brigade in a twelve-mile pocket around Gaza which took the name, Faluja, from one of the villages within it. More than five thousand men were pinned in this sector while the Israelis, with their newly-acquired guns, tanks and aircraft poured fire into their trenches. The men of the Faluja Pocket became heroes in Cairo; they did something to repair the shame of seeing thousands of troops trickling back from Palestine. The soldiers' hero of Faluja was Colonel Sayyid Taha, a giant Sudanese whom the troops dubbed Black Wolf; but Gamal Abdel Nasser, Abdel Hakim Amer and several other Egyptian officers also held on to their positions. Their stand at Faluja had raised their status among the younger officers, a fact they exploited in recruiting members of their Free Officers' Society, the organisation which aimed at reforming the army which had done so badly in Palestine. The Egyptian hero of the war was Major-General Mohamed Neguib; in the seven months of fighting he had received three wounds, the last so serious that they gave him up for dead. A quiet, loyal soldier, Neguib had been sickened by what he saw in Palestine. Poor training had contributed to the débâcle, but so had obsolete equipment like the shells which failed to explode and the grenades which did – prematurely. The Egyptian high command had bungled by insisting that the country was ready for war, then letting fighting men die for want of support. At this point, the soldiers did not blame the king, nor did they envisage over-throwing him. They merely thought of strengthening the army.

Now the army, demoralised, was retreating before the Israelis who had by-passed Faluja and were penetrating into Sinai; at Rafah and El Arish they had bottled up Egyptian units and were preparing to strike into Egypt. Within a few days they might have crossed the desert and worked down the coast to the Suez Canal. Had that happened, Farouk's history as King of Egypt would have ended there and then. But the Jews had forgotten that Egypt had a treaty with Britain, a country which was touchy about the Canal. On the last day of 1948, a telegram from the U.S. State Department landed on the desk of James Grover McDonald, American Ambassador to Israel; it ordered him to hand Israeli Prime Minister, David Ben Gurion, an ultimatum stating that if his country did not immediately withdraw from Sinai, Britain would enter the war on the Egyptian side. McDonald had only a few hours to act; it was mid-afternoon and they told him that Ben Gurion had gone to the Sea of Galilee for a rest-cure and could not return. The ambassador had to undertake the journey himself, skirting the Arab lines and taking his chance with minefields before reaching Galilee. The ultimatum angered Ben Gurion, but McDonald stressed that the British meant what they said. Finally the premier said, 'Well, we can take on six Arab countries but we really can't take on the British Empire, too. There will not be a single Israeli hoof on Egyptian soil in forty-eight hours.'

Thus ended the Palestine War. On the twenty-fourth of February, at the Rhodes armistice, Israel won the right to the Negev; Abdullah got his hands on Palestine, though he paid for it with his life, dying at the hands of one of the Grand Mufti's followers. Egypt had to withdraw from Judea, having lost everything she had gained in prestige among the Arabs and emerging from her adventure shaken and facing grave internal problems.

Long before the signing of the armistice, Cairo had boiled over with riots largely instigated by the Moslem Brethren. El-Banna's men were running amok, their ranks expanded with the over-spill of students from the two universities, their terrorist arm now aiming not only at the foreigners but at Egyptians who had betrayed Islam. In October, the commandant of Cairo police, Selim Zaki pasha, fell to an assassin's bullet; after him, the governor of Cairo. Nobody felt safe. Farouk, who had flirted with the brotherhood in its early days to counter the *Wafd*, now realised they were tilting at organised government, even his throne. The premier, Nokrashi, went further, insisting el-Banna was bidding for absolute power; he drew up a decree outlawing the movement, banning its newspaper and the various organisations in which it had a financial interest. Before he signed the decree Mustapha Amin, the publisher, sought him out with a message from the leader of the terrorist arm. This brother had told him, 'We do not want to kill Nokrashi since we do not believe he is a traitor. But we will have to if he signs the decree.' Nokrashi laughed off the warning. 'I was supposed to die when I joined the 1919 revolution,' he said, no doubt referring to his trial after the murder of Sir Lee Stack. 'I have therefore had an extra thirty years.'

El-Banna, himself, met Thabet to make a final appeal through him to Farouk to rescind the decree; he undertook to stop interfering in politics and back the king in his fight against Communism and other subversive factions. By now, neither the king nor Nokrashi trusted the Supreme Guide's word; the decree proscribing the brotherhood was signed on the eighth of December. El-Banna kept his promise on one matter. Three weeks later, Nokrashi was stepping into a lift at the Ministry of the Interior; from a corner of the building several men sprang, one emptying a revolver into the prime minister.

In Nokrashi's place, Farouk appointed his own cabinet chief, Ibrahim Abdel Hadi pasha, ordering him to stamp out the brotherhood at any price. The new premier used the police ruthlessly against the movement. From the evidence they uncovered it became clear that el-Banna meant to stop only at the presidency of an Egyptian republic, that he even saw himself as a new caliph. His cells had proliferated throughout Egypt and other Middle East countries, and he had linked these with his own secret radio network. The quiet, enigmatic priest now commanded an army big enough to set Egypt and several other countries ablaze and looked as though he intended to give the word soon. At the beginning of 1949 his faithful were estimated to number nearly two millions, his terrorist organisation several hundred thousand. Abdel Hadi cracked down on the fanatics; the prisons filled with Brethren leaders who found themselves, ironically, occupying beds which Jewish prisoners had vacated only a few hours before, having been released by the government. If Abdel Hadi and the king required proof of the Supreme Guide's motives they unearthed it in the homes of these prisoners, and even of peasant families.

Thabet entered the king's study one day to sound him out about a pact with el-Banna and observed that Farouk was glowering over a calendar.

'Do you want to see the picture of the new king?' Farouk demanded.

'The new king!'

Farouk handed the calendar to the press councillor. 'This is only one of hundreds of copies which the police seized at Damanhur. They have all had my photograph removed and el-Banna's stuck in its place. Nokrashi was right when he assured me these people wanted to rule.'

Though driven underground, el-Banna could still stage his revolution. Millions agreed with him when he declaimed against the Jews and the British, against corruption in the government and the palace; when he cited the Koran as a testament to revolt. Early in 1949, his disciples secretly proclaimed him Caliph of Islam, and it seemed that even political organisations would rally round him.

On the twelfth of February 1949 the Supreme Guide was conferring at the Young Men's Moslem Association in El Malika Street. As he quit the building, a group of men who lay in ambush opened fire on him from a car, and he fell. No one has ever found el-Banna's assassin, though several people were brought to trial after the revolution. It is thought that the wife of a prominent Moslem Brother revealed the details of his secret rendezvous to her lover, a member of the secret police. This man, one of the police who guarded Nokrashi, had vowed to kill el-

207

Banna; he planned the ambush and probably fired the bullets which killed the religious leader. The Revolutionary Council believed this, since they were on the point of arresting the man when he committed suicide. However, suspicion naturally fell on Farouk and his prime minister. The story that the king had ordered the assassination gained credence when one of his aides openly boasted that he had shot the Supreme Guide. No one has ever produced evidence that Farouk ordered the execution; he did not, however, disguise his pleasure and relief when someone brought him the news.

Without el-Banna, the brotherhood never again wielded the same power. The singer was always greater than the song. No more did the brethren rant about Koranic law, or revolution, or spiritual direction of the Moslem world; its new leader, a parched character called Hasan el-Hodebi, made a pact with Farouk, and while the king remained, his followers kept quiet.

CHAPTER SEVENTEEN

*When ye divorce women, divorce them at their special
times. And reckon those times exactly, and fear God your
Lord ...* (LXI: 1)

In the middle of the Palestine fiasco, Farouk decided he would
divorce his queen. Nokrashi lamented that he could hardly have
chosen a worse moment; he reminded him he would lose all
public sympathy and repeated the arguments which had previously
deflected him. This time Farouk would have none of them. Farida
wanted the divorce as well, he said. It was true. For four years
they had shared their four palaces, but rarely saw each other;
Farida and the children kept to their apartments, Farouk to
his. For the sake of her children Farida had forced herself to
remain queen, though disliking every moment of the life Farouk
led, the company he kept and the gang which had attached
itself to him. Finally, her patience ran out.

Nokrashi still insisted that it was a bad moment. The king,
however, had a brilliant idea. Why not let the Shah of Persia steal
some of his ignominy by persuading him to divorce Fawzia at the
same time? It took months to convince the Shah that he should
divorce his wife, who had remained in Egypt, though eventually
he consented and Farouk could therefore proceed with his
plan. Accordingly the double divorce was arranged; on the
seventh of November 1948 both rulers went through the simple
ritual of Moslem divorce, one in Teheran, the other in Cairo.

Farouk had chosen the second and more solemn method of
divorce in which a man repudiates his wife before Allah. This
necessitates concrete grounds and, as Farouk commented later,
the failure of a wife to produce a son does not entitle a man to
divorce her under Koranic law. Farouk intended to make his parting from Farida final. And yet he had qualms. At the last minute
he appealed to the queen to return to him, sending first her

father, then Husain Sirry, his grand chamberlain and former premier, to plead with her. She refused. The king, thereupon, went through the formula of repudiating his wife three times, then signed the divorce papers. When the ceremony had finished, he disappeared. Several hours later, two of his sisters, Fawzia and Faiza, found him in one of the palace rooms, sobbing like a child.

The announcement from the palace said, 'The will of Allah, our Supreme God, has decreed that the sacred ties between the two noble spouses be loosened, and he has turned the heart of His Majesty, King Farouk, and that of Her Majesty, Queen Farida, to this act, notwithstanding their mutual dislike of a separation by repudiation.'

Farida reverted to her maiden name, becoming Madam Safinaz Zulficar. To the villa she had built near the Pyramids, she took her youngest daughter, Fadia, and her English governess, Miss Anne Chermside. The other two daughters remained with their father at Kubbah Palace, though they were allowed to visit their mother once a week.

With his divorce, Farouk alienated himself further from the Egyptian people for whom Farida had always proved a popular figure; he also widened the rift between himself and his mother, who knew nothing of the double divorce until she heard a radio announcement in America. Any chance he had ever entertained of inducing Nazli to return to Egypt had now gone. Their final break came when the queen mother renounced her religion and converted to Roman Catholicism after having been nursed through illness by nuns. Two years after his divorce, the king promulgated another decree depriving his mother of her titles and possessions in Egypt.

Most people in touch with the court imagined that Farouk would now marry Princess Fatma Tussun. But Fatma had fallen in love with someone else. At a party one night in the Brazilian Embassy in Cairo, she met Prince Juan of Braganza, a descendant of the old ruling family of Brazil, who was passing through the city. Within thirty-six hours, Dom Juan, director of a Brazilian airline, had flown back to Cairo to phone Fatma and ask her to marry him. She said, 'Yes,' then made her plans to leave

Egypt. As the king, Farouk had to grant his relative permission to leave the country, though she had already had his consent to take her daughter to Switzerland to have treatment for asthma. Suspecting nothing, Farouk said goodbye to her and she departed, to meet Dom Juan in Europe. A few weeks later, Farouk was informed that she had become engaged to the Brazilian nobleman, news which sent him into a fury. He would move heaven and earth to stop this marriage and bring her back. First, he dispatched his acting cabinet chief, Hassan Yussef, to the Brazilian ambassador to ask him to intercede and prevent the wedding. Hassan Yussef explained that Moslem women were not permitted to marry outside their religion if any member of their family objected. The bewildered ambassador agreed, but was it a matter for him? What could he do to influence Dom Juan, or Fatma? Next, a mission went to Paris, where the couple intended to marry, to plead with Fatma to return. Alive or dead, she must be brought back, Farouk instructed the head of the mission.

'His Majesty begs you to return and meet him for a short time to discuss the matter,' the official said. 'If you do not agree with him you can then come back to France.' Fatma replied that she had too many commitments and would be unable to travel for some time.

'His Majesty would have liked to tell you this in person, but could not leave the country. He has authorised me to say that he will make you Queen of Egypt if you will return.'

'He must know that this is not possible, since I am engaged to marry another,' Fatma declared.

Seeing that his arguments were having no effect, the official took another tack. 'His Majesty says that, if you do not return, he will take away your titles and confiscate your wealth. You have two thousand feddans (a feddan is roughly an acre) and your daughter has eight thousand feddans. You can lose ten thousand feddans by this marriage.'

Fatma retorted that wealth did not interest her.

'He will prevent you from seeing your daughter.'

'When my daughter is grown-up and understands the circumstances which made me leave her she will come back to me.'

So Fatma resisted every argument. Even the hostility of her own family, inspired in some measure by the king, would not change her mind. She was married soon afterwards in the house of the Comte de Paris and went to settle in Brazil. The day of the marriage no one, not even Pulli or Thabet, dared approach Farouk. Now he felt persecuted, that everyone was betraying him; this intensified his sense of sexual inadequacy, his security as a king. The pretence of ruling – that, too, seemed beyond him. The further he withdrew into the labyrinthine wastes of Abdin, Kubbah, Ras el-Tin or Montazah, the more furious his night life became, as though he were determined to prove that he did not care. State business he shrugged wearily aside, his private cabinet irked him. But contact with these people was rare, not surprisingly since he and his staff were working different shifts. When they were lunching he was sitting up in bed, gulping down orange or guava juice, reducing Pulli's serried ranks of eggs, moving on swiftly to fish cakes, steak or chops, a kidney, coffee, toast and marmalade. His barber would then shave him before he stepped a few stately paces to his bathroom where he would spend fifteen futile minutes presenting his paunch, his fleshy chest and hips to the latest American vibrating machine which never appeared to make a millimetre of difference. His valet would then dress him while he cast an eye over his appointments for the day. Audiences he cut to a minimum; orders to his staff would be transmitted through the valet, Mohamed Hassan Suleimani, or one of the Italians. From this period dates the formation of what Neguib later christened the 'kitchen cabinet'. State secrets, coded messages, commands and reprimands – almost every communication to and from the king passed through the valet or another of the servants.

He had renounced the practice of sitting at his study desk. Papers piled up under the clenched bronze fist his father had bequeathed him as a paperweight, with its Arabic inscription, reading, 'I will do'. The king's private secretary, Husain Hosni, admitted that, in the last three years of his reign, he seldom met Farouk and never had a private audience. A note dictated to the valet, signed or unsigned, would arrive on the desk of the cabinet chief, whether it concerned some new gadget the king wanted from Europe or America, or an instruction to his prime minister. If the mood was on him, Farouk might empty his in-tray at any hour between midnight and dawn, then dispatch a servant to wake up senior palace officials with the documents.

He gave the impression of having abdicated responsibility, of wishing to live like a rich sybarite. Yet, even in this role, he failed. He had never parted willingly with money, but now his mean gestures were written into his legend. He would purloin a gold lighter, a new type of razor, or something as mundane as a matchbox; he would lift a valuable book from someone's shelves, or leave holes in a stamp album to fill gaps in his own. In a sense, his collections reflected his character, his restless, inconsequential spirit. His exquisite Fabergé ornaments, his priceless watch and clock displays lay cheek-by-jowl with a stock-pile of cigarette cards, post-cards, cheap ashtrays, walking sticks, razor blades. His famed hoard of erotica varied from artistic nudes to shabby representations of female nudity in corkscrews, cocktail glasses and statuettes; the pulp paperbacks with garish covers also proved that his taste in pornography had not developed beyond the adolescent stage. His jackdaw complex, his instinct for acquiring what other people prized was all very sad.

He split his time between the gambling table at the automobile club and half a dozen night-clubs. At one time, people passing along Kasr el-Nil street could tell Farouk was playing cards; his loud, constrained laughter reached as far as Suleiman Pasha Square; now that the laughter was more muted, they had another proof, with his bodyguard lounging outside or taking up discreet station at the windows of surrounding houses. Since the death of el-Banna and the Palestine débâcle they could take no chances with his safety. Inside, the king played obsessively, his face empty of expression or brooding over his cards; occasionally, his jowls would wobble at some joke he or Thabet had made. He gambled badly, relying like his father on luck rather than probability, and losing with ill grace. Once, with a large pot on the poker table, someone with three aces decided to call the king. 'Full house,' Farouk said grandly, and everyone waited for him to table his cards. He threw them, face-down, to the dealer, looked at the man and said, 'Parole du roi'. On another occasion he was called when holding three kings to a full house. 'I am the fourth king,' he insisted. Wit apart, such royal jokes were not always appreciated. He was credited with observing, more seriously, to King Zog of Albania, 'Soon, there will be only five kings left: Spades, Hearts, Diamonds, Clubs and the King of England.'

However, one man laughed in the right places and lost to Farouk as though the king were conferring a great favour on him. Elias Andraos had wormed his way into the royal fraternity by donating money to the Moassat Hospital in Alexandria where the king had a top-floor *garçonnière,* well-stocked with foreign nurses who walked the wards rarely. Andraos, a fleshy-face Copt, had built his fortune out of wartime scrap and invested some of it buying royal patronage. Farouk rewarded these gifts and the economic advice Andraos gave him by creating him pasha, a decision to which even his most servile palace officials took exception. By then, the title, like everything that Farouk seemed to touch, had been devalued. Even the king's jeweller, Ahmed Naguib, was now a pasha. Andraos capitalised on his title and his royal contact to increase his fortune; and every shady deal which involved him also, by implication, involved the king. It must be said that Farouk often remained ignorant of how the Copt was using him and his name. Nor did he profit much financially from Andraos's jobbery.

Everyone knew of Farouk's topsy-turvy life. When he entered a club with his gambling friends, those who could escaped, or faced the prospect of being trapped by protocol until the king took his leave. A woman cousin of Farouk, and her friend, were caught thus in Alexandria. Finally, the cousin approached him, curtsied and said, 'Your Majesty, please go home so that we can all leave.' He gazed at her through his tinted spectacles. 'Home?' he muttered. 'Home? I have no home.' He could hardly call Abdin or any of his other residences 'home'. As though they symbolised his failures or the duty he was growing to hate, he stayed away from them as much as possible.

Instead, he would spend aimless hours in his favourite haunts. Camelia was singing at the Auberge des Pyramides and, at the Scarabée, there was a new French singer called Annie Berrier who had captivated him. Annie became his new companion; she would finish her act, come and sit with the king then make the rounds with the royal party. Night after night, he would squat on the perimeter of the stage, pensive between outbursts of laughter, his eye roving the dance-floor or other tables, his gaze travelling slowly from female ankles to face. He fancied himself an authority on women, reading charm and character in their legs and their way of moving, criticising this or that girl. So there he sat, this bloated satyr putting his cloven hooves on show, intent on the next adventure. His clique vied with one another to indulge him. A new girl or a new party piece and they had the king's approbation. But now it took more than a new face to stimulate his flagging sexual appetite. His medicine cupboards brimmed over with bottles, phials, pill-boxes, many of them- aphrodisiacs; he drew the line at powdered rhino-horn which someone brought him, though he would try amphetamines, mixed hashish and honey, caffeine tablets. His obesity, always an aesthetic embarrassment, further complicated his attempts to make love.

Whatever they found him – a singer, belly-dancer or some- one nearer his own class – he never varied his romantic formula. The girl of the moment was stranger than anyone he had ever met; he saw something mysterious and remotely beautiful in her; if he were not a king with all his responsibilities, he would escape somewhere, anywhere, with her. Later, the dancers, the night- club entertainers might make fun of the king's corny line, but at the time they were flattered, half-believing him. After all, he was a king. He would put his words of love into French, which he contended was the only language for them; he could, how- ever, switch his unoriginal patter into any of his seven languages.

His women friends discovered him to be sentimental, romantic. Late one evening in early 1950, he picked up a dancer outside the Auberge des Pyramides. He had just attended a religious ceremony with some of the government ministers, and hungered for some excitement. He turned the red Cadillac south, then east towards the Suez road. The dancer asked where they were going, and he said, 'To a romantic place. To Al Maza.' Everyone in Cairo knew Al Maza, their lovers' rendezvous. He reached the spot, halted the car; the desert was quiet at that hour and the moon had come up full.

As though waiting for them to embrace, someone threw a strong beam of light on Farouk and his girl friend; several men sprinted from a parked car close by. The king ran to his own car, grabbed a pistol and began firing in the air. All of a sudden, the men halted. They had recognised Farouk. He had been caught by the morals squad which, every now and then, swooped on couples as much at the king's insistence as anyone else's. Worse still, that night a writer from Al Mussawar and a photographer from Al Assas had accompanied the police to report their raid; the cameraman had already taken some flashlight pictures of the scoop. As Farouk stepped fully into the headlights one of the policemen fainted. The king grabbed the camera and smashed it against a stone; he fired several more revolver shots over their heads, climbed into the car and drove off.

Two days later, Akhbar el-Yom published a story about an anonymous Great Man whom the police had ambushed in the act of love. He had, according to the report, suppressed an investigation into the incident which the newspaper described. Furious the king ordered the seizure of the paper, even demanding that every sold copy should be traced and confiscated. However, he made no secret of the story among his own friends, joking and guffawing about the discomfiture of the police, and acting as if he wanted them to spread the gossip.

This curious quirk in his nature (which Edward Ford had perceived so long ago) still impelled him to glorify himself and impress even those who did not matter. He told one British ambassador that Egyptian secret agents had arrested two Jews who were trying to poison the Sweet Water Canal. 'Of course they confessed when they were tortured. I was there.' The schoolboy echoes through it all. He needed no such propaganda. His goodwill had vanished; legend now conferred on him the title, Farouk the Damned, and he himself was beginning to believe it. Foreigner and Egyptian gave credence to any story about him, however far-fetched. Tales like these, patently fabricated, leavened the coffee break at Groppi's or the Thé-Dansant at Shepheard's:

'*You know what really happened about Captain* ——*?*'

'*That's the medical officer who died . . . the one the newspapers keep on mentioning so mysteriously?*'

'*The king was having an affair with her, of course.*'

'*Her? But she's not his type. Always reading the Koran. And not very pretty.*'

'*Anyway, he was in bed with her; Farouk, that is. The husband came back, opened the door and saw them. He ran and got a pistol and would have shot the king, but they shot him first.*'

'*Who shot him – the king?*'

'*Well, some say Yes, and others say it was that little ADC, what's his name? – Omar Fathi.*'

Another fragment of aprocypha which probably owed something to Farouk's own sense of melodrama:

The other night he was driving back from the desert with one of his girl friends when the car was stopped by robbers who had set up a road block. They were ordered out, the king and his girl. Their car was ransacked and they took their jewels. They even stripped them of their clothes. One of the robbers suggested shooting them so that they couldn't tell the police, but the others wouldn't have it. When they got back, Farouk sent a squad of police to the village, had the robbers rounded up and brought before him. He asked for the man who had wanted to shoot them to step forward. One of them stepped forward, and the king shot him. Just like that, in cold blood.

Such anecdotes did him enough harm; another rumour did much more to damage his reputation. The army was still smarting at its defeat by the Israelis, and was searching for any excuse, any scapegoat. They blamed everyone and everything, but themselves. It was the defective arms the government had procured for them; in fact, these were no better nor worse that the Israelis had. The Egyptian army did not want to admit that it lacked training, experience and leadership more than weapons. But the arms scandal became an obsession with senior officers. Men like General Neguib came out of Palestine determined to expose the racketeers who had profited from the war. Suspicion fastened on General Husain Sirri Amer and several members of the royal family, as well as Farouk's gambling associates. Undoubtedly, profiteers had been busy, and the investigation demanded by Neguib and his colleagues would have exposed men uncomfortably close to the king. Not unnaturally, he quashed attempts to open an inquiry, leading the younger officers to suspect him. Neguib, who had carried out his personal crusade against arms dealing, said later, 'Even I was unaware of the fact that the king himself was involved in the arms racket until the spring of 1950. In the meantime, I had foolishly kept Farouk informed of my efforts to put a stop to the racket by seizing all the arms I could find and arresting everyone who attempted to hide or sell them.' Thus, Farouk became a scapegoat when he had taken no personal part in supplying the army. Though, perhaps, as one diplomat put it, 'He gnawed the bones that other people placed at his feet.' The arms scandal helped to drive Neguib into the circle of Free Officers which Gamal Abdel Nasser was forming to agitate for army reforms.

CHAPTER EIGHTEEN

They will ask thee concerning wine and games of chance.
In both is great sin, and advantage also; but their sin is
greater than their advantage.   (II: 216)

Despite the scandals and his loss of face, Farouk imagined he
could conjure his way out of trouble; his pride had suffered, but
nothing had dented the illusion of royal infallibility. Could he
not always fall back on the people who had cheered him when
the British and the *Wafd* threatened to destroy him? A few public
appearances, another government manipulation and the country
would settle down. But the newspapers went on muttering about
the arms racket and successive governments failed to quieten the
riots in the streets. Had Farouk listened to his own cabinet or
read between the lines, he might have grasped the fact that the
accusations and the unrest were aimed at him. The frivolous
mind discarded any such implication. He chortled when he ran
his eye over an article in *Akhbar el-Yom* about an anonymous
scoundrel, under the title: Who is He? The writer, also unnamed, said:

'Is he intelligent? Is he an idiot? Nobody knows, for he
sometimes acts like a genius and at others like a madman.
His face looks innocent, then criminal. Is he good? Is
he wicked? ... He has the furious eyes of a tiger yet runs like
a rat. He sees and still appears to be blind; he lives, though
sometimes he is believed dead. He belongs to heaven
and hell. He has gained everything only to lose it. He is only
interested in what he still does not possess. He would like to
take the shirt off everyone's back. His greatest pleasure is to
steal what everyone holds dear, whether it is precious or worth-
less. He is a thief by nature. He falls over himself to steal his
neighbour's scrawny sheep, then the moment he has a thing,
it ceases to interest him.

'He steals from everyone, even his friends, even his family. Such is his voluptuous way, such is his vice. He fancies that no one notices, believing himself to be surrounded by thieves. Is he crazy?

'He reminds us of Lon Chaney, the man with a hundred faces. If he looks in a mirror, it blows up and distorts the successive portraits of himself: the great nationalist, the man of destiny, the thief, the ringleader. These, at least, are the parts he has given himself. He never hesitates between virtue and sin, for sin lures him irresistibly and gives him more pleasure than virtue. His friends have given him up. They attempt to excuse him by saying. "He is a sick man". But the people are not mistaken. They say, "He is the greatest thief".'

Farouk could not contain himself with laughter. He must know who this man is; he called in his chief Press censor, Thabet, and sent him round to the newspaper to demand the blackguard's name from the editor. Of course, the Lebanese returned with a fictitious name. Farouk never once suspected he was reading a caricature of himself, or more important, that this was his public portrait.

While newspapers sought ways round the censorship to reflect public discontent with the king, Farouk suddenly discovered that his most bitter enemy had suddenly become his ally. Nahas was now telling *Wafd*ist crowds that their sovereign represented their aspirations and they should look to him for leadership. The king remained sceptical as, in one speech after another, the *Wafd* chief praised him. 'I shall never believe that those words have come out of the mouth of Nahas,' he repeated constantly to Thabet. The Press councillor, who had been intriguing with the *Wafd*ists to back the king and resume government, assured him they did. 'Well,' said Farouk, 'It seems that six years have taught them a lesson.'

Those years in the wilderness would have appeared to change Nahas. What had happened to the old firebrand who had fought every line of the constitution in the early days? A recent stroke had slowed him down. But, like others, he witnessed popular feeling turning against the king; beneath the surface, the Moslem Brethren, Young Egypt extremists, the Communists and the army were all conspiring to topple him. Even Nahas, hardly the political genius, could predict that the *Wafd* and ordered government might founder if the dynasty fell. So, he listened to Thabet, allowing the Press councillor to hold secret meetings with his secretary-general and right-hand man, Fuad Serag-ed-Din, to devise a rapprochement between the party and the king. To prove their loyalty, the *Wafd* joined the coalition formed by Husain Sirry to prepare for elections at the beginning of 1950.

Farouk and Sirry fancied they could rig the elections to apportion the seats between the three main parties so that no one would have a clear majority. That way the palace would hold the balance. Several times the king said to Thabet, 'If destiny decides one day or another that Nahas comes to power, you will never see me again in Egypt. I shall have packed my bags and quit the country.' Now, when he had acceded to four *Wafd*ists in the Sirry cabinet, he returned to the theme. 'If the *Wafd* wins the election and is called to govern, it will never be Nahas who presides over the cabinet.'

However, the elections in January 1950 gave the *Wafd* the expected majority with two hundred and twenty-eight out of three hundred and nineteen seats; to everyone but Farouk, the obvious choice for premier was Nahas. The king petulantly threatened to abdicate if the party decided to nominate Nahas. 'If they do that, I shall refuse to recognise the elections,' he told Thabet. 'I shall then dismiss the parties and form a military government with General Haydar at its head, and assume the responsibilities of government myself.'

Soon, the crowds which gathered to celebrate outside Nahas's house in Garden City convinced him that he had no alternative but to accept him as premier. Nahas he expected would immediately resume the struggle for constitutional power; but when he met him, he realised the fires had burned out; at seventy, Nahas had become a doddering, indecisive old man whose political shrewdness had deserted him, leaving little but the ringing voice and the cry of independence and the unity of the Nile Valley.

For Farouk he represented no more than a talisman which might keep a section of the Press and the public silent; he was able to twist him round his finger like the scarab ring he wore. With so many political debts to pay, so many promises to make good during the six barren years, Nahas soon became embroiled, despite himself, in the shady dealings which had ruined his party so many times before. His wife, Zeinab, more than atoned for the lost years, auctioning promotions, dealing out contracts, using the cotton exchanges to enrich herself and her friends. Not even the cotton boom which Egypt owed to the Korean War could buffer the effects of the price-rigging in Cairo and Alexandria. The opposition parties made free with the scandals which followed each other, feeding the extremists with facts about government corruptions and its attempts to bury the arms racket. One example they gave was the fact that a hydro-electric scheme, started in 1948 at an estimated cost of just over ten million pounds, would now take nine years instead of five and cost nearly twenty-five million pounds. It was only one of many. The soaring cost of existence was hitting the villagers who were complaining of real poverty for the first time since the early days of the world war. Yet Nahas made no real effort to reduce this misery, and the pashas concerned themselves even less.

In the past, Nahas merely needed to intone his anti-British slogans to deflect the discontent of the masses; but in his foreign policy, too, he fumbled. As a new prime minister, commanding a real majority, he might easily have re-opened negotiations with Britain on the basis of the Sidky-Bevin talks. The Attlee Government had then conceded total evacuation by 1949; surely it could do no less than take up where those discussions had broken down. He might have repeated the triumph of 1936. But, no, he had to raise the old bogy of the Sudan. When Ernest Bevin passed through Cairo at the end of January, the *Wafd* leader seized the opportunity to demand the scrapping of the 1936 treaty and the resolution of the Sudan issue, in Egypt's favour. Farouk, whom Bevin met at this time, backed these proposals. But the British Foreign Secretary could hardly agree to such suggestions, or even the resumption of talks; for one thing, his party faced a general election the following month; for another, Communist moves in Europe and the Far East had made it essential to keep Egypt as a base.

Thinking the king might see that his interest lay in contesting Communism, that he might temper Nahas's intransigence, Britain attempted to improve its relations with Farouk. They played on his respect for the royal family; so in 1950 he had visits from the Duke of Edinburgh, the Duke of Gloucester, and an invitation from Lord Louis Mountbatten to lunch on board H.M.S. Liverpool at Alexandria. He had to manoeuvre his paunch sideways down the ranks of the ship's guard of honour; he was delighted when one of his staff, who imagined himself unobserved, pinched a ship's matchbox for his collection. The King of England conferred the rank of General of the British Army on him, the presentation being made ceremoniously by the new ambassador, Sir Ralph Stevenson. Farouk commented to Thabet that he thought the rank 'compensation for the incident of February the Fourth'. He could not resist the irony of putting on the uniform and inviting British officers stationed at Fayed to a banquet in Inchass Palace, so that they would have to salute him. And the British finally gave him his trinket, a brand new helicopter for his private use. 'Ten years too late,' he grunted.

If he went through the pretence of friendship with Britain, it did not extend to politics, for he let Nahas rant on about Suez and the Sudan. The *Wafd* seemed bent on a showdown with Britain, even though Sir William Slim, Chief of the Imperial General Staff, and Sir Ralph Stevenson tried to convince the premier that Britain would not budge, especially since the fighting in Korea. On the sixteenth of November, Nahas read the king's speech at the opening of parliament. He said:

"My Government considers that the 1936 treaty has lost its validity as a basis for Anglo-Egyptian relations, and it deems it inevitable that it should be abrogated. It is also necessary that future relations should be founded upon new principles which you should approve – immediate and com-

223

plete evacuation and the unification of the Nile Valley under
the Egyptian crown ...

'My Government is therefore proceeding without hesitation
or undue delay with the task of realising these national objectives
– the proclamation of the termination of the 1936 treaty
– with the further proclamation of the abrogation of the two
agreements concluded on the sixteenth of January and
the tenth of July 1899, establishing a dual government in
Sudan.'

The speech provoked riots, which the *Wafd* were believed
to have inspired with the idea of lending weight to their political
arguments. The situation drew this editorial comment from the
New York Times:

'The violence that accompanied yesterday's opening session
of Parliament is indicative of a precarious international
situation. The *Wafd* Government has been a great disappointment to those who hoped for social progress and economic
reconstruction in Egypt after the fiasco of the Palestine war.
There has been no less inefficiency and corruption than usual;
the arbitrary expulsion of twenty-nine opposition senators in
June was contrary to all democratic practice; the activities of
King Farouk have brought him world-wide criticism; economic
distress, already acute, has been increasing steadily ... Out-
siders will find it difficult to believe that the present agitation
is not a tactic to divert popular feeling from grave internal
abuse and neglect.'

The Foreign Office reacted blandly to the king's speech. His
Majesty's Government could not approve any move that would
leave the Middle East without adequate defence at such a time;
the Sudan was making great progress, politically, socially and
economically and this could not be disturbed; the Sudanese
must be allowed to decide their own future when the time was
opportune. Bevin did say, however, that there might be a gradual
agreement about withdrawal of troops, provided that both

countries could define the circumstances in which the troops could re-enter Egypt.

To add to the problems of the government and the king, news came from America that Farouk's sister, Fathia, intended to marry Riad Ghali, a Copt and former diplomat who had acted as secretary to the queen mother and her daughters in the U.S.A. Marriage of a royal princess to a non-Moslem would cause a sensation in Egypt. Farouk therefore dispatched an aide, Brigadier Ahmed Kemal, to America to try to stop the wedding. The brigadier, the palace police chief, was urged to take any steps, even to persuading the U.S. Government to deport Riad Ghali. Despite the king's emissary and the warnings he transmitted, the marriage took place on the tenth of May 1950; for days the Egyptian Press forgot everything else to play up the scandal. Since Farouk had not given his blessing as head of the family and she had married outside the faith, he had to deprive her of her titles and confiscate her property. His mother acquiesced in the marriage, so she, too, was accorded the same treatment.

In the middle of the wrangle with Britain, during the late summer of 1950, Farouk decided to take his first trip to Europe since the war. With the *Wafd* government in trouble at home and cold war intensifying in Europe, his timing was hardly diplomatic. He could rely on Thabet's Press censorship to protect him in Egypt, and he had dreamed up an ingenious scheme to balk criticism abroad. He would travel incognito! He would go as Fuad Masri pasha, with a false passport. From the moment he stepped off the quay at Marseilles he presented a target for newspapermen and photographers. The roly-poly outline, the moon face, the bushy moustache – who could fail to identify these when they had appeared in the world Press? Yet Farouk believed he could hide behind a flimsy disguise of dark glasses, when three Albanian bodyguards shadowed him everywhere, when he led his whole troupe into night-clubs along the Cote d'Azur. Photographers ambushed him as he shuffled in and out of casinos at Cannes or Monte Carlo. No one who lost as much at roulette or chemmy could go undetected. Night after night he sat, pushing one-hundred-pound counters in piles on to the roulette table, backing Number Nine which appeared to have some mystic significance for him. In several casinos he had his special table with no maximum stake.

He granted no interviews, and several times snarled at journalists and cameramen. But the stories appeared; the newspapers knew, to the nearest kilo, how many chickens he had eaten for his midnight snack, how many litres of raspberry juice he had swilled after his gambling marathons, how much money he was up, or more often down. When he took to the road, the world knew. How could they fail when Fuad Masri pasha headed his caravan of seven Cadillacs flanked by motor-cycle outriders? When his private plane preceded him and a secretary commandeered whole floors of hotels for him and his staff. So, when austerity still gripped Europe and the tension between the West and the East mounted, Farouk was stealing the headlines with his massive spending spree and his playboy life.

His destination was Deauville. Annie Berrier was singing at the Ambassador, and he had invited Samia Gamal, his favourite belly-dancer, to join the party. He had also sent word to Camelia, now something of a name in Egyptian films, to meet him at the Channel resort. When his convoy arrived at the Hotel du Golf a crowd had collected. He looked at them, grinning. 'You know I'm incognito,' he said. It took twenty-five rooms to accommodate his party. He had to drop the assumed name because of the advance publicity and the numerous other celebrities at Deauville. There were the Aga Khan and his Begum, Prince Aly Khan and Rita Hayworth as well as a list of international names. Farouk did his share of entertaining and more than his share of gambling; now, he used chips worth a thousand pounds each which he could not place quickly enough himself, so he employed his staff as runners between tables. In one evening alone, he lost fifty-five thousand pounds at Deauville Casino.

For his friend, Annie Berrier, he had a brilliant notion. He persuaded a French composer to write a song for her, called the *Chanson du Nil*. He would act as her publicity agent. He hired the Casino and invited every famous name in the place to hear the premiere. The song never caught on, though the publicity helped Annie Berrier to make her reputation. One afternoon, Farouk waddled out of the hotel in bathing trunks, his body-guard and the French police round him, singing the *Chanson du Nil* in his flat, tuneless voice.

He was looking forward to meeting Camelia who was flying from Cairo on the thirty-first of August, then motoring from Switzerland to Deauville. He had sent a chauffeur and a secretary to Geneva to meet her. On the day she was due, the secretary telephoned to say the plane had crashed near Cairo and Camelia was dead. Farouk hung up on him. It could not be true, for he had not felt it. She could not be dead. He ordered a member of his staff to ring Cairo and refute this piece of nonsense. But Cairo could only confirm the news. A Constellation had crashed in the desert half an hour after taking off from Farouk Airport. Yes, Camelia, also known as Lilianne Cohen, was among the fifty-five people who died.

Farouk had to glean every detail about her. What she was wearing, where she was sitting, who was with her and the exact moment of the crash. They told him how she had been trapped by the fuselage and burned to death; how her jewels and trinkets lay scattered around her. They repeated the story (which she and Farouk had previously agreed) that she was travelling to Switzerland on her doctor's orders. She was twenty when she died. Even when he had every detail, the king would not accept the fact that she was dead; he went on believing that nothing could prevent their meeting. Days later, when forced to acknow-ledge the truth, he said that her death was an ominous por-tent. He repeated to his friends that she had brought him luck and now his *baraka* was deserting him. As if to endorse this feel-ing, the Press in Europe and America began to criticise his gross behaviour and his lavish spending: from Egypt he learned that the Press there were making veiled attacks on him. One of his staff, suspected of profiteering during the Palestine war, had been arrested at the airport and Cairo magistrates were issuing search warrants against other members of his entourage. Farouk con-tacted Nahas, who was in Europe for medical treatment, and demanded the reason for these actions against his staff. He hinted that, unless the *Wafd* leader intervened and stopped the inquiry, he might have to govern without a king. Nahas promised to have the charges quashed and to try to stifle the Press campaign against Farouk.

No one could do much about the world Press. In eight weeks Farouk had earned himself the reputation of a playboy, a buffoon, a callous man who made free with his country's wealth while his people struggled for their existence on three pounds a month. He also won himself the name of a lecher, who did not stop at open procurement of women but even sent his minions to embarrass women sitting in company in hotels and night-clubs. Europe, which had previously known him as a slim, shy boy in 1937, was shocked at the transformation thirteen years had wrought in his appearance and manners. He was now an obese faun with boorish humour and vulgar habits.

Egypt, too, was losing patience with him and his seedy clique of Italians, Lebanese, his Albanian bodyguards, his graft experts like Elias Andraos. A few days after his return, the opposition parties banded together to deliver a petition to Abdin Palace. Signed by leaders of the *Saad*ists, Liberals, Nationalists and Independents, the manifesto came close to denouncing the king as well as his advisers. It said:

'Egypt today is passing through a stage which may be considered the most critical in the country's history. It is regrettable that, whenever the country looks towards the palace, obstacles are put in the way for no apparent reason. Circumstances have placed in the palace certain officials who do not deserve the honour. These men offer bad advice and mishandle affairs. Some of them have even come under suspicion – now being investigated – that they are implicated in the arms scandal affecting our valiant army.

'The belief prevails that justice will be incapable of touching these officials . . .

'The World Press describes us as a public that bears injustice silently, and says that we do not know that we are being maltreated and driven like animals. Allah knows that our breasts are boiling with anger, and that only a little hope restrains us . . .

'The country remembers the happy days when Your Majesty was the honest, good shepherd. All the hopes of the country were concentrated on Your Majesty.'

The joint statement indicted the non-Egyptian clique around the king and urged him to rid his court of such people. But the note, with its overtones of revolt, was significantly written in the past tense, as though the political leaders had renounced the idea of reforming Farouk. Paradoxically, it was Nahas who jumped to defend him, shrugging aside the petition and acclaiming the king as the 'protector of the faith and a generous benefactor'. But then he, his wife, his lieutenant, Serag-ed-Din had all come under attack from the opposition on charges of corruption. To turn over any stone between Abdin Palace and *Wafd* headquarters was to uncover some worm-ridden scandal. The *Wafd* and the king appeared to have entered into a pact to connive at each other's misdemeanours.

The names of Andraos and Thabet evoked anger and resentment throughout the country; in every murky piece of finance the Copt's hand could be seen; as economic adviser to the king, he was teaching Farouk tricks which his father, or his grandfather, Ismail, might have scorned as beneath them. Produce from the royal estates fetched the highest prices merely because the king had clapped customs duties on imports which would have competed favourably with his own goods. Acting on Andraos's counsel, he persuaded the docile *Wafd* to release him from his obligation of paying taxes on his profits, his income and even his annual revenue; he sold off one of his yachts, the Fark el-Behar, to the government, had them refit it at enormous expense, then appropriated it for his pleasure trips. Andraos now sat on the board of scores of companies in which Farouk had interests and which, even in the shaky Egyptian economy, never failed to prosper. Where did Farouk stop, where was satiety? When he owned a twentieth of the arable land of Egypt and his palaces bulged with bought or stolen treasure, he was plotting new methods of increasing his fortune. A ruse he tried on hundreds of his friends became known as Farouk's Treasure Box. One of its victims was Ali Amin, twin brother of Mustapha, the publisher. He had just married when he received a call from Karim Thabet. 'You know there's a custom in Egypt whereby you give a box of chocolates to your friends. The king's a friend, aren't you going to give him a box of chocolates?'

'Of course,' Amin replied.

'Well, there's a box which the king likes at Ahmed Naguib's (the royal jeweller). He would like you to fill this box and send it to him.'

Ali Amin visited Naguib's and asked for the box; the jeweller showed it to him and he looked at the price tag: six hundred and fifty pounds! Amin walked out without the box. Making enquiries, he discovered that hundreds of Farouk's friends had been duped into buying the same box. When the king had eaten the chocolates, back it came and another six hundred and fifty pounds went into his account. Amin bought an expensive china box, filled it with sweets and had it delivered to the palace. The king was furious when he realised someone had seen through his trick.

No one really fathomed what motivated him – cynicism or stupidity, avarice or the insane wish to possess what belonged to other people. Did he collect money for the sake of collecting it, just as he gathered pebbles from the beach, regardless of their shape or worth, and piled them in his vault? It seemed aimless, irrational, like so much of his life. However, something still counted. For instance, one of his friends came to him. 'I can get you seven million dollars from an American dealer for your stamps and place the money abroad.' The king turned on him. 'What! Sell things that my father took so long to build up.' He appeared immune to the sullen protests of politicians and people yet reacted like a touchy, sensitive child when something pricked his vanity. One night he summoned Karim Thabet from Cairo to Alexandria with such urgency that the Lebanese thought another goverment crisis had blown up. Farouk's round face was suffused; he flourished an American magazine, open at a page showing a picture of King Fuad. Thabet saw, portrayed beside Fuad, a prominent Alexandrian surgeon who had grown the dead king's type of military moustache, turned up and waxed to needle-point. 'He must cut it off,' Farouk was bawling. 'It is a royal decree.' So Thabet had to rouse the chief of police who took the royal order to the medical man, forcing him out of bed and waiting until he had shaved off the moustache. Only when he heard the decree had been executed did Farouk retire for the night.

CHAPTER NINETEEN

Know ye that this world's life is only a sport, and pastime, and show, and a cause of vainglory among you! (LVII: 19)

How much longer could this melancholy hedonism go on? And how to stop the pointless parade round night-clubs? The casual charade of women through the palaces and rest-houses? The capricious despotism? The drift into such despondency that he might renounce his throne as well as his royal function? His influential allies had quit him. With the British he no long counted for much. His greed and gross behaviour had alienated and disillusioned friendly politicians and pushed him into an uneasy alliance with Nahas. Soon, the people would disown him. Lose them and everything would crumble.

Some of his friends felt that another marriage might redeem him. Seeing him dejected one day, Edgard Gallad, proprietor of the royalist newspaper, *Journal d'Egypte,* said, 'Majesty, what you need is a great love.' Farouk looked at him, bitterly, 'In life you only have one great love, and I have had mine.' But Farida, whom he still loved, resisted every attempt at reconciliation. Fatma had deserted him. At one time, the mothers of the 'fifty families' who ruled Egypt would have fallen over each other to present their daughters; now, there was no rush, except perhaps to keep them away from this bloated lecher. As usual, it was Thabet, now virtually the chief of the royal cabinet, who dreamed up a plan to save the king's reputation. 'If Your Majesty marries, it should be a commoner, for in this way you will win back the love of the people.' Farouk grabbed this lifeline. At least it might produce the son and heir that he and the throne needed. The word went out, unofficially, that the king was looking for a new bride.

One of the men to keep his eyes open was Ahmed Naguib,

the crown jeweller. In his shop, one day in November 1950, came a couple looking for an engagement ring; when he glanced at the girl, Princess Fatma came to mind. Not that she strongly resembled Fatma, but something similar in their profiles struck him. He decided to help them choose their ring and make enquiries about the girl. She answered his questions quite naturally. She had become sixteen on the thirty-first of October; she was attending the Princess Ferial School and her name was Narriman Sadek; her fiancé was a diplomat called Zaki Hashem. The jeweller gathered up the rings on the counter. 'You need something better than these,' he said. 'I have a special ring in Alexandria which is beautiful and very cheap. Give me your address and telephone number and I shall have it in two days.' When they had gone, Naguib put through a call to Mohamed Hassan, the king's valet, to inform him he had found the right queen for Farouk. He described Narriman, saying she would visit his shop at three o'clock the day after tomorrow when the king could judge for himself. The valet passed the message to Farouk, who consulted Thabet (it was the night he spotted the surgeon's moustache).

Cancelling his appointments, Farouk ordered the royal train to take him to Cairo. At Naguib's shop in Abdel Khalik Sarwat Street, Narriman was trying on several rings when the king entered. His questions overawed the girl: were there any pashas in the family? Did she speak any foreign languages? But his interest in Narriman began to deepen when he saw she had chosen the engagement ring. Thabet and other members of the court clique had guessed correctly. She was engaged; therefore he would want her. In the transaction, the jeweller, the valet and the Press councillor had forgotten one thing: Zaki Hashem. Even if the girl agreed, he might cause trouble. Farouk solved this problem simply. He ordered the girl's father, Husain Fahmy Sadek, to go to the fiancé and make the announcement, to tell him his marriage had been quashed by royal decree. 'I am sorry,' said Husain Sadek, 'but there has been a change of plans. The king has decided to marry Narriman. Give me all her pictures and we shall arrange to send back all your presents. We have been asked not to speak to you or telephone you. I'm sorry, but it is the king's command.'

Still, no one knew officially about the king's engagement, though in the hotels along the Nile, the cafés in Suleiman Pasha and Kasr el-Nil streets they joked that the king's kleptomania had finally extended to stealing another man's fiancée. At first, the Cairo set refused to believe it. A sixteen-year-old girl with no background as Queen of Egypt! On the eleventh of February, Farouk's thirty-first birthday, the palace made an announcement which put it beyond doubt. Thabet had written the royal hand-out in his best, sugary prose. 'Rendering praise to Allah, His Majesty's cabinet is happy to announce to the noble Egyptian people the good news of the betrothal of their King, who has given them his heart and his love.

'On this blessed day, when the country celebrates with gladness and joy the glorious anniversary of the royal birth, there took place, by the grace of Allah, the betrothal of our well-beloved Sovereign with the descendant of an illustrious and noble family, Mademoiselle Narriman Sadek, daughter of Husain Fahmy Sadek bey. In announcing the news of this happy betrothal of the great Farouk, His Majesty's cabinet thanks divine providence for its beneficence, and prays that it may surround His Majesty with its high solicitude, secure his happiness and felicity, and make of this blessed betrothal a source of happy omen for be-loved Egypt and for the august royal family.'

Narriman had been sent to Europe to spend almost a year being groomed for her role as queen. She had French and Italian ladies to teach her languages, deportment and to chaperon her. But when she returned, shortly after the palace announcement, Cairo society still considered her gauche and out-of-place among them. Once again, the royal decree was invoked to summon them to meet the future queen; Nahas and his cabinet lined up dutifully to be introduced to Narriman; no one dared ask Prince Mohamed Ali, then in his eighty-third year though still heir-apparent, what he thought of the king's choice. Farouk himself appeared in-souciant of their opinion; it seemed to many that he had even lost interest in the wedding; some of his officials contended that his enthusiasm evaporated as soon as Narriman had accepted him. Whereas he had immersed himself in preparations for his marriage to Farida, he now thought only of one aspect of his forthcoming ceremony – what it would bring him in presents.

In fact, the king did not much mind what anyone gave him – as long as it came in gold. Thabet and his lackeys put the word around that His Majesty favoured gold, adding that Farouk did not care if it came plain or fancy. Ingots would save Andraos the bother of melting it down for him. Farouk reckoned to make a tidy fortune out of the wedding by the time he had sold off his presents and smuggled the gold out of the country. 'If we could only marry him off half a dozen times we should all die millionaires,' Thabet quipped, cynically, to one of his friends. To smuggle the gold out of Egypt, Farouk had decided to spend his honeymoon abroad. He passed hours calculating minutely what the wedding would cost him, down to fractions of a piastre. It came to seventy-three thousand four hundred and eighty-three pounds and fifty-nine milliemes, which included the ring from Ahmed Naguib, Narriman's pearls, the wedding gown and private receptions; it also covered the free food and gifts for peasants on the day of the ceremony. Even Pulli's expenses for buying Narriman's clothes and paying her hotels were carefully estimated by the king to parts of a piastre. For example, in 1951 the Italian received five thousand five hundred and five pounds and thirty-two milliemes for Narriman, and the king ordered him to reduce her spending.

On the sixth of May, fifteen years from the day he became king, Farouk went through the marriage ceremony in the Ismail Room of Abdin Palace. He had decreed that the wedding would outdo the splendour of his first marriage. Cairo blazed with neon-lit triumphal arches, illuminated portraits of Farouk and Narriman; the Nile reflected thousands of fireworks. In a sudden fit of generosity, Farouk doled out three thousand acres of his own land to selected farmers, promising them a house, a gamoosa, a donkey and crop seed; from his own money he gave more than fifty thousand pounds to the poor. For the day of the marriage, the newspapers declared a truce, and many carried laudatory articles about the king and his new queen.

It should have outshone his wedding to Farida. But no royal decree could compel people to acclaim a king who had abused his position and their trust, or a queen who might have been any one of their daughters. Few people cheered when Narriman rode through the triumphal arches, wearing a gown with six thousand sequins which had cost Farouk four hundred pounds in Paris. No more than two thousand were scattered around Abdin Square to wait for the couple appearing on the balcony. The streets of the capital carried the extra traffic without much interruption. Compared with his first marriage, this had flopped.

The next month, Farouk and his bride boarded the Mahroussa to sail to Europe on their honeymoon. Again, he had quit the country during Nahas's treaty negotiations with the British; but what struck many Europeans, and Americans, as worse was the fact that Farouk had chosen to act the flamboyant, free-spending potentate at a time when Russia had closed off Berlin and the cold war threatened world peace. His own palace cabinet might have deterred him, or a few words from the British Embassy might have sent him elsewhere on his trip. But, had they advised, would he have listened? He had to unload his spoils. Unknown to anyone, except Pulli and Thabet, most of the wedding gifts in gold had been melted down and packed into the hold to pay for his honeymoon, for his gambling or to swell the numbered accounts in Switzerland.

The first stop was Taormina in Sicily. There, they lazed for six days before sailing for Capri where the king had booked a whole floor of the luxury Caesar Augustus Hotel at Anacapri. 'Have you any Zionists here?' he called loudly to the director as his party of sixty were being installed. He had a horror of Jews who might spy on him or poison his food; he also detested newspapermen, and scanned every hotel register to ensure he would have immunity from them. At Capri, he refused all interviews, taking a childish delight in keeping the scores of correspondents kicking their heels outside the hotel. It merely

236

increased the avidity of the Press to report the progress of the honeymoon.

He soon proved that marriage had not altered his ritual; he rose after his midday feast, flipped through the papers and looked at any documents which had arrived in the diplomatic bag from Cairo. Then he dressed in a grey flannel blazer and white ducks, set his yachting cap on his balding head and drove to his favourite spot on the island, the Canzone del Mare, run by his friend, Gracie Fields. There, he would attire himself in a floppy, cotton hat, tennis shoes and bathing trunks to lounge at the edge of the pool or porpoise up and down in the water until the sun was low. His appetite, too, had diminished none. The hotel chefs wondered where he put their best offerings. *Vol au vent*, sole, mutton chops, fricasséed chicken, lobster, grilled steak, potatoes, vegetables, fruit, ice-cream – all this would vanish at one sitting while Narriman and his entourage fidgeted at the long table the hotel had arranged specially for the royal party. His coffee arrived from the Mahroussa and was served in golden cups and saucers.

With his bride of one month beside him, his eye still roved round the dining, and drawing-rooms, almost as though he wished to offend the young queen or provoke scenes. Once or twice he did cause trouble by sending one of his servants to invite some lady who had taken his fancy to join the party, without her male escort.

From Capri he moved to Rapallo for several days, then to Venice Lido, into Switzerland and back into Italy. Following the royal caravanserai came droves of reporters and photographers who spared no detail in the progress of this gargantuan rake. How could they when he ordered a hotel in Lugano to build a high wall to keep them out? When one of his bodyguard assaulted a cameraman? When he lounged on the Lido beach, a great walrus, with two pretty girls manicuring his hands and feet? When he flew his barber from Paris in the middle of the morning to give him a shave? Suddenly the adverse comment in the British and American Press alarmed him; he raged at the accounts of his trip in the English and Continental newspapers, tearing them up and strewing them across the floor of his suite. More disturbing, some of the reports were percolating into Egypt, where editors were defying the censorship to give diluted versions of the king's exploits. He wired Thabet, ordering him to stop these stories; the Press councillor drafted a tighter law which he persuaded a *Wafd*ist minister to push through parliament. But where censorship ended, the Egyptian genius for rumour-mongering took over. Thabet's law merely increased the circulation of foreign magazines and newspaper cuttings from hand to hand and magnified talk about Farouk's farouche and vulgar behaviour.

Their tour of Northern Italy over, the party made its way to the South of France. He was now reported to be trailed by two Moslem Brethren who were keeping Cairo informed about his doings; he feared them less than the Zionists. 'I don't want them putting a bottle of whisky and a pork chop on the table, then taking my picture,' he joked. But he believed they might, and use such a picture to denigrate him.

So the honeymoon continued, at a cost of one thousand pounds a day. Farouk spent most of this. He put up at the Carlton in Cannes, but flitted from one end of the Cote d'Azur to the other, sight-seeing with Narriman or appearing for his nightly session at one of the casinos. Wherever he sat, the No-Limit sign went up, and his pudgy hands pushed one thousand-pound chips across the baize as fast as croupiers could handle them. His eight-inch cigars and his lust for gambling earned him the nickname of The Locomotive. If he won, he would bellow in French, 'Ah, had you that time!' If he lost, more frequently the case, the room would still reverberate with his schoolboy chortling.

The papers which arrived in the diplomatic pouch or were ferried direct from Cairo by private plane twice a week might have reached him from another planet for all the notice he took. The gloomy news from his palace about government corruption, the inability to keep food prices down, the abortive negotiations with the British did not appear to bother him, nor did it detain him more than a few minutes from the gambling tables, the Eden Roc pool or Riviera night-clubs. Only towards the end of his honeymoon did he grow dejected at the prospect of returning to trouble in Cairo. The Aga Khan, who had an hour or two with him, said: 'I was immediately aware of a great change in him. He was enveloped in a mood of depressed fatalism, an atmosphere of, "I cannot do what I wish – very well, let them do what they want".'

But one thing heartened him and gave him new confidence to return to Egypt after his thirteen weeks of honeymoon. Narriman was pregnant. He began to take a more active interest in running the country. He felt he could not long connive at the greed and corruption of the *Wafd* which had broken every one of its election promises. Its pensions scheme, which the king himself had launched by issuing the first books with several pounds in each, was costing too much and had to be curtailed; the cost of bread, beans and the oil for cooking them, was rising when Nahas had pledged himself to ease the burden of the fellahin; the unemployment figures were mounting alarmingly. Crowds might collect round Nahas and kiss his hand, but Farouk knew how much they got from party funds for this service while the doddering *Wafd* leader did not. The mass of the peasants were growling about the government and the king.

In the midst of this economic crisis some people carried on with courageous indifference. Fuad Serag-ed-Din, now virtual ruler of the *Wafd*, and Nahas's wife, Zeinab, were making themselves fortunes out of cotton and other deals. Serag-ed-Din, with two ministries, Finance and the Interior, dispensed patronage and cynically took advantage of the cotton boom to enrich himself and his brothers. His close friend, Zeinab, also built up her bank account. But it could not last. The slump came in cotton, the government intervened to keep up prices and left itself with almost all of the 1951 crop unsold. The country found itself facing bankruptcy.

At the first audience he gave Nahas, the king stormed about the conduct and corruption of the *Wafd* administration. The old premier broke down in front of Farouk, crying, 'You say this to me who have sacrificed so much for you.'

'Not you, pasha – the others,' Farouk replied. It was a moment that might have dissolved their enmity, but it soon passed.

Even the traditional safety-valve for resentment, the cry of Suez and the Sudan, failed to rally the unemployed and the hungry. Playing on the emotions of peasants and workers, trained agitators were exploiting the unrest and shouting against the king and the government. Earlier that year Egypt saw the first hint that Communism was infiltrating these extremist movements; communist-front newspapers were circulating openly, attacking everything and everyone in authority, including the British and Americans. Above all else, Farouk feared Communism; its appearance in Cairo demonstrated to him, more than the economic chaos, that the *Wafd* had failed and must be removed. Communist and general agitation caught Nahas, too, in a dilemma. On the one hand, he wanted to force Britain out and establish Egyptian sovereignty over the Sudan; on the other, he feared that, if the British went, he might fail to control the riots he himself had done so much to instigate.

He had an inspiration. Why not counter the Communists with those who hated them, the outlawed Moslem Brethren? When he put the proposal before Farouk, he waved it aside angrily. But, argued Nahas, members of the Brethren are already secret agitators. So, why not make peace with their leaders, reinstate the organisation and use it against Communism? That sort of reasoning appealed to Farouk who agreed to legalise the Brethren. Banning the movement for two and a half years had done nothing to temper its self-righteousness, its uncompromising nationalism. At once it tabled its demands: a state of war with Britain; confiscation of all British property and severance of all cultural, political and economic ties; release of imprisoned Brethren with official permission for them to carry arms; legal immunity for those who were fighting against the British and the Jews. The declaration even suggested that Farouk would be classed as an enemy of Egypt and an accomplice of Britain if he rejected the demands. How could he accede to such impractical proposals? As a sop to the Brethren, he allowed Nahas to Egyptianise the Gezira Club and dismiss some British officials

– mainly schoolteachers – from government posts. Without in any way appeasing the Brethren, he convinced the British that the Brethren had palace support during the incidents and riots which plagued the Canal Zone in the autumn of 1951.

It was obvious that Nahas could not solve the country's economic problems, nor extricate his government from the predicament his demagoguery had created; he had set the stage for a collision with Britain who now felt that to pull out of Egypt would leave the Canal open to Russian infiltration. The Labour Government stalled while Nahas stalked the country, making speeches which did nothing but provoke violence and attacks on the British and their Embassy. The *Wafd* leader warned Britain, bluntly, that he would fulfil his threat to denounce the 1936 treaty and with it the fifty-two-year-old agreements on the Sudan. Meanwhile, his henchman, Fuad Serag-ed-Din, was secretly re-arming the Moslem Brethren and recruiting its members and other extremists into the auxiliary police force to wage terrorism against the British forces in the Canal Zone. These commandoes, or *fedayeen*, trained at Zagazig, had already clashed several times with troops near Ismailia.

Britain proposed a diplomatic solution, suggesting that Egypt should become part of a Middle East Defence Organisation which would embrace France, Turkey, the United Kingdom and the United States; this only seemed to strengthen Nahas's determination to tear up the treaties unless Britain conceded total withdrawal and Egyptian sovereignty over the Sudan. However, the *Wafd* was resorting to its old game of baiting Britain in public, though its leaders were prepared to talk reasonably with the British Ambassador, Sir Ralph Stevenson, in private.

Two factors precipitated a crisis: The *Wafd* government had observed how Dr Mossadeq had forced the evacuation of the British by nationalising the Anglo-Iranian Oil Company, a legal precedent, it seemed to them, for rescinding the treaties; nearer home, the king had once more aligned himself with the opposition parties and was bidding to expose government corruption in order to gain a pretext for sacking Nahas. Farouk had decided to press for a law enabling an investigation into the fortunes acquired by *Wafd*ists. Such an inquiry would have exposed the premier's wife and Serag-ed-Din, among other government members and supporters. When Nahas attempted to balk the proposal it led to a blazing quarrel with Farouk which left the *Wafd* leader in no doubt that the king would dismiss him unless he pulled off some coup to forestall him. A coup such as abrogation of the treaties with Britain!

Had Farouk known that Nahas was drafting legislation to denounce the treaties he would have opposed it, fearing that the British might again humiliate him and his government by using force. Or worse still, that they might accept the necessity to evacuate the Canal and leave him at the mercy of the *Wafd*. He knew nothing of Nahas's manoeuvre until it lay before parliament in the form of two decrees. When the king protested that this was folly, Nahas taunted him with the alternative of resigning and, at the same time, denouncing the king as unpatriotic for refusing his signature to the decrees. Farouk was trapped. On the fifteenth of October 1951, the *Wafd*ist parliament voted the abrogation decrees. Twelve days later, Britain learned officially that Egypt had torn up the treaties and that King Farouk had been proclaimed King of Egypt and the Sudan.

Anthony Eden, Foreign Secretary in the Conservative Government which had been returned in the October election, immediately dispatched a stern warning to Egypt, pointing out that the 1936 treaty contained no provision for unilateral denunciation. The action was therefore illegal and contrary to the United Nations Charter. 'Meanwhile,' the note said, 'His Majesty's Government regard the Treaty, and the Condominium Agreements of 1899, as remaining in force, and intend fully to maintain their rights under those instruments. In addition, they hold the Egyptian Government responsible for any breach of the peace and any damage to life or property that may result from their purported abrogation of these instruments.'

Nahas had saved himself and his government. The king could hardly dismiss the patriot who had flouted British authority. In their conflict with Britain, Farouk and Nahas gained an unexpected ally: the United States ambassador, Jefferson Caffery.

A career diplomat for forty of his sixty-five years, Caffery had arrived in Cairo two years previously. Most of his service he had spent in Latin America, and had once joked to Edgard Gallad, 'Wherever I've been, revolutions seem to break out.' In the post-war years, the Americans had discovered the strategic importance of the Suez Canal and the economic influence of the Middle East oil-fields; they were determined that the Communists should not gain dominance in that area. The Communist menace worried Caffery much more than it did the State Department; he had convinced himself that the Russians meant to get their hands on the Middle East oil. He saw Britain and Egypt at loggerheads over Suez and the Sudan and believed that he, the honest broker, might help to resolve the differences and bring peace and security to the area. Though Caffery no doubt genuinely felt he could mediate in the quarrel, his attitude was strongly tinged with distaste for Britain as a colonial power, and with contempt for the corrupt ruling class in Egypt. He held to the simple thesis that if poverty were not lifted from the fellahin, that inchoate, inarticulate peasantry would turn Communist. On good terms with the king, he nevertheless disliked the life he led and the gang which was inspiring his actions. The ambivalence of Caffery and American policy had a strong bearing on subsequent British action. As one senior official observed, 'The British were fed up taking all the kicks in Egypt while other nations, with equally vital interests, refused to share the burden yet would interfere in policy-making.'

Caffery's interference was resented. Eden scarcely viewed the American ambassador's pressure for a plebiscite on the Sudan as a friendly or helpful move, while he seemed to want Britain to walk out of the Canal without adequate guarantees that it would be defended in case of war. To the Foreign Office, it appeared that the ambassador was trying to push them into conceding Farouk's sovereignty over the Sudan in return for assistance in negotiating some vague formula on Suez. Farouk and Nahas now imagined that, whatever difficulties they got into with Britain, they could always rely on the American ambassador to resolve them.

For the moment, however, Britain had determined to stay in the face of a hate campaign whipped up by Nahas and Serag-ed-Din. Mobs of students and unemployed factory workers surged through Cairo streets, shouting, 'Down with Britain. Long live Nahas.' In the Canal Zone, the guerrilla units were using guns, grenades, dynamite and petrol bombs against the Erskine Line, drawn round the Canal Zone by the British commander, Lt-General Sir George Erskine. The fedayeen put a thousand pounds on Erskine's head; they offered a hundred for any other British officers and this was too often collected. In mid-November, three officers died in an ambush set by Egyptian auxiliary policy; a few days later, another officer and nine men were wiped out in a raid. On the eighth of December, Erskine razed a huddle of mud huts at Kafr Abdu which were giving the fedayeen cover from which to shoot British guards on the water-filtration plant which supplied the forces. In Cairo, the Press demanded retribution and Nahas recalled the Egyptian ambassador from London.

Worse than murder and sabotage was Serag-ed-Din's move to starve the base of food supplies and labour. More than sixty thousand Egyptian civilian employees had orders to quit Suez, and Britain had to draft in military reinforcements to keep the military and civilian installations going. If it threw another discontented mob on to the streets, the boycott also convinced the British that they could never operate the Suez base without Egyptian goodwill and aid. By the end of the year, some eighty thousand British troops and their ancillaries occupied the base, and their patience was running short.

On the nineteenth of January 1952, in broad daylight, Egyptian fedayeen attacked the biggest munitions dump in the Middle East, at Tel el-Kebir; two days later they used the tombs of a Moslem graveyard in Ismailia as a springboard for another assault; later that week they detonated an arms dump. In every case the men came from the two barracks of the Buluk Nizam (auxiliary police) at Ismailia. Deciding the guerrillas had gone too far, General Erskine moved in with tanks and infantry at dawn on the twenty-fifth of January; his men called to the Buluk commander to surrender. This man, Major-General

Ahmed Raif, telephoned Serag-ed-Din in Cairo, getting him out of bed to ask for instructions. They were brief. 'Resist to your last bullet,' said the *Wafd* secretary-general.

Just after seven o'clock, the Buluk opened up with rifles, sub-machine guns and shot-guns. A blank round from a Centurion tank did not quieten them, so the tanks punched a hole in the barracks and the Lancashire Fusiliers went in behind them. At noon the battle had ended; forty-six military policemen had died, another hundred were wounded and about eight hundred surrendered. The Lancashire Fusiliers lost five killed; nine were wounded. It need never have happened. But Serag-ed-Din had been seeking a pretext to bring Britain to the conference table over the Sudan. Now he had it, or so he thought. For their part, the British had shown reckless, even ruthless repression, and too much efficiency. Had they left an escape route, the Buluk would never have had to stand and fight.

Cairo newspapers called it the Egyptian Stalingrad; the city exploded with anger and humiliation. The *Wafd* youth demanded a massive protest march the next day, and Serag-ed-Din agreed, providing they left the king alone. Even as late as the sixteenth of January, Farouk had been openly insulted by jeering crowds on the occasion of the birth of his son and heir, Prince Ahmed Fuad; the *Wafd* did not want a repeat of this, or other previous insults. By the evening of the Canal battle, the protest had gathered weight. More extreme *Wafd*ists had decided to join the Communists, the Moslem Brethren and Young Egypt members in a meeting at Fuad University the next morning; the Buluk ordered a strike of volunteer police in Cairo; factory and office workers organised a boycott of British businesses; the Council of Ministers emerged from an extraordinary session with the decision to break off diplomatic relations with the British. That evening, the British Embassy passed a warning to British subjects to keep off the streets and stay at home until after the demonstrations; Egyptian servants whispered the same advice to British and other foreigners. In the Canal Zone, an alert went out to all troops.

As darkness fell, Cairo had the febrile tranquillity of a city under curfew; its streets emptied, as though for once the demonstrators had something more important to do or the mass of its citizens had been stunned by the events. Farouk, too, had decided to forego his night rounds and retire early. Tomorrow he had invited six hundred army and police officers to a banquet at Abdin Palace in honour of the birth of his son. Did he, or anyone apart from the plotters who were already preparing their weapons, suspect that dawn on the twenty-sixth of January would see the genesis of a revolution?

CHAPTER TWENTY

And in the city at noon he was full of fear, casting furtive glances round him: and lo! the man whom he had helped the day before, cried to him again for help. Said Moses to him, 'Thou art plainly a most depraved person.'

(XXVIII: 17)

AT seven o'clock on the day which became known as Black Saturday about three hundred Buluk Nizam strikers marched across the city from their barracks to Fuad University where Communists, *Wafd*ists and Moslem Brethren were gathering to start their demonstration. The first sign of trouble came when the police, ordered to keep the meeting quiet, joined the mob and fraternised openly with its leaders. An hour later, a huge procession made its way across the Nile bridges to converge on the parliament buildings. In their thousands, they piled up in the courtyard shouting, 'We want arms to fight for the Canal'. Turning to Princess Shevikiar's pink-and-grey baroque palace, now cabinet offices, they roared for the *Zaim* (leader) of the nation. Instead of Nahas, out stepped the portly Minister for Social Affairs, Abdel Fattah Hassan, who began to harangue them from a balcony. 'This is your day,' he cried. 'You will be avenged. We will expose ourselves to the enemy's fire in the front rank.' For three hours he filibustered, promising them anything – arms from the Russians, a battle for Suez, a British boycott. Perhaps he hoped the crowd would disperse peacefully. But the mass in front of him swelled until groups commenced to break away from its edges and lead a mob towards Abdin Palace. There, for several ominous minutes it paused to hurl slogans accusing Farouk and the British of the canal massacre before thrusting on to Opera Square.

It was now eleven-thirty. At the Badia Cabaret a policeman was lounging at a table, drinking whisky with one of the dancers.

247

'Aren't you ashamed when your brothers are dying in Ismailia?' a voice bellowed at him. The policeman snubbed them with an angry insult while the dancer sneered. It was enough. As though waiting for some signal, some excuse, the crowd erupted into the cabaret, overwhelming waiters and servant boys; they stacked tables and chairs on top of each other; several people then materialised with paraffin cans to spray the spirit over the piled furniture; someone flung a blazing rag on to the bonfire. Within minutes the cabaret was blazing. Firemen pushed through the screaming throng, running out their hoses, but before they could couple them a gang had slashed them. The brigade chief appealed to the police, and they merely laughed. Emboldened by this, the crowd surged along Fuad Street to the Rivoli Cinema.

If the first fire was caused by a spontaneous outburst from Moslem youth, the second was organised. Jeeps, loaded with men, scattered the mob; out of them leapt squads of men armed with every instrument of the fire-raiser – crowbars and battering rams, steel-cutters and picks, petrol in cans and bottles. Like demons they worked, as though drilled to the second; a bunch of them broke down and prised open the cinema door; others sloshed paraffin and petrol over the auditorium; the third group lit the rags and lobbed them on to the stage and among the seats. That fire lit, they moved on to start others, surfacing among the crowd, performing their grim work as though to some military plan. All over the city that day, the sweating, soot-grimed faces of these fanatics were spotted. But no one ventured to stop them, no one remembered even seeing them.

After the Rivoli, the arson squads set the Metro Cinema alight before barging through the mob to the Turf Club, to them the hallowed symbol of British oppression. Eighteen people were sitting in the club just after mid-day when the rabble swarmed over the wall and charged through the door. As the Britons, men and women, rushed for the garden the fire-raisers met them in the foyer, clubbing them over the head with iron bars; the club secretary, a Greek, was dragged out by the necktie and managed to stammer in Arabic that he was not British. He did not interest them. As though following a blueprint they doused the leather

248

chairs and the curtains, then the portraits of the pro-consuls – Cromer, Gorst, Kitchener, Lloyd – with petrol; they smashed and soaked the mementos of seventy years of British rule; they deluged the dining-room and the library, even the books. Nothing must survive. Soon the building was an inferno, but the fire-raisers still had one grisly task to do. They picked up the dead and dazed Britons from the foyer and slung them into the heart of the fire. Four men, their clothes blazing, staggered from hiding towards the door; they, too, were bludgeoned and heaved back into the blaze. One man tied sheets together to attempt an escape from a top-floor window; flames burned through the sheets and he fell to be trampled to death by the crowd. Ten people died in the Turf Club, including the Canadian Trade Commissioner and James Ireland Craig, a government official and a well-known Arabic scholar.

As the flames spread, the hatred and hysteria of the crowd mounted; they bulldozed their way down Suleiman Pasha and Kasr el-Nil streets towards the banks, the airline offices, the luxury shops and restaurants. Anything capitalist. Anything foreign. 'Let them play a bit,' said one of the political police, leaning passively against Suleiman Pasha's statue. The frenzied mob needed no such encouragement. Shopkeepers might bang their grills shut and fade away; the fire-raisers cut or pick-axed the doors open and, in minutes, had the shops contributing to the pall of flames and smoke over the centre of Cairo. In one door. Out again. In another. No thought of looting, yet. Just burning. So quickly did they operate that several of the incendiary squad were trapped by fires of their own making.

At first they chose their targets carefully. The cinemas, with their garish hoardings and Western sex symbols; after that, places of decadence in Moslem eyes, like the Cecil Bar, the Ritz Café, the St James's, the Parisian. When they had fired the bars and night-clubs and stoked the flames by bursting bottles of liquor over them, they turned to restaurants like Groppi's, meeting place of the élite, and Jewish stores like Cicurel's, Robert Hughes and Adès. But with each street they tackled, each fire they lit, their discretion gave way to the mad urge to set everything on fire. Up in flames went the TWA office. Then Fords, with its gleaming new models. British or American? What did it matter now? The Twentieth Century French Art Gallery, Chryslers, Weinstein's stationery shop – one burned as brightly as another. A crackling of gunfire came from one street, causing the mob to duck instinctively. No, it was neither police nor army, merely exploding cartridges in a gunsmith's shop in Kasr el-Nil street.

For three hours, unmolested by authority, the rabble had taken possession of the city; around them the flames crackled; above, smoke palled over the capital, over the Nile and blotted out the wan January sun. Had there been a wind, even a Nile breeze, Cairo could never have survived. So far, the fire-raisers had steered away from two strategic centres of authority: Abdin Palace and the British Embassy. For how long?

Sir Ralph Stevenson, his staff armed and ready to resist, must have asked that question a hundred times between eleven-thirty and two-thirty. How long, too, before the government acted? Several times before noon the British Ambassador had tried to contact cabinet ministers, but that day no one wanted to talk to the British. Nahas, they told him, was having a pedicure and could not be disturbed; the foreign minister was on equally urgent business. And Serag-ed-Din, that devious man? He was buying a new piece of property, presumably at knock-down prices in Cairo. Sir Ralph decided to cross the street and discuss the situation with Jefferson Caffery in the American Embassy; he poked his nose out of the door, ordering the security guard to unlock the chain on the front gate. A burst of machine-gun fire made them duck. 'More better inside, Excellency, I think,' said the guard. 'More better inside, you're right,' replied Sir Ralph.

What should he do? He had heard about the holocaust at the Turf Club. How many other Britons had died he had no means of telling. Should he pick up the telephone and order General Erskine into Cairo to crush the revolt and stop the mob from butchering British and foreign subjects? Erskine had his First Division and the 16th Parachute Brigade sitting astride the Suez Road. 'Twelve hours if unopposed, six hours if opposed,' he had retorted when asked how long he would require to take Cairo. It was no tongue-in-cheek quip. He meant that, if the Egyptians fought in the open they would make things easier than if they used guerrilla tactics and did not clear the streets of the capital. All this Sir Ralph appreciated; he was also aware that action by Erskine would constitute an act of war, and those six or twelve hours would give the crowd time to kill several hundred foreigners. On the other hand, Farouk could order his army into the streets within an hour. The British Ambassador could not imagine that the king wanted to lose either his capital city or his throne. So he sat and waited.

At one-thirty, by the time the royal banquet started, the centre of Cairo was burning fiercely, and Farouk had been informed. With him was his army commander-in-chief, General Haydar, and almost every senior officer in the Egyptian army. Yet, the king made no sign, except to motion his six hundred guests to sit down for the eight-course lunch to honour his heir. From the palace windows, the guests could observe the smoke pluming over-head, could catch the dull growl of the crowd. Serag-ed-Din – according to his own account – had telephoned the palace, re-questing the king, through Haydar pasha, to order out the army. Still Farouk did nothing, apart from instructing Miss Anne Chermside, the English governess, to take his son, Prince Ahmed Fuad, up to the roof of Abdin Palace and stay there.

Among the senior officers were General Mohamed Neguib and his brother, Ali, who had forced their way through the rioters to the palace. Neguib later recounted what went on at the lunch. 'Farouk and Haydar seemed pre-occupied throughout the banquet, but neither had even so much as mentioned the riots. Their frequent whispered conferences with various courtiers, however, indicated that they were aware of what was happening.' Why did Farouk ignore the riots, the threat to Cairo? Why no concern? Because he had decided to gamble and roast the *Wafd* in their own fire. Let it burn a little longer and he could drive Nahas out of office. That triumph would justify the desperate throw he was making by giving the mob its head. And the *Wafd* had begun to react. Fuad Serag-ed-Din presented himself in person at the palace just before two-thirty to plead for troops to quell the riots. Haydar and Farouk's cabinet chief, Hafez Afifi, did not appear to share his fears, though they promised army support.

So far, the mobs had left Shepheard's Hotel alone; three times they had passed this building by the Nile, one of the finest pieces of arabesque architecture in the Middle East. For a hundred years it had housed almost every foreign dignitary to visit Egypt; it was part of the country's history. The arson gangs would surely leave that alone! While the frantic crowd swirled round it, dragomen in royal blue robes kept their station outside, perhaps hoping to deter the fire-raisers; waiters and staff, in caftans, cleared the lounges and advised guests to stay in their rooms. Just after two-thirty, the crowd broke its stride before the Arabic arches of Shepheard's; as usual, the incendiaries struck first, stacking the priceless ivory-inlaid furniture in the middle of the vaulted lounge and adding carpets and curtains before hosing them with paraffin and applying a lighted torch. As the flames and smoke rose, clients ran for the rear entrance or groped their way through the fumes to the front door. One woman, trapped in an upper storey, jumped to her death before the passive crowd. Farouk's current foreign mistress escaped with her life but lost her clothes and jewels. Within half an hour, the graceful dome of the hotel crumpled and sank into the inferno; in two hours nothing but blackened walls had survived. Fire had consumed everything – the knapsacks and revolvers deposited there by officers who fought at Omdurman and never returned; kitbags and uniforms mouldering from the 1914–18 war, along with the unclaimed baggage of the more recent world war.

At four o'clock, the gang of fire-raisers had finished their work in Cairo and headed for Mena House, near the Pyramids, to set that ablaze. There, however, they met their first opposition from dragomen who defended the old building and drove them off. It was after this that the main mob took a hand on its own and a new element was added to that cataclysmic day. Looting and plundering. Shop windows gaped open, those which still stood. So the crowds grabbed handfuls of merchandise, from jewels to cheap trinkets, silk dresses, gold, silver, something to eat. They swarmed over the smouldering buildings seizing whatever came to hand.

In Abdin Palace, at that hour, the banquet was finishing. Suddenly, Farouk made up his mind to act. First he sent for the American Ambassador who arrived within minutes. Did Mr Caffery think the British would intervene if the riots got out of hand? To Caffery he seemed a frightened man who behaved as though he wanted the British to order their troops into action. When the ambassador explained the predicament over the delay, the king then instructed Haydar to call out his own army. Half an hour later, he sent for Nahas and his cabinet ministers to tell them to declare a state of emergency. When they had done that, therefore accepting responsibility for the unrest, he sacked the whole government. To Nahas, he said, 'You have shown criminal negligence in not maintaining order and security in the country. I withdraw my confidence from you, since you are no longer capable of governing.'

At five o'clock, the first detachments of troops arrived on the banks of the Nile, five hours too late, They scattered the mobs and looters from the city centre to make way for the firemen. Dozens of buildings still blazed, sending glowing cinders spiralling into the twilight and the fireglow, like kite-hawks. To bring the flames under control and clear the rubble from shops, offices and streets took the fire brigades and the army another two days.

More than four hundred buildings were destroyed in the fire, and some twelve thousand families lost their homes or their livelihood. The dead? No one knew how many Egyptians had died in those five and a half hours. Twenty-six foreigners, mostly British, had perished and the hospitals dealt with about six hundred wounded foreigners and Egyptians. Even estimates of the damage were vague, though British businessmen reckoned to have lost between three and four million pounds. The official figure for the damage was twenty-five million pounds but observers would have put it at six times that amount.

Who started and fuelled the fire? Of course, the British were blamed. They had started the fire, so ran the accusation, to give them an excuse to occupy the whole country. But whom did they hire to carry out the crime? Had there been any real evidence for this ludicrous suggestion would any Egyptian have withheld it? Bracketed with the British was Farouk, though here we have a better motive. He wanted the fire to burn long enough to singe the *Wafd* and give him his pretext for sacking them. But he never really envisaged himself in the role of Nero. When the rioters ran amok he became as alarmed as the rest. That afternoon, according to one of his trusted courtiers, he was secretly terrified, fearing for his crown, his capital and his ten-day-old son. As a last remedy he would have called in the British. No, Farouk might have warmed his hands at the blaze, but he stood to lose everything had the army failed to restore the situation.

The culprits belonged to three groups: the *Wafd* must accept most of the guilt for having ignited fanaticism and making no move to control the result. Like the king, Nahas and his cabinet were waiting in the wings. The Communist-inspired peace movement is believed to have organised the first arson squads, abetted by Ahmed Husain and the National Socialists. Then, as the pattern of the incendiarism proves, the Moslem Brethren took a hand, exploiting the opportunity to destroy every trace of the foreign infidel and the iniquitous pasha as it was represented by cinemas, night-clubs and hotels.

Farouk gained most from the fire; it looked as though he had gambled and won. He had *bust* the *Wafd* for good; he had acted as a man of decision by quelling the riots with the army; in Egypt and abroad he was praised for having demonstrated courage and sagacity in averting a revolutionary situation. The evening of Black Saturday, he called several advisers together to help him choose a new government. The question was, who was strong enough to lead it, to root out *Wafd* corruption and set the economy right. Farouk and his *chef de cabinet*, Hafez Afifi, came up with the name of Neguib el-Hilali, a beaky-faced lawyer and mystic who outdid the zealots of the Moslem Brethren in puritanism and would therefore relish finishing the rout of the *Wafd*. Hafez Afifi with Farouk's entrepreneur, Elias Andraos, drove through the ruins of Cairo in the early hours of Sunday morning to wake Hilali with the momentous news that the king had appointed him prime minister. Hilali met them in a dressing gown and red, woollen night cap. He thanked the king, then told both men, 'How could I form a cabinet while guns are still sounding...me, who cannot stand to see anyone wringing a chicken's neck? You had better go and see Ali Maher.'

That old fox was still awake, as if expecting a summons. He said 'No' as well, but changed his mind with a little persuasion from the king's emissaries. He had even listed the members of his new cabinet in a notebook, though he took Andraos's advice about Farouk's likes and dislikes in his prospective cabinet. That Sunday, Ali Maher was driven through Cairo in a white ambulance to interview members of his new government. To his credit, nevertheless, he brought order back into the city, called off the *fedayeen* and recommenced negotiations with Britain; for the first time in years the cost of living went down and one government appeared to be doing something for the Egyptian poor.

Left to himself, Ali Maher might have conjured Egypt out of its difficulties. Ironically, it was Farouk who ruined his chances. Not the Farouk he had known as the callow boy king to whom he had given the primary lessons in political intrigue, but a cynical despot in the hands of Thabet and Andraos, a man bent on enriching himself at the expense of everyone and everything even if it meant destroying the semblance of constitutional rule. Ali Maher is too dangerous, Thabet and Andraos whispered to the king; he is plotting with the *Wafd* instead of breaking it up. They whispered, too, that the premier had lost the king's confidence in his negotiations with the British. So, on the second of March, four weeks after assuming office, Ali Maher handed in his resignation. Farouk accepted it without a word of gratitude for his old mentor.

The king now imagined he could run the country himself. After all, hadn't he swatted the *Wafd* on Black Saturday? He

255

had shown everyone that day. He boasted about the fire of Cairo as though it had been a personal triumph. He no longer needed to fear Nahas, and those who had fired Cairo now realised their error. He was the real hero of the crisis. He could make or break politicians as he willed. He had proved he could count on the loyalty of the army. Or so he believed.

CHAPTER TWENTY-ONE

Even so have we placed in every city, ringleaders of its
wicked ones to scheme therein: but only against themselves
shall they scheme! and they know it not. (VI: 123)

In fact, with control of the army Farouk could appoint or dismiss
governments at his whim. Neither he nor his palace cronies
had reason to suspect the loyalty of the services. Not with his
own generals, like Haydar and Husain Sirri Amer, in charge.
British and American intelligence men were also convinced
that the Egyptian army would take the king's part as it had
done during the fire of Cairo. In December, the House of
Commons heard Anthony Eden declare the friendship of the
Egyptian army for Britain and describe it as the most peaceful
group in the country. Yet, the signs of discontent, even of revolt
were there. On the twenty-seventh of December, when the Officers'
Club, the focus of army influence, held its elections, the king's
nominee, Sirri Amer, was opposed by General Mohamed Neguib,
hero of Palestine. Farouk rightly interpreted this as a direct
snub and reacted by adjourning the meeting and postponing the
elections.

The key to Neguib's nomination was a group known as the
Free Officers. Its leader: Gamal Abdel Nasser. The election was
the first time that Nasser had dared, publicly, to confront
authority. With the exception of two or three close friends, no one
realised that he had been planning an army coup since the
Palestine war. But it stopped with the army. As late as Black
Saturday, Nasser had no thought of overthrowing the king or
organised government; he had set his sights, as Arabi before
him, on army reform. What sort of man was this Colonel who
had created a secret cabal of regimental officers prepared to tilt
at their chiefs of staff? Of fellahin stock, Nasser was born
in Alexandria in 1918, though his family hailed from Beni Mor

village on the edge of the Nile in Upper Egypt. As a boy, he would look up at aircraft and chant, 'Ya Azeez, Ya Azeez, Dahiya takhud al-inglez'. ('Almighty Allah, may disaster overtake the English') Before he was out of school he had come under the influence of the Young Egypt fascist movement and had tangled with authority during anti-British demonstrations. As he said, much later, 'In those early days, I led demonstrations in the Nahda Secondary School, and I shouted from my heart for complete independence, and many others behind me shouted, too. But our shouts only raised dust which was blown by the wind, and produced only weak echoes which shook no mountains and shattered no rocks.' Thinking he would make a lawyer, his father who was a district postmaster, enrolled him in a law school; he stuck this for a few months before deciding to enter the Military Academy. There, as a cadet, he met Abdel Hakim Amer, Sadat and a handful of young men who shared one thought: liberate Egypt from the British.

The humiliation of the king in 1942 affected some of these men profoundly; much worse was the shame of returning, defeated from Palestine, even if some had acquitted themselves bravely. They had to blame someone; their self-respect demanded it. The general staff, they said, had let them down, with the help of the royal clique which was lining its pockets while soldiers died for want of equipment. That fiasco orientated Nasser and his group towards rebellion, though only an army rebellion. Of the group, Anwar el-Sadat proved himself the firebrand, keeping contact with the Moslem Brethren, plotting political assassinations, devising schemes for blowing up British military installations. Nasser abjured violence, preferring to work patiently and cunningly to build up five-member cells of young officers who would back the eventual revolt. No one penetrated his secrecy. He divulged nothing: his aims, his method, his part in the plot. Since he was only an obscure colonel he had to find a man popular with the army and known to the people. Mohamed Neguib agreed to become president of the Society of Free Officers, Nasser's group.

His horror of violence turned Nasser to pamphleteering to gain his ends. One morning, Farouk entered his study to find a crude document headed, 'The Army say No to Farouk.' It outlined why the officers would not elect General Sirri Amer to the presidency of the Officers' Club. Like previous pamphlets, it enraged the king without achieving anything. For the first time, Nasser began to listen to his collaborators who were urging the assassination of the king's puppet general. He agreed to organise the attempt. One group would shoot Sirri Amer, another would cover the first, and a third would stage the escape. They spent weeks studying the general's movements. On the night, they hid outside his home until his car drew up. Describing what happened in his book, *The Philosophy of the Revolution*, Nasser said, 'As soon as he was sighted, he was met with a volley of bullets. The execution squad then withdrew, covered by the protective force, and we hurried to safety. I started the motor of my car and drove away from the scene of our carefully-planned "positive action". But suddenly there rang in my ears the sounds of screaming and wailing. I heard a woman crying, a child terrified, and a continuous frightened call for help. While speeding away in my car, I was overwhelmed and excited by a multitude of emotions. A strange thing was happening to me. The sounds were still loud in my ears: the screaming and wailing and the crying and the frightened calls for help. I was now too far away from the scene to hear the actual sounds, but nevertheless they seemed to be chasing me – following me.'

Nasser spent a remorseful night. He need not; they had fired fourteen shots at Sirri Amer and failed to hit him. Only his driver was wounded.

The attempted assassination had one important result. A member of the group, Lieutenant Abdel Kadar Tahar, was arrested, only to be released for want of evidence. A fortnight later he was invited to a deserted spot at Roda, between two Nile bridges, by one of the king's men. A car drove up and its occupants fired a fusillade of bullets at him. Before he died, Tahar stammered to a doctor in the hospital, 'It was Farouk who had me assassinated.' No one will ever know whether the king gave the order; none the less, the accusation stuck. One newspaper repeated an obituary of the lieutenant several times, without comment, to add substance to the story. Everyone blamed the king. When the election to the Officers' Club was resumed in January, Nasser cleverly arranged a two-minute silence for the dead officer, and General Neguib swept the poll with two hundred and seventy-six out of three hundred and thirty-four votes. The result so angered Farouk that he declared the election void, appointed a committee to revise the bye-laws and with-held funds for new premises in Fuad Street.

Now the king went in fear of his own life. His visits to the automobile club he had to cut to two a week; while he gambled, the place assumed the look of a military headquarters with soldiers and police ringing it. In night-clubs he never appeared without his Albanian bodyguard, and he sat with his hand shielding a small, silver pistol. He would scribble the names of people whom he fancied wanted to assassinate him on pieces of paper which he would stuff into his wallet so that the police would discover them on his body. The names changed every week; the list grew with his terror. One day, a bullet was fired through his bedroom window at Kubbah. His guards searched the ground, found nothing and concluded that the marksman had hidden outside the palace walls and hoped, by some fluke, to hit the king. After that, Farouk took to wearing a bullet-proof shirt and driving with a sub-machine gun on the front seat beside him. As his red car passed, the people stood sullen; some even jeered openly. He shunned official functions, inviting only his gambling friends and people like Thabet and Andraos to the palace. He had become a despot who governed by royal caprice, without real power to solve the country's problems; he was the richest man in Egypt, but impotent in mind and body. To one of his woman friends, a continental cabaret artiste, he expressed his sense of resignation, of futility in a scribbled note on which he had doodled his favourite letter F twice, and added the words, 'Farouk Foutu'.

In such a state of mind, Farouk listened to no one. The election of Neguib should have warned him that his final source of authority, the army, was disgruntled. He ignored it. Shortly after the burning of Cairo, the new Minister of the Interior, the capable and energetic Mortada el-Maraghi pasha raided the barracks at Madi, rounding up members of Nasser's group who were printing pamphlets attacking the king and the government. When he reported this to Farouk, the king rebuked him. 'Leave my army alone and don't interfere in its affairs,' he said. Gossip from his Italian pedicurist and a woman journalist meant more to him than information from his ministers. They told him what he wanted to believe – that Communism was the real menace. El-Maraghi listened, astounded, to Farouk reiterating the phrase, 'When I go the Communists will take over.' In vain, the minister tried to convince him that the threat would not come from Communism, rather from the army and the people. 'What do I care? said Farouk. 'The Egyptians hate me and I hate them. When the Communists take over I shall go and live in Europe.' El-Maraghi pointed out that his cousin, Khedive Abbas Hilmi, had spent most of his life exiled in Europe, regretting Egypt. 'He was a fool,' Farouk snapped. These moods baffled his court and his government. One moment he was planning to salvage his crown and the country; the next he had lapsed into a petulant humour and was threatening to renounce everything.

When Ali Maher resigned, he turned again to Hilali, thinking this ascetic – called the Don Quixote of the Nile – might rally the country behind a programme of reform. Hilali began well, placing Serag-ed-Din and other *Wafd* leaders under house arrest and initiating an inquiry into government corruption; he suspended parliament, promising elections under a reformed system by the end of the year; he even managed to ease Anglo-Egyptian tension by opening talks with the British, though these soon reached deadlock again over the Sudan issue.

But it was not international friction that finished Hilali's bid to clean up the country; he had threatened to expose government graft, thereby incriminating *Wafd*ists. Hilali promulgated a decree obliging every Egyptian to declare the source of his fortune. Even the king signed the decree. *Wafd* politicians, however, made it plain to Hilali that if he so much as printed one word of scandal about the party they would retaliate by revealing everything they knew about palace corruption – cotton rigging, arms trafficking, land seizure, everything. Hilali's decree frightened three other men: Elias Andraos, Karim Thabet and Ahmed Abboud pasha, one of the richest industrialists and landowners in Egypt. Andraos and Thabet, their pockets well-lined by Abboud, drove Hilali out of office by a series of intrigues. Thabet and Andraos went to the U.S. ambassador with the suggestion that Hilali would never carry the country with him if they wanted a defence pact; the only party capable of signing such a pact was the *Wafd*; at the same time they appealed to *Wafd* leaders who were under threat of exposure to approach the Americans. Though Caffery and the State Department were pressing Britain to resolve the Sudan question in Egypt's favour, they would have none of this double-dealing. Hilali was informed and immediately resigned in such terms that they could not be published without arraigning the king. Though his letter of resignation was banned by the censor its contents became the small change of bazaar gossip and Farouk lost more credit.

Farouk had few qualms about losing Hilali. Andraos had given him a share of the reward – one hundred thousand pounds in gold. In any case, he could never have submitted to any investigation about the origins of his wealth. How would he have explained the sums he had received for ministerial appointments under the Maher government? Or the trips which certain of his staff had been making to Europe to bank money in his Swiss accounts? Or the appointment of his friend, Andraos, to a directorship of the Misr Bank? The web of corruption had too many threads attached to him and his clique for him to weep over Hilali. The victor of Black Saturday could govern alone. If it came to the worst, he could always fall back on his friends, the Americans, whose ambassador had been so helpful over the Sudan. Caffery, he knew, feared Communism just as much as he did. As for the British, he no longer needed them unless there was a real revolution; then they would come running as they had always done.

Thabet was whispering in his ear again, this time another scheme which would recapture some of his popularity. The great Farouk, he was sure, could trace his descendance back to the Prophet Mohamed. He recalled that one of the older chamberlains always insisted that Queen Nazli's grandfather had been accorded the title of El Sayed. Did that not prove that the queen mother and the king were descended from the founder of Islam? Thabet's arguments appealed to Farouk's vanity. Without further prompting, a day or two after Black Saturday, the king delegated the task of confirming this theory to one of his ministers. The minister enlisted the aid of Sheikh el-Biblawi, of Al Azhar, and began the long inquiry which, of course, could lead to only one conclusion. In the first week of May, the Press and radio made the announcement that the king could trace his line directly back to Mohamed and had therefore adopted the title of El Sayed in addition to his others. The royal commission did not bother to cite evidence supporting its statement. Cairo and Alexandria laughed and scoffed at the king's presumption, at his lickspittle court; the *ulema* deemed it blasphemy. Who, even among the ignorant *fellahin,* could consider it valid for a moment? For the people, it confirmed one thing: the king's madness, his stupidity or his cynicism; it squandered the slight influence Farouk still had with the leaders of Islam. Even in the army, as Neguib related afterwards, it dented his prestige. Neguib said, 'Farouk as everyone knew, was a descendant of Albanians and Circassians on his father's side and of Turks and Frenchmen on his mother's side... If there was any Arabic blood in Farouk's veins it was so diluted that it couldn't possibly have been traced back to Mohamed, and it was a sacrilege for anyone to have tried to do so.'

But he, the king, was the only government since the abrupt departure of Hilali. Farouk did not realise it then, but the fall of Hilali, the man who had honestly attempted to buttress the crumbling structures of authority, was his own ruin. Neither the British nor the Americans believed that Farouk could act responsibly. The king remained oblivious of this. With his shabby baggage of royal sycophants, pimps, procurers and double-dealers, he fled the torpor of Cairo for his summer holiday on the beaches of Montazah, leaving the unfortunate Hafez Afifi the task of shoring up the government with yet another premier. It was as though the king was retreating from his duty as he had once escaped from his lessons and run into the servants' quarters. He had much the same people around him, his famous Kitchen Cabinet: Pulli, Mohamed Hassan, the valet, Thabet, Andraos, Abdel Azziz, the butler, his Albanian guards. These people governed the country by proxy, translating, interpreting, anticipating the royal whim.

By day, Farouk wallowed in the swimming pool while girls whom he scarcely knew paraded before him; or he shambled from his rococo palace through the pines to the beach to brood over the Mediterranean and stoke himself with rich food for the evening exertions. In the gold evening, a convoy of Cadillacs, most of them red, sped along the corniche to the automobile club, or a night-club, or his cabaret on the top floor of the Moassat Hospital. It was all so pointless, a form of mental and physical anarchy. But everything reflected it; the country had no government, although this made little difference to the masses; only the pashas and politicians realised something was missing. They trundled after the king, to the swimming pool, the beaches, the gambling tables, hoping that he would interrupt his pleasure long enough to give them a tired audience or a hint about the next administration.

For a week this charade continued before he sent one of his valets to Hafez Afifi, asking him to summon Husain Sirri. He had saved Farouk before, after the Palestine débâcle; he might again, if given the chance. He presented his ministerial list to Farouk, who glanced at it and struck out two names, substituting others. One of these was Karim Thabet, most despicable of the villains around him; the other was General Sirri Amer, hated by Neguib, Nasser and the Free Officers for his part in the Palestine arms swindle. He was the new Minister of War. Husain Sirri had, in fact proposed Neguib, the man he knew to be leading the campaign conducted by the young officers against the king and his army chiefs. Now, with two of the king's nominees in his cabinet, Sirry found that able men like Maraghi refused office; they realised this was the end. As Anthony Eden said,

'There were to be no more attempts to root out corruption. Egypt was back in its dirty financial groove.'

The cabinet of Husain Sirry was denounced with such vehemence by the Press that even Farouk became anxious. Instead of listening to his prime minister – whom he rarely met – he took his cue from Thabet and Andraos. Neguib, the ringleader of the officers, should be posted to a remote garrison in Upper Egypt, they said. Husain Sirry managed to annul this royal order. But, on the tenth of July, Farouk scrawled a note in pencil which he handed to Abdel Azziz (his butler) who handed it to Hafez Afifi (his cabinet chief) who handed it to Husain Sirry. It concerned General Haydar, the army C-in-C, who had some sympathy for the Free Officers. 'Haydar must be removed within five days unless he dissolves the executive committee of the Officers' Club and removes the twelve officers who have been conspiring against His Majesty the King.' Five days later, Farouk himself suspended the committee.

Now the Free Officers had to act. Sirri Amer's appointment, the proposed posting of Neguib and the suspension of the Officers' Club Committee all hinted ominously at an army purge. Nasser had already fixed the beginning of August as the date of the army revolt, but still had no precise plan. Some of the original Free Officers thought the only way to achieve their ends was to massacre the country's leaders; three days after Farouk's warning about Haydar, they drew up a list of thirty traitors they meant to assassinate, including the king. American Central Intelligence Agency officials in Cairo heard about this plan and went immediately to Nasser, with whom they were in contact, and argued him out of it. He, in turn, dissuaded Sadat, Amer and others.

Although Nasser had taken every precaution to keep the movement secret, British Intelligence and the C.I.A. had gleaned word of the officers' plot. The Americans actively encouraged Nasser to strike at the king whom they had abandoned as a depraved and dissolute weakling who was allowing Communism to take a grip on Egypt. The British agreed about the king, though they knew less than the Americans about Nasser and his bid for power.

Egyptian army intelligence officers had also gathered the names of several of Nasser's close colleagues and knew something of their aims. When Husain Sirry received information that the officers were planning a coup, he telephoned the king from Cairo. First, he tried Montazah, then Ras el-Tin, and finally tracked him to the gambling room of the automobile club. He explained the situation, adding, 'We know what is coming in the course of the next forty-eight hours. We know the men behind the revolt. Have we your authority to step in and arrest them?'

'Who are these men?' Farouk listened as the premier recited the names. 'A bunch of pimps (moarrassin),' he shouted, banged down the phone and went back to his cards.

That meant the end for Sirry, who resigned on the twentieth of July. To whom could Farouk now turn? Everything around him appeared to be disintegrating. In desperation, he again sent for Hilali and agreed to all his prior conditions. Hilali demanded a free hand to deal with corruption and stipulated that Karim Thabet and General Sirri Amer must be removed. At four p.m. on the twenty-second of July, Hilali presented himself at Ras el-Tin with the fifteen men he had selected as ministers. In their grey morning-suits, they paced across the ebony-and-ivory floor of the Throne Room to where Farouk, in admiral's uniform, had wedged his massive body into the leather chair on the dais. Suddenly, Hilali noticed another figure, dressed in black, enter the room and join his cabinet. Farouk's laughter rang from the arabesque ceiling. 'Gentlemen,' he said, pointing to the sixteenth man, 'I give you the new Minister of War.' It was his brother-in-law, Ismail Shereen, husband of Princess Fawzia. The king was still chortling on the way to his afternoon swim at Montazah. He had, it seemed, learned nothing from the previous crisis.

CHAPTER TWENTY-TWO

Wherefore let them flounder on and disport them, till they come face to face with their threatened day.   (LXX: 42)

While Farouk was splashing in his pool, the news that he had appointed his brother-in-law minister of war had travelled a hundred and twenty-five miles to Nasser's house in Manshyat el-Bakri, an eastern suburb of Cairo. To the rebels, this move implied imminent arrest. Eight of the original group of Free Officers met immediately and set to work drafting the time-table of the revolt; within an hour they were scanning six closely-typed pages, the blueprint of the uprising. In shirt sleeves, on that sweltering afternoon, they finalised their plan which they intended to carry out in two stages; first, they would take over the army by capturing the general staff; second, they would seize the king. *Nasr* (Victory) was the password. Even at this stage, the ever-cautious Colonel Nasser decided that, of his membership of three hundred Free Officers, he could trust only ninety. And these he would have to alert by word of mouth. In his jaded black Austin he travelled from house to house, briefing the men singly, swearing them to absolute secrecy.

Not many revolutions can have depended on so few men, on such flimsy preparation. If Nasser's officers miscalculated and blundered at times, this was offset by the chaos and indecision of the men in authority. His security measures broke down. One of the Free Officers told his wife to pray for him that night and she drew the whole story of the projected coup out of him. Frightened, she rang her friends and, within a couple of hours of Nasser's visit, the general staff had summoned its members to an urgent meeting at Kubri el-Kubbah, near Abbassiah Barracks. Hearing news of their meeting on his briefing round, Nasser went into a panic; he drove to Major Abdel Hakim Amer's home to tell him. It was eleven-thirty, ninety minutes before their Zero Hour. Amer said, 'We must get some troops. We can't capture the general staff single-handed.' But when the two officers reached the military compound they saw the gates were heavily guarded by M.P.s. Now they were both scared. As they retreated through Heliopolis they suddenly ran into an army convoy and halted, thinking the general staff had already ordered out troops. Too late, the leader of the contingent had spotted them and started interrogating them. As they were trying, desperately, to talk their way out of being shot a voice shouted Nasser's name. It was Colonel Yussef Mansur Sadek, one of the most trusted of the Free Officers, leading men of the Thirteenth Machine Gun Battalion. He had mistaken the Zero Hour and ordered his men out for midnight instead of one o'clock, an error which cost Farouk his throne. Quickly, Nasser explained about the general staff. 'We can use your company to capture them all together,' he said.

Inside an hour they were marching twenty general officers out of the headquarters. Armoured cars and tanks had taken up their stations at key points – the Chamber of Deputies, Abdin Palace, Abbassiah Barracks, the Citadel, Farouk Airport, the Nile bridges, the city entrances and exits. Special squads had seized Cairo Radio and other broadcasting stations, the telephone exchanges, the electricity stations. By three o'clock in the morning, while Cairo slept, Nasser's troops had occupied almost every strategic point. Whoever has Cairo, has Egypt, runs the military adage. The Free Officers were now beginning to think in those terms.

Just at this moment, General Mohamed Neguib had a telephone call from Mortada el-Maraghi, Minister of the Interior, who said, 'I appeal to you as a soldier and a patriot to put an end to this affair.'

'What do you mean?'

'You know what I mean. Your boys have started something in Kubri el-Kubbah, and if you don't put a stop to it the British may intervene.'

'I don't know what you're talking about. And besides, how do

I know you're Maraghi? For all I know, you may be only trying to find an excuse for arresting me.' And Neguib put the phone down.

Two of the Free Officers, Wing Commander Ali Sabri and Colonel Abdel Moneim Amin, were despatched to tell the British and Americans that the revolution was not directed against any foreign power. Abdel Moneim Amin woke up the British chargé d'affaires, John Hamilton, who informed him that the British had no intention of intervening. They then sat chatting about Moneim's days at Larkhill gunnery school. The Americans declared, too, that they had no thought of bringing pressure on the revolutionaries.

It was all but over, with no resistance, no bloodshed. Neguib moved into revolutionary headquarters. '*Mabruk* (Congratulations)' he said to Nasser and the other leaders. It had been so simple that they could hardly believe it. But what about Farouk? The officers convened a meeting to decide how they should deal with the king, still in Alexandria. There was one man to whom he might still listen: Ali Maher. Anwar el-Sadat went to see the old statesman to ask him if he would head a government, at the same time dropping the hint that he might eventually become president of a new republic. Maher agreed provisionally.

Sadat then returned to Cairo Radio at seven a.m. to broadcast the revolutionary proclamation to the nation:

'People of Egypt. Egypt has lived through one of the darkest periods in its history. The army has been tainted by the agents of dissolution. This was one of the causes of our defeat in Palestine. Led by fools, traitors and incompetents, the army was incapable of defending Egypt. This is why we have carried out a purge. The army is now in the hands of men in whose ability, integrity and patriotism you can have complete confidence. The former army chiefs, who are now under arrest, will be released when circumstances permit.

'Egypt will greet our movement with hope and joy, and she can be sure that the army is pledged to protect the national interest. I take this opportunity to warn the Egyptian people against its enemies, and to ask them to allow no acts of violence or destruction to be committed. Such acts can only harm Egypt. They will be regarded as acts of treason and will be severely punished. The army, in co-operation with the police, will be responsible for law and order.

'I particularly wish to reassure our friends, the foreign nationals in Egypt, that the army considers itself entirely responsible for the protection of their persons and property. May God sustain us.'

People took the news calmly. It seemed the army merely wanted to purge the corrupt men in its own ranks, in government and the royal entourage. Which was what everyone wanted. There was nothing in the broadcast about the king, as though the men behind the revolution had not yet made up their minds what to do with Farouk. People gathered round the smiling figure of General Neguib as he toured the city, but the White Revolution created as little excitement as it had spilled blood. Only the twenty-five pounders and the armoured cars around Abdin Palace hinted at the trend the quiet coup d'etat was taking.

While the Free Officers were taking possession of Cairo on the first night of the revolution, Farouk was asleep at Montazah Palace. Between one and two o'clock in the morning, he was wakened by two officers of the royal guard who gave him news of the capture of his general staff and key points in the capital. 'You, Sire, and your family are in danger. We have received word that in a few hours, Alexandria will be under martial law.' Immediately, the king contacted Hilali and members of his cabinet; he roused Pulli, giving him instructions to take a car to Cairo, to contact the British commander on the Suez Road and plead for troops; if that failed, the Italian should ask the British Embassy. Looking out to sea from his balcony, he spotted an Egyptian army bomber sweeping in low over the palace, then a warship swinging its guns on to the plane. At least the navy had remained loyal. A moment or two later that hope vanished; he heard that his other warships were lying trapped under the fortress guns of Colonel Wahid Shawki, one of the Free Officers. He had to act.

Anne Chermside, governess to the baby prince, Ahmed Fuad, was wakened and told to get herself and the infant ready. Ras el-Tin, at the other end of the corniche, had a stronger guard, better communications; from there, he might rally the navy and the loyal section of the army. At just after two o'clock, he drove his Mercedes out of Montazah; in the back seat were Miss Chermside with Fuad in her arms; his personal pilot, Hassan Akif, took the front passenger seat, arming himself with a sub-machine gun. Narriman and his daughters would follow the next day. In the twelve-mile dash they saw hardly any sign of the uprising, only two armoured cars which had posted themselves in Arabi Square. Ras el-Tin had not been touched, though it sat dangerously beneath guns of the Quait Bey fort. Farouk ordered his guards into position at barricaded windows.

Now he really needed the British. But he could not ask them directly. He telephoned his friend, Jefferson Caffery, at the summer embassy in Alexandria; the ambassador made it clear, however, that the Americans could not help, and he did not believe the British would. Describing the events of that morning, Eden said, 'From eight a.m. onwards the king was frequently on the telephone to the United States Ambassador. He repeated, each time more clearly, that only foreign intervention could save him and his dynasty. He did not ask explicitly for British military action, but the implication was obvious. I had frequently indicated to our Embassy that British forces would not intervene to keep King Farouk on his throne.'

Desperate now, Farouk sent Narriman's uncle, Mustapha Sadek, to Cairo to meet Neguib and ask what his conditions were. He had still heard nothing from Pulli, and could hardly know that the Italian had fallen into the hands of the revolutionaries. British headquarters had referred Pulli to the Embassy and, once in Cairo he was trapped, since all roads in and out of the city were blocked. At midday, Farouk had a call from the queen's uncle: Neguib, he said, was making few demands; the main one was that Hilali must go and the king must appoint

271

Ali Maher prime minister. That afternoon, Hilali handed in his resignation. The king wondered why neither the British nor the Americans had acted to stifle the coup; he himself attempted to counter the movement by appealing to Wahid Shawki to take his side and stop menacing the navy with his guns. But Shawki refused.

When news of the king's action reached Cairo, Neguib and Sadat made plans to fly to Alexandria to balk any attempts at a counter coup and force the king's abdication. Before they left they were aware that they could turn their revolt into a coup d'etat by deposing the king. British intervention – the one factor they had feared – would not halt them. Just before midnight, John Hamilton arrived at Neguib's headquarters with the text of Eden's message which stated that the British would not support Farouk. As he wrote it down, slowly in longhand, Neguib raised his head and grinned at the diplomat. 'You know, this reminds me of taking down dictation at Gordon College,' he said.

Arriving in Alexandria, Neguib predicted no great problem in capturing the king whom they had isolated and cornered in Ras el-Tin. But what to do with him when they had taken him prisoner? The question exercised the younger officers more than the plan to surround the palace. So, in their army barracks, Neguib and half the members of the revolutionary council sat down to one of the most bizarre trials in history, to give judgement on one issue: should they or should they not execute Farouk? For hours, behind closed doors, the trial dragged on. The self-appointed prosecuting counsel, Wing-Commander Gamal Salem, argued vehemently and eloquently for the death penalty. 'He is a murderer,' he shouted, 'and has to be hanged as we hang murderers. He is a leader who betrayed his army and has to be shot as traitors in the army are shot ... We here represent justice; the courts hang the ordinary man who murders one man, so how in fairness can we let a man go free who has murdered a whole people? The law sentences the thief who steals a loaf of bread, so how can the revolutionary law let the man go who has robbed a whole nation?' Farouk would use his smuggled funds to fight against the revolution from exile, he contended. The imperialist, would use him as their cat's-paw.

Other officers maintained that abdication and exile were punishment enough. As for Neguib, he commented that he did not care whether Farouk lived or died; if the interests of Egypt necessitated his death, he would die; if it were not in Egypt's interest, he would be spared and sent into exile. Suddenly, the general realised that this crucial verdict depended on the votes of only half the revolutionary council; the others, in Cairo, must have their say. He therefore ordered Gamal Salem to fly to the capital and put the question to Nasser and his collaborators. Nasser, in turn, sought advice from Farouk's old tutor, General Azziz el-Masri, who simply grunted, 'A head like Farouk's interests me only after it has fallen.' But then, the old rebel was urging a purge and a blood bath to clean out all the ruling class. The majority sided with Nasser, who dictated a message to Neguib counselling him to seize the king and get him out of the country as soon as possible. 'We cannot execute Farouk without a trial,' he wrote. 'Neither can we afford to keep him in jail and preoccupy ourselves with the rights and wrongs of his case at the risk of neglecting the other purposes of the revolution. Let us spare Farouk and send him into exile. History will sentence him to death.'

Still unaware that he had been judged and condemned to exile, Farouk waited in Ras el-Tin for the rebels to put their demands to him. The worst of the storm had blown over, he told himself. When Ali Maher arrived in Alexandria on the morning of the twenty-fourth of July, the king felt sure enough of himself to quibble because his old premier had brought a military escort. 'They will think it is February the Fourth all over again,' he complained. Ali Maher persuaded the three armed officers to retire while he discussed the crisis with the king. The irony of this interview struck both men: the dandified little *entrepreneur* who had guided Farouk's first steps in autocratic government was now acting as an instrument of the new order; for his part, the king fancied he might outwit the new premier. But Maher had received detailed orders from Nasser and Neguib. 'The revolutionary council demands that you dismiss eight men in your court,' he said, bluntly. 'They are Antonio Pulli bey, Karim Thabet pasha, Elias Andraos pasha, Mohamed Hassan, General Mohamed Hilmi Husain, Hassan Akif, Yussef Rashad, the palace doctor, and General el-Yel Nasr.'

'And what if I refuse?'

'The army is in a position to force you to acquiesce.'

'That means they will depose me.'

'Unless I can give them the assurance that you will co-operate.'

'Very well then, I agree to those demands.'

The king also had to submit to the sacking of his favourite army commander, General Haydar pasha, and authorise the appointment of General Neguib as commander of the armed forces. The interview ended on the understanding that Farouk would remain King of Egypt, that Maher would form a new government. But, at eight o'clock the following night, an armoured column had reached Alexandria from Cairo; it surrounded Ras el-Tin within half an hour and infantry moved into the palace courtyard; in the skirmish between them and the royal guard two men were killed and several wounded before the building surrendered. The king, now realising he was fighting for his life, ordered a messenger to contact the American ambassador. 'I am besieged in my palace by rebels. Will you please use your influence and that of your country to save our lives?' Caffery promised to do what he could. Soon afterwards, he met Ali Maher to say he had a guarantee that the king and his family would not be harmed.

At nine a.m. on the twenty-sixth General Neguib and Colonel Sadat handed Ali Maher the text of their ultimatum to the king; Maher scanned it, his face going pale. It said:

'In view of your misrule, your violations of the Constitution, your contempt for the will of the nation, which has gone so far that no citizen can any longer feel his life, property or dignity to be safe; and because, under your protection, traitors and swindlers are allowed to amass scandalous fortunes by wasting public monies while the people are dying of privation and hunger; and since these abuses were aggravated during the war in Palestine which gave rise to an abominable traffic in arms and munitions, the army has authorised me to demand that Your Majesty abdicate in favour of the heir to the throne, His Highness, Ahmed Fuad on this day, Saturday, the twenty-sixth of July 1952, and that you quit the country on the same day before six o'clock. In the event of a rejection of this ultimatum, you will be held responsible for the consequences.' Neguib had signed the document.

At ten forty a.m. Ali Maher had his final interview with Farouk at which he handed him the ultimatum. The king read it, sitting on a wooden chair outside the Rotunda, a circular room with a domed roof which had been used for official receptions. 'I am sorry, Your Majesty,' Maher murmured when Farouk ended his scrutiny of the document.

The king then made his requests. 'I should like to take Pulli with me. I have known him since I was a child and it means a great deal to me.' Nasser refused that favour, though he did grant the king permission to take some of his personal wealth with him; he allowed him to leave the country on the royal yacht, Mahroussa, on condition that the ship returned as soon as he had reached exile. Did Ali Maher think he might return to Egypt as a private person? he asked. 'The Duke of Windsor sometimes returns to England,' the premier suggested.

The king then signed the ultimatum and gave it to Ali Maher. For a moment he looked at the premier. 'And what have they promised you, Ali pasha? The presidency?' The premier did not reply; he bowed and left.

While Farouk waited for the abdication document to be presented to him, he got word to his sisters that he would be leaving at six o'clock. Joseph Simpson, secretary to the American ambassador, managed to penetrate the revolutionary guard to tell the king they had assurances about his personal safety. 'I have never been so glad to see anyone,' Farouk said. Half an hour later, Caffery arrived to confirm the guarantees.

At twelve thirty, Suleiman Hafiz brought the abdication document which he and another Supreme Court Justice, Abdel Razek Sanhuri, had drafted; the revolutionary council had made changes, stipulating that it should contain a reference to the will of the people. The final version read:

'We, Farouk the First, Whereas We have always sought the happiness and welfare of our people, and sincerely wish to spare them the difficulties which have arisen in this critical time, We therefore conform to the will of the people. We have decided to abdicate the Throne in favour of Our heir, Prince Ahmed Fuad, and in the present rescript to give our orders to this end to His Excellency, Ali Maher pasha, Prime Minister, that he may act accordingly.'

In a note to Ali Maher, the king's reaction to this document was later described by Suleiman Hafiz. 'He cast a brief glance over the text and asked me what the Act was based on. I replied that provision had been made for it in the preamble to the Constitution. He appeared calm, but judging from his slight coughs and the shuffling of his feet, he was terribly nervous and trying to control himself. He read the document twice, then begged me to add to the phrase, "the will of the people," a reference to "Our will". I pointed out to him that the text was drafted in the form of a royal rescript. He asked me whether that meant that the royal will was understood. I said that it was. He signed, and said: "I hope that in view of the circumstances you will excuse this signature. I had better sign it again." He did.'

The document, in Arabic, no bigger than the page of a book, bears two signatures, one at the top, the other below the text. They are not noticeably different.

Farouk supervised the packing of his baggage. But what could he take, except personal belongings? He had been trapped in Alexandria when all but a few of his possessions lay in the vaults of Kubbah or the museums and private rooms of Abdin. At Ras el-Tin he had a small part of his stamp collections and some gold coins. The gold he loaded into twelve ammunition boxes and the stamps went into suitcases; he sent servants to

Montazah for the queen's jewels. Compared with the vast wealth he had acquired in sixteen years it was petty.

His sisters, Fawzia and Faiza, had arrived with their husbands to bid farewell. While her father dressed in his white admiral's uniform, Princess Ferial, his eldest daughter, wrote her mother a note which she confided to one of the guards. It read:

'My very dear mother, it is heart-breaking to have to leave Egypt and not to kiss you goodbye. I hope God never again makes me go through the experiences of these past few days, having to say farewell to so many whom we love, and to so many beloved things.'

Neguib had promised to escort the king to the jetty in the forecourt of the palace. At five forty-five, Farouk gave up waiting for him and walked into the courtyard. To Jefferson Caffery, he turned and said, 'I want you to realise this, that my children are accompanying me of their own free will.' The palace guard and his personal Sudanese guards had formed a last guard of honour; he walked slowly down the line, stopping now and again when he recognised a face and muttered a word of farewell; he stood while the national anthem was played, his flag lowered and handed to him. Then he took the few paces to the jetty and to the launch of the Mahroussa. There, he paused for a moment to shake hands with Ali Maher and Jefferson Caffery before crossing the gangway. Narriman followed him, carrying the baby king in her arms; no sound was heard except the lamentation of his servants.

On the deck of the Mahroussa he stood, fidgeting, looking at his watch and at the sailors who were casting adrift. A minute or two and Neguib, whose jeep had taken the wrong turning, would have missed him; the jeep bored through the crowd on the quay, and a launch picked up the General and three other revolutionary leaders and took them to the yacht. Neguib later recounted what happened at that last meeting:

'Farouk was waiting for us on the bridge. I saluted and he returned my salute. A long and embarrassing pause ensued.

277

Neither of us knew what to say. We were both gripped by a mixture of emotions that brought us close to tears.

"*Effendim*," I said at last, addressing him politely as a private citizen rather than a king. "You remember that I was the only Egyptian officer who submitted his resignation in 1942."

"Yes, I remember," said Farouk.

"I was ashamed of the humiliation to which the King of Egypt had been subjected."

"I know."

"We were loyal to the throne in 1942, but many things have changed since then."

"Yes, I know. Many things have changed."

"It was you, *effendim*, who forced us to do what we have done."

Farouk's reply will puzzle me for the rest of my life.

"I know," he said. "You've done what I always intended to do myself."

I was so surprised that I could think of nothing more to say. I saluted and the others did likewise. Farouk returned our salutes and we all shook hands.

"I'm sorry not to have received you at the quay," he said, "but you ordered me to be out of Egypt by six o'clock. I kept my word."

We nodded and prepared to leave the bridge. But Farouk had not yet finished.

"I hope you'll take good care of the army," he said. "My grandfather, you know, created it."

"The Egyptian Army," I said, "is in good hands..."

"Your task will be difficult. It isn't easy, you know, to govern Egypt."

Such were Farouk's last words. I felt sorry for him as we disembarked. Farouk, I knew, would fail as an exile even as he had failed as a king. But he was such an unhappy man in every way that I could take no pleasure in his destruction, necessary though it was.'

At seven o'clock, the Mahroussa, a shimmering white shape

278

with its royal pennants flying, eased its way through the grey naval ships and the freighters in the harbour. On the upper deck, Farouk stood, bareheaded, gazing over the bow towards the sea. Every ship in the harbour hoisted flags as a farewell signal. Seeing this, the crowds went suddenly quiet, as though only at this moment the significance of the past three days had penetrated; there was no tumult; only the hollow thud of the twenty-one-gun salute from the frigate Malik Farouk. It was the king's last request.

How had they made it, this incredible revolution? A handful of officers, not more than two thousand men had taken over Egypt. In one of the least bloody revolutions in history only two soldiers had died and seven others had been wounded. Even its leaders seemed daunted by their success.

A close investigation of the Free Officers' plot makes it manifest that, at that moment, they did not intend to carry out a national revolution, but merely act to save themselves from the arrest and trial which they believed the king was planning. Nasser himself has said he does not act, he reacts. In those three days he saw one obstacle after another collapse before him; his tactical sense convinced him that he could convert revolt into revolution. Before the coup, how could he have hoped to win? He had ninety trusted officers. Against that were several thousand loyal officers and more than twenty thousand troops, as well as the navy, at the king's disposal. They could have snuffed out Nasser's revolt before it started had he not captured the whole of the general staff and left Farouk out of contact in Alexandria.

Would Nasser ever have begun his bid for power unless he had received secret assurances that Britain would not use troops to prop up Farouk? Such promises did not come from the British Embassy, or its intelligence, before the army revolt. The American ambassador denied all prior knowledge about the revolutionary plot except to say the embassy 'knew something was going on in the army'. The Central Intelligence Agency, however, were active and did have contact with Nasser and several of his Free Officers. El-Maraghi, Minister of the Interior, discovered that CIA men were distributing reports about the Cuban revolution, and urging Nasser to follow this pattern to overthrow Farouk. Still, Farouk knew better, and ignored the warnings.

But, even after the Free Officers had taken Cairo, he might have attempted to crush the rebellion. He might have appealed to the navy, or rallied the Hilali government to confront the rebels; he might have fled to continue the fight from a friendly Middle East Country. Instead he dithered in Alexandria, thinking he could still buy off Neguib with a portfolio or even the premiership, knowing nothing about the strength of the Free Officers. Decision and action – this was asking too much from a man who had never faced up to reality throughout his life. Many people who knew Farouk intimately have remarked, 'He never acted like a king.' Or, 'He had ceased to want to be king.' The sibylline dialogue which so puzzled Neguib in his final interview, gives the hint; long before the Free Officers envisaged revolt, Farouk had abdicated; he had weighed the responsibilities of kingship against the life of the leisured sybarite. And he had prepared himself for the latter.

CHAPTER TWENTY-THREE

Woe on that day to those who charged with imposture!
On that day they shall not speak,
Nor shall it be permitted them to allege excuses.
Woe on that day to those who charge with imposture!
This is the day of severing, when we will assemble you and
*   your ancestors.*
If now ye have any craft try your craft on me.

(LXXVII: 34 to 39)

LIKE Ismail before him, Farouk set course for Naples. The three uneventful days and nights on the Mahroussa he elaborated into a fantasy in which he had dodged two aircraft and a torpedo boat, pursuing him on instructions from the revolutionaries to scuttle the ship and the royal family. He persisted in narrating this fairy tale in the face of logic which should have convinced him that the leaders of the coup d'etat were too mindful of world opinion to attempt a massacre at sea. Indeed, Mohamed el-Tabeh, the writer, expressed surprise to Nasser that he had allowed Farouk to take so much money out of the country. 'If he had asked us for our wallets we would have given them gladly to get rid of him,' Nasser told him.

On the twenty-ninth of July, the Mahroussa – stripped during the voyage of all its valuables – put Farouk and his entourage ashore at Naples; they transferred to a charter boat and sailed for Capri. As soon as they stepped ashore, Farouk went to the Canzone de Mare. Boris Alperovici, husband of Gracie Fields, caught sight of the immense figure, still in admiral's uniform, striding towards him. 'Boris, my friend,' he said, grinning. 'I am no longer king and I am here with only one pair of pants. Please take me to your tailor.'

At the height of the season he also had difficulty getting rooms for his party of twenty-nine. However, Nicolo Farace, the enterprising proprietor of the Eden Paradiso, at Anacapri, compensated the guests on the third floor of the hotel and installed the exiles there. Farace noticed they had brought only two or three dozen large suitcases and twelve wooden boxes which looked as if they contained arms and ammunition. Farouk appeared concerned about nothing other than the boxes, hardly glancing at the accommodation but specifying that one room should be reserved for the boxes and should have only one bed. The boxes arrived in a car from Capri guarded by the three Albanians, Shaker, Yacob and Abdel, who carried Tommy guns. One posted himself by the lift, the others unloaded the boxes and put them into the room. Several suitcases were placed in the same room.

For the first three days no one ventured down from the third floor. More than three hundred reporters were besieging the hotel and finally Farouk was compelled to hold a press conference. Sitting on a swing seat, on his sun terrace, with the infant king of Egypt on his knee and Narriman by his side, he read a statement in French and English.

'I hope you will forgive me if I do not speak as freely as you would like me to. While I am no longer king, I still have several grave responsibilities, and one of them is towards the Italian Government which has courteously given me hospitality here. I want to carefully avoid saying anything that might possibly embarrass them. I repeat, I am no longer king, but I do have with me the King of Egypt and I owe him a responsibility. So that you can see, with all the problems that have fallen on my shoulders, I would not like to add to them by any unguarded remark. So far as the present government in Egypt is concerned, I wish them all the luck in the world, because they need it. Governing a country in these days of world crisis is no easy matter. When I became king at sixteen years of age, I was hopeful that I could improve the position of my country in its relations with other nations of the world, and my love for Egypt and for the people of my country, even though I am in exile, is as great today as it was then.'

He asked the reporters to leave him and his family in peace

282

to move around and behave as private individuals. He admitted that, judged by ordinary standards, he was still wealthy.

Wherever he went on the small island, the Italian police and his three Albanian guards never strayed far away. Farouk still believed that the revolutionary government would try to assassinate him and his son. The Eden Paradiso staff vetted everyone at the reception desk; people with Middle East passports were politely told, 'Sorry, no rooms.' Their vigilance broke down one day, and the horrified Signor Farace discovered someone from the Lebanon in the room directly below Farouk's dining-room. For an uncomfortable half an hour, he and the police searched the room, listening for the bomb they thought the man had planted before leaving for a stroll in town. They persuaded the king to dine in Anacapri that night, took the room apart, and found nothing. Another evening, Farouk was eating in the Canzone del Mare when the lights suddenly failed along the Marina Piccola; no more than thirty seconds later they came on again; in that time the king and queen were flanked by their Albanians whom no one had spotted before. They had obviously rehearsed the drill to perfection.

The ex-king suddenly developed toothache and had to visit a Neapolitan dentist; he amazed Boris by chatting in the dialect of Southern Italy. 'Where did you learn that?' he asked. *'Con una piccerella al letto.'* ('With a little bird in bed.') He seemed content to live quietly, spending most of his time between the hotel and the swimming pool. He was half-amused, half-angry with the stories that newspapers printed about him. Capri, which has to import water, ran short that summer; several newspapers blamed Farouk for the drought, alleging he used too much water in his bath. 'Ah, these twerps. You would think by this time they'd have some understanding of the principle of Archimedes. Don't they know a fat man displaces more water than a thin man and can't fill his bath up?'

They also declared he was broke and could not settle his hotel bill. It did not worry Farace that the king might be a day or two late paying his account. He had finally solved the riddle of those boxes. The hotel proprietor became friendly with Pietro della Valle, who had fled with the king, and with Pietro had gone into the guarded room one day. The ammunition boxes were full of gold coins, while the suitcases had some stamps in them. Italy, as Farace well knew, had a law enabling hotel proprietors to confiscate the property of guests who failed to meet their bills. He would willingly have settled for the gold and stamps. But Farouk paid regularly.

The hotelier had to earn his money. No one had warned him Farouk turned normal living inside-out, that his fabulous regime meant breakfast at midday and dinner at midnight. The lift to the third floor never halted; decrees showered on the staff which caused panic in the kitchen. The king must have special fruit, pigeons or quail for breakfast, a rare fish which had suddenly taken his fancy, steak, lamb chops. At any hour of the day or night, the exile would expect his whim to be honoured immediately, as though he still played the potentate in Abdin or Kubbah.

To Gracie Fields, he confessed his liking for girls. 'I can't help it. It's a family weakness. We all fall in love very easily and very deeply,' he said. Narriman scarcely concealed her disgust as his eye roved round the restaurants and the swimming pool. He was sitting with her one evening in the Canzone del Mare watching a dress show staged by the Italian designer, Emilio Pucci. Seeing the royal interest in one of his dresses, Pucci sent the model gyrating several times round the table while Farouk applauded. 'Are you admiring the dress, Your Majesty?' the designer asked. 'The dress? Oh, the dress! I was thinking how much better she would look without it.'

For the first week or two, Farouk enjoyed his exile. Egypt he had left far behind, and never discussed his sixteen years as king. In a floppy hat, crumpled slacks, sleeveless sports shirt and sandals, he wandered round the square in Anacapri every evening, or sat drinking sweet fruit juice at a cafe. Apart from his shape, he might have passed for any tourist holidaying with his wife. But the idyll had to end. He made plans to transfer his gold to Switzerland through an Italian bank, to sell his stamps and to settle himself and his entourage nearer Rome. No one knows how much Farouk had banked before his dethronement, but the gold coins and his few stamps brought him about two million pounds, enough to keep him and his staff for the rest of his exile.

Early one morning, Carlo d'Amelio, a Roman lawyer who had many royal clients, received a phone call from Capri. It was Ahmed Faim, the ex-king's secretary. 'His Majesty wants to see you immediately in Capri,' he said.

'Immediately! But it's two o'clock in the morning,' the lawyer protested. He argued an adjournment and met Farouk the following day on Capri. The ex-king recalled his friendship with King Victor Emmanuel, who had died in exile in Egypt, and the fact that d'Amelio had acted for the Italian king. 'Since friends of friends are friends, I would like you to represent me as you did him.' When they began to chat, Farouk told him that the revolution had hit him like a *coup de tonnerre*. Its leaders, he was certain, would have killed him and his family had he not signed his throne away. 'They even held a gun at my head,' he said. The real villains were the Communists who had exploited the international situation to take over Egypt. 'The Soviet Union,' he said, 'could do no more in Europe so it had turned to Africa. It wanted a free hand in Egypt so that it could take over the rest of North Africa, carry out a huge pincer movement and make the Mediterranean a Russian lake.'

D'Amelio arranged for Farouk and his family to rent the Villa Dusmet, a square, red-stucco mansion with forty rooms in the wine country of Frascati, half an hour from Rome. At the end of October they moved in. Farouk now styled himself Prince Farouk Fuad. He was thirty-two, an exile with a court of twenty-five people. How did he plan to spend the rest of his life? He might have easily deployed his intelligence, his business talent, his languages in some enterprise; he had his two million pounds, plus the money he had banked before the revolution; he could have had access to the best of European society; he might have interested himself in social work. Not Farouk. He still slept half his life away. (When he quit the villa, the most dilapidated piece of furniture was the double-bed in his room.) He would sit for hours in the afternoon beneath the massive, knotted wistaria on the terrace, dangling Fuad on his knee or watching Narriman wheel

285

him through the stepped gardens. He still stuffed himself, amazing the Italian staff with the number of pigeons he could consume at one sitting. In the evening, he would take off for Rome. It was invariably the Via Veneto. He would dine at the Café de Paris, then dive into several of the numerous strip clubs or night-clubs just off the avenue. Now that he was spending his own money he stayed away from casinos, though he did gamble in a small club near the Piazza Barberini. He also spent a few shillings a week on Italian football pools, and sometimes several pounds a night on fruit machines into which he would feed lira by the hour.

He did write his memoirs which were published by a British Sunday newspaper and several continental journals. A few thousand words of moral whitewash which fooled few people; it was too late to blame the *Wafd* and Lord Killearn, to criticise Farida and his mother, to accuse Neguib of having been the tool of the Communists and the Moslem Brethren. Farouk, fantasist to the end, probably could not untangle truth from falsehood in the stories that he spun. Can we really imagine him sprinting for a cold shower at The Shop before reveille had faded away? Can we picture him menacing his mother and her lover (Hassanain) with a revolver? Or poised to shoot Sir Miles Lampson in the stomach? Or rallying the royal guard at Ras el-Tin? No, these memoirs are about the person he wanted to be and might have been. Having spent the best part of his life fabricating myths could he hope to demolish them with a few newspaper articles?

At the Villa Dusmet, he drifted as pointlessly as he had done in Cairo. A British peer, who knew him in the old days, visited him at Frascati and discovered a sad, morally-eroded figure who behaved for all the world like some retired stockbroker, solely preoccupied about his son and his daughters, for whom he hoped to attract good Moslem husbands. Even Roman journalists and photographers, noted for their uninhibited quest after material, had to work hard. They hardly expected the great gambler to try to beat fruit machines, or fill in the pools, regardless of whether he sent them to the local tobacconists with a liveried servant in his green Mercedes. He was good only for trivia. He had pinched a contessa's bottom and almost provoked a duel with the husband. This earned him a paragraph. He successfully sued a Milan chocolate manufacturer for calling their Turkish delight, Farouk, and displaying his photograph. He was being sued by Bulgari, the jewellers, for seventeen thousand pounds, the balance outstanding on two 18th-century German snuffboxes which had belonged to Frederick the Great, and which Farouk had brought before the revolution. Bellini, the fashion house, was also claiming payment for dresses which Narriman had bought during the honeymoon. Farouk gave them both the same reply: they should sue the Egyptian Government who had appropriated the articles. Besides, he said, he had no money.

Soon, however, Farouk was back in the headlines. Narriman was wearying of exile and the role of the dethroned queen. She began to protest plaintively about Farouk's way of life, his excesses, his incessant pursuit of women. Before this, her memoirs had spoken of the king's fascinating shoulders, the dark virile hair on his arms and powerful wrists. Now she was accusing the dispossessed monarch of caring only for his reserved places in gaming houses and restaurants; she was seeking escape, so she said, from all this luxury and mental torture. But was there another reason? A *fetwa* (religious decree), issued by Al Azhar, had just deprived the ex-king of the custody of his children and ordered him to return them to their mothers. Farouk construed this as pressure upon him to give up his son, the King of Egypt. Narriman might then be coerced by the revolutionary government into returning with him to Egypt where he would become a pawn of the new government. His suspicions deepened when Narriman started to hint at divorce; they became truth for him when the formidable person of his mother-in-law, Mrs Assila Sadek, descended on the Villa Dusmet. Thus began the tussle between Farouk and the two women, with Fuad as the prize. The quarrel ended with Narriman and her mother storming out of the villa without the child. Farouk openly accused Mrs Sadek of abetting his wife in her decision to leave him but said, through his lawyer, that he was 'awaiting every new development with full faith in the justice of Allah'. The same *fetwa* which had decreed the children's return was used as a pretext for Narriman's divorce. Farouk shrugged when he heard the news: Narriman had meant little to him and never again did he discuss her with any of his friends. She had given him his heir, and did he not still have him? If he imagined this amounted to anything in Egypt he was to be disillusioned quickly.

When the Calf falls a Thousand Knives flash. So runs the Arabic proverb which Farouk often quoted. He and members of his former clique did not appreciate its implications until the Revolutionary Command Council began its purge. First, on the eighteenth of June 1953, they officially deposed King Ahmed Fuad and declared Egypt a republic. It was the end of the Mohamed Ali dynasty which had lasted one hundred and forty-eight years. They had pushed through an agrarian reform act, which led to the resignation of Ali Maher after only two months in office. This laid down that no one could hold more than about two hundred acres of Nile land, and meant that the Fifty Families who had ruled Egypt lost all but a fraction of their possessions. The land and property belonging to the three hundred and seventy members of the Mohamed Ali family was confiscated in this way, ninety thousand acres of royal land thus passed to the *fellahin*. The royal property fetched seventy-five million pounds which the new government spent on rebuilding the gutted centre of Cairo.

Determined to discredit and obliterate traces of the old régime, Nasser decided, in October 1953, to stage revolutionary tribunals which would judge politicians and courtiers for their part in corrupting the government of the country. Nahas, who had sped back from Europe thinking the revolution would reinstate him and the *Wafd*, found himself under house arrest and indictment. With him were his wife, Zeinab, and Fuad Serag-ed-Din. The presence of Colonel Anwar el-Sadat on the tribunal suggested that the finer judicial arguments would not get much of a hearing. One by one, the princes, pashas, politicians and palace servants paraded before the three-member tribunal. As they pleaded for their lives or freedom, it seemed that beside each of them in

288

the dock, stood the massive silhouette of Farouk, the absent head of the organisation.

Prince Abbas Halim, his cousin, testified that he was effeminate and impotent, a man who merely posed as a woman chaser; also, he cheated at cards; he borrowed money from the Jews to gamble. The prince walked out of the court with a fifteen-year suspended sentence.

As a sop to the Moslem Brethren, eight members of the royal guard were arraigned for the murder of Hasan el-Banna. Farouk, the prosecution stated, had planned the murder. The Egyptian public read, too, that the ex-king had ordered ten cases of Pepsi-Cola to be flown from Egypt while on his first trip to Europe after the war. His affairs, his part in the arms scandal, his property deals, his wild orgies in the 'cabaret' at the Moassat Hospital – no sordid fact was with-held from the Press, no excuse for execrating him missed. The former king could hardly appear in his own defence and no one who valued his life or liberty could act as his advocate.

For treason, corruption and the abuse of power, Karim Thabet received a life sentence. The tribunal ordered him and his wife to return all the property they had acquired from May 1946 when he became Press Councillor. The Lebanese served only two years in Turah; he emerged from prison into house arrest with a hefty manuscript which, curiously, Nasser gave permission to be published in his own newspaper, *Al Gumhuriyah,* and in English and French newspapers under state control. No wonder though, since it smeared every politician who had served in any government since 1937. In this poisonous blend of recrimination and self-justification, Thabet appeared as the man of principle beset by rogues and villains; however, he cleverly underplayed Farouk's misdeeds. Had he not acted as the king's political adviser from 1946?

General Mohamed Hilmi Husain, formerly the king's chauffeur and Dr Ahmed Nakib, who ran the Moassat Hospital, both got fifteen years for corruption. Nahas was acquitted, though his wife was deprived of three hundred and thirty acres of land; Serag-ed-Din received fifteen years in prison for corruption.

Ibrahim Abdel Hadi who had done nothing dishonest except break the Moslem Brethren, was sentenced to death. But none of the public figures was executed. Having pilloried them, the government later released them.

The person everyone expected to hear was missing from the tribunal. In house arrest since the revolution, Antonio Pulli had confessed everything and therefore escaped public trial. Pulli knew every secret and it would therefore have been easy to use him to blacken Farouk's name. He had managed the king's spending money, had arranged much of his private amusement; he could have told how much Farouk smuggled abroad, down to the account numbers. With that brain which forgot nothing, however trivial, Pulli could lead them to every valuable object which Farouk had cached throughout his palaces and rest-houses. But, there were some things the new government wished to keep to itself. Pulli, placed in the dock, might have talked too freely; he might even have divulged the pathetic truth about the great impostor Farouk was.

The end of the trials led directly to another phase in the dismantling of the old order. Towards the end of 1953, the government announced plans to auction the royal treasures. The sale would include everything, from the priceless *objets d'art* which Ismail and the khedives had bequeathed and Fuad and Farouk had augmented down to the rubbishy bric-à-brac which the exiled king had stowed in every palace. At last, the wondering universe would see the fabulous treasures of the jackdaw king – or so the Egyptian Government suggested in its advance publicity. Farouk tried to intervene to prevent the auction and the sale of rare antiquities which, he declared, should be displayed in Egyptian museums. Neguib's government ignored him and approached Sotheby's in London to catalogue the collections and organise the auction.

It took Sotheby's experts more than three months to sift and arrange the hoard which Farouk had assembled and the sedulous Pulli had stored; they had to sell the largest stamp collection in the world, some eight thousand five hundred coins and medals in gold, and one hundred and sixty-four in platinum, and one thousand two hundred and sixty-one works of art in gold and silver which included exquisite boxes, clocks and ornaments by the great Russian jeweller and goldsmith, Carl Fabergé. Farouk's famous collection of silver and glass, his library of rare books and illuminated Korans, his hundreds of watches and time-pieces – all went into the auction. Only the Egyptian antiquities were spared and sent to national museums.

Some of the specialists recoiled when they noticed how the army guards were treating the collections. With a Fabergé Easter egg which realised six thousand four hundred pounds in the sale they were playing football. The mechanism of several rare Swiss snuff-boxes which showed lovers in various postures had almost been exhausted by the soldiers who had given them more to do in three months than they ever had in the king's possession.

Farouk appeared to have some grounds for his contention that the army and the Moslem Brethren had gone out of their way to brand him an immoralist and a lecher. Hundreds of reporters had a peep show of Farouk's erotica. Few of the journalists were excited by what had shocked the sensitive Islamic element in the revolution. The showcase of pornographic books, opened at the most titillating page, had as its centre-piece, *Lady Chatterley's Lover*. Mellors, the gamekeeper, was one of the king's favourite literary characters, or so they said. The rest were mainly French novels which would not have raised a Parisian eyebrow, or 'pulp' romances which spoke more eloquently for the king's lack of culture than his prurience. But, when the mosaic semi-nudes over his bathroom doors are labelled erotica almost every-thing comes into the same category: the American playing-cards with 'topless' women, the art drawings by Fabiano, the trinkets which tourists can buy in Italy and France. Even the gold holder (*zarf*) for his Coca cola bottle evoked moral censure.

A pair of stage handcuffs came to light in Montazah, and soon Egyptian mythologists were declaring that these were the very manacles which Farouk had used to fetter women to his bed; the fact then appeared in an official guide. Almost anyone could see that they were trick handcuffs, probably acquired by Farouk the practical joker. But all this erotica was sieved from his futile

291

collections of razor blades, match boxes, bottle tops, toothpaste tubes and placed in a separate room where the army had hung a notice, reading 'The Secret Museum – Farouk was a man of sensuous, often vulgar taste; we have taken his collections of pornography from his chambers; they may be seen inside.' Just before the auctioneer, M. George Lee, started the bidding at the end of February 1954, an army spokesman stood up to announce that anyone bidding over five thousand pounds during the sale would have a free tour of the pornographic museum. Those who got the biggest kick out of the erotica were three American spinsters who ran in horror to their ambassador to protest at such filth.

The dismemberment of Farouk's treasures and his junk had its poignant side. A huge marquee floated over the lawn at Kubbah. Sudanese waiters, in caftan and tarbush, dispensed sherbet while a brass band played hit songs from musicals. It had the flavour of Open Day at some eastern Sandhurst. Inside, groups of people were patrolling the miles of corridors, examining the lots. They threw a harsh sidelight on the personality of the man who had gathered them. There was the jewelled rattle he had been given as a child, his 'stinks' sets and his language primers; in another room were Geiger counters, inscribed, 'Measure Nuclear Energy Yourself,' and lumped with these, some nude statuettes in alabaster with jokes ('Is that Fanny Browne?') written on them, and the long lipstick holders he would dish out to his friends. A room full of roulette wheels, playing cards, dice and Maj Jong sets testified to his gambling mania; another contained the electric vibrators and the keep-fit rowing machines which he used too seldom. In the bathrooms stood his refrigerators and hot-plates for early-morning snacks, and a pharmacopaeia of medicaments. In one room hung a signed portrait of Hitler. One box of Syrian sweets, a relic of his marriage to Narriman, also found its way into the sale.

The government enjoyed itself auctioning the royal possessions. It made no attempt to preserve the best of Ismail, Tewfik, Fuad and Farouk. Officers tramped through the sale rooms, sneering at his private correspondence, joking about his love philtres (in fact, mediaeval perfumes). On the day that Sotheby's men were leaving, the army staged a *coup de palais* in reverse. The experts got a whisper that something important was happening, and waited for it. In the late afternoon, an army major came to them with the news, 'The king is here. The government has brought him secretly into the country.' The man looked exactly like Farouk, with his white admiral's uniform and dark glasses. Until the Egyptian army officers burst into laughter, the Sotheby staff believed it was the king. He was an Egyptian actor called Arqero, one of the sixteen known 'doubles' that Farouk had.

In the end, Farouk's legendary treasures fetched no more than about seven hundred thousand pounds. Many observers regretted the dispersal of the finer pieces in the royal museums. And the final cut of the knife.

CHAPTER TWENTY-FOUR

Oh that death had made an end of me. My wealth hath not profited me! My power hath perished from me!
(LXIX: 28, 29)

WITH Narriman gone, Farouk gave up the villa and moved to an apartment in Rome. He now spent most of his time in the Italian capital, though he visited his son and daughters three times a year at Cully, on Lake Geneva, where he had sent them with their governesses and his Albanian guard, Abdel Rostum. Occasionally, he took a trip to Monaco where his friend, Prince Rainier, had conferred honorary citizenship on him and his family. By law, this denied Farouk permission to sit in at the roulette and chemmy tables in the Casino, but what did that matter? Besides the five shillings he wagered each week on the pools under the name of Mr Omar, his gambling days had finished. So had the orgies of his free-spending days as king. He still had a yacht, La Favorita, in the port at Monaco, but his friends in the yacht club noticed that it grew shabbier, that the ex-king could not afford its upkeep.

In Rome, the Via Veneto no longer lured him, or his table at the Café de Paris. Not, as some wag remarked, because the Israel Tourist office moved into the suite above the café, but because he had less to spend and Italian photographers irritated him. Roman society largely ignored him and he made no effort to cultivate his equals; he resented people who brazened their way into his company and found a new secretary, Lucien Gallas, a former French actor, to help him keep his privacy; he now chose his restaurants for their seclusion and muted his famous laugh to avoid attracting attention. He could still be spotted in the company of women, but they were Rome's *ragazze facile*, and even they did not rush to spend a profitable night with the morose exile who played schoolboy pranks and bored them with his talk of loneliness and need for friendship.

One evening, in a restaurant called the Belvedere delle Rose, he met Irma Capece Minutolo, the eighteen-year-old daughter of a Neapolitan taxi driver, who had come to Rome to break into films. She was appearing that evening in a beauty contest. When she lost, Farouk protested loudly, and after the show invited her to his table. That casual encounter developed into a friendship which lasted until his death. Irma was gay, unsophisticated; she reminded some people of a larger edition of Narriman. But she supplied something in Farouk's dreary existence. He began to interest himself in her career. She should give up the idea of films and become a serious singer. He paid for her lessons, and when he moved to the Via Archimede on Parioli Hill, he moved her into the apartment beneath his. When she made her debut in Naples, he broke his rule about public appearances to act as her escort. The Verdi recital ended in fiasco when the lights failed and they had to borrow candles from a church next door. Farouk wept openly. But he had launched Irma and lived to see her make something of a name as a lieder singer.

Though he still considered himself very much a king, he meddled little in politics. In 1955, however, he condemned the Egyptian government for instituting a reign of terror and failing to resolve the economic problems. The solution, he thought, lay in restoring the monarchy. Then, soon after the Suez crisis, in a confidential letter to the heads of the American, British and French states, he wrote:

'We have never ceased to follow developments in our country with the greatest attention and We have never forgotten Egypt's supreme interests. Although unwilling to discuss and judge the policy of our country since our departure, We must, alas, realise that We have foreseen and predicted the grievous developments shown by the recent events.

'With the greatest compassion are We considering the dangerous march of our country and choose this moment to raise our voice and to ask you, knowing the deep humanity of your country and yourself, to try by all possible means to devise a peaceful solution of the problems which now divide your government from the Egyptian people, who cannot be held responsible for the mistakes of their leaders.

'We invoke God, praying that the voices of reason and of heart should prevail, and that our beloved people and the whole of mankind should be spared the horrors of conflict which, We are sure, can still be averted.'

He had signed it, 'Farouk of Egypt'. His statement and his plea had little impact; he must have realised that Nasser and his Arab socialism had finished with the monarchy for good. He never again attempted to influence events in Egypt.

He still liked to be addressed by his old rank of 'Majesty' and expected his staff to jump at his orders. His lawyer, Carlo d'Amelio, complained to him once when he telephoned after midnight. 'Please, Majesty, ring me tomorrow in my office. It is not a very important matter.' Farouk said nothing, but several days later, his secretary rang at the same hour, ordering the lawyer to come and see the king. 'I am in bed,' said the lawyer. 'I shall come tomorrow.'

Half an hour passed, and his phone started ringing. It seemed that every newspaper in Italy was asking questions about Farouk's gift to some girl who had appeared on television that evening. When the lawyer protested he knew nothing about it, the journalists replied, 'But Farouk says he has given you five million lira (two thousand eight hundred pounds) to present to the girl.' D'Amelio had no sleep that night. He rang Farouk's secretary to discover that the ex-king had been watching a programme called *Double or Nothing* which featured a young woman who was competing for money to put her sick mother through an operation. When she lost, the ex-king had instructed his secretary to phone the studio to tell the sponsors he had given the sum to his lawyer. Next day, when d'Amelio rang Farouk to find out why he had done it, he said, 'Because you did not wish to speak to me the other night.'

With his gaggle of servants and bodyguard, he patrolled Rome from eight in the evening until dawn the next day. From Parioli to the Piazza Barberini, to the Piazza di Spagna, to Via del Corso and back to the side-streets off the Via Veneto, he did the nightly tour, like that schoolboy on the look-out for thrills who could not stay away from Piccadilly. Only now he looked like a roué who had experienced everything, a voyeur who had seen everything, a man grown bored and blasé. Or, like some somnambulist groping round the same beat without real awareness of what was happening to him. When his few acquaintances filtered away, tired of his stale humour and his shaggy-dog stories, he would finish the night sitting lugubriously in the Flying Dutchman café at the main station, waiting for the girls to appear after their night-club acts, hoping he could induce them to join him and his bodyguard and often wandering home disappointed. He became a prey to publicity men who foisted their starlets and cabaret stars on him, thinking that a picture or two with Farouk would produce a few column inches in the Press. None of them stayed long. As for the Egyptians who were a sizeable colony in Rome, he met only a few; even they felt he did not matter any longer.

There were stories that the bailiffs had tried to evict him from Via Archimede for failing to meet his rent; his lawyer admitted that Farouk had little money left, that his fortune had run through his fingers since abdication. However, he still kept his staff of twelve, his three cars, the small yacht and a villa in Switzerland. For his son and three daughters, he had established a trust from which they drew about twelve thousand pounds a year. But where had the millions gone? Farouk answered the question indirectly when he phoned an exiled Egyptian politician in 1963 to plead for financial advice. He confessed he had lost very heavily on the European stock exchanges, that he had been badly advised. Since the politician refused to help, he never discovered how badly off Farouk was.

His staff, and those who acted for him professionally, never found him generous. His daughters also thought twice about asking him for money; he even quibbled about new clothes for them, or a course of riding lessons. For a man of such evil repute

297

he was astonishingly strict about Moslem discipline. Each of his daughters had to seek his sanction to cut their hair or varnish their nails. Never would he permit them to go out unchaperoned; he even reproached his secretary, Lucien Gallas, for allowing his daughter, Francoise, to venture out alone in Rome. It took Fawzia, his second daughter, months to pluck up courage to ask her father's consent to study at an interpreters' school in Geneva; he would only hear of Ferial teaching at a secretarial school in Lausanne if she did not reveal who she was. But he sent his son to the village school at Cully. He visited the school himself and took the trouble to meet and chat with boys of Fuad's age. Perhaps he was recalling his own lonely childhood when he observed to one of the governesses, 'I think it will be a good thing for my son to meet children like these'.

Drinking was another practice which offended against his code. He criticised an exiled Egyptian who liked whisky. 'Do you not know it is a *haram,* forbidden by the Koran,' he scowled. To placate him and keep his friendship, the man had to produce the Mohamedan bible to prove that, in certain cases, their religion waived its laws on abstinence.

Towards the end of 1964, Farouk suffered a minor coronary attack. No more than a sharp, stabbing pain in the chest, but a warning that his heart and arteries were reacting to the strain that his rackety life was imposing on them. He weighed nearly two hundred and eighty pounds, but the flesh which had once been firm, now sagged on him; his face looked puffy and plethoric; his vision was bad. Though only forty-four, he had the slow gait and the appearance of someone twenty years older. Dr Luigi Donati, who had treated him for the best part of thirteen years, advised him to visit the Cecil Clinic in Lausanne for an examination, and accompanied him to ensure that he travelled by train. In Switzerland, they told him that, unless he shed several stones in weight and stuck to a diet, his heart would give out. His glandular trouble added to the weight problem, but for this they could do little. He had digitalis to steady his heart and other drugs to reduce his blood pressure.

His attitude to dieting amazed his friends. At breakfast he

would be surrounded by a dozen different meats, from steak to roast pheasant. 'This is my new diet,' he explained. But he continued to eat pastries and swallow sweet drinks. When they put him into hospital to enforce the diet, his staff would smuggle his chocolates and cakes into the private room. He came out and went to see a friend. 'If I don't watch myself, I haven't much longer to go,' he said. Then he asked for a bottle of lemonade; he put his thumb over the top and shook it. He laughed. 'I like to watch it fizz,' he cried. Even his doctor decided that he was too much an autocrat to alter his habits.

He still had an eye for a beautiful woman. At the beginning of 1965 he met Sonia Romanoff, a Yugoslav actress, aged twenty-two, who was introduced by a girl friend. He invited her for a drink in his apartment, receiving her dressed in a flowing arab cloak with sandals on his feet. He was sitting in semi-darkness, watching television ('My only contact with the world'). Islamic green was everywhere – the carpets, the upholstery and the curtains. He had cages of exotic birds which he looked after himself. There he sat, eating chocolates and sipping orange juice until eleven o'clock when he called for his Mercedes. He made for his favourite restaurant, the Île de France on the Via Aurelia Antica on the outskirts of Rome. Every mile or so he would jam his foot on the brake and they would lurch forward. 'A braking test,' he would explain, as though he did not trust cars.

As Miss Romanoff got to know him she discovered that, beneath his adolescent jokes, the fun he appeared to have throwing paper balls at people in restaurants, he was a sad, isolated figure, with few real friends. Sometimes it was difficult to believe that this was a playboy of international renown, especially when he would take her to a restaurant run by some Hungarian friends where their companions were six cats. Farouk would feed them from his plate, then gorge himself on *apfel strudel*.

Through his staff and one or two Egyptian friends he kept himself informed about his old clique. Pulli, whom he always claimed had been tortured, had been released from house arrest within two years of the revolution. First, he had run a club on a Nile boat – one of Farouk's old possessions – but this failed. The government had also trusted him enough to grant him permission to go abroad twice and visit relatives in Italy. Though he spent some time in Rome and looked up his old friend, Pietro Della Valle, he made no attempt to contact Farouk. The Italian, to whom the great used to truckle for favours, was now managing a cake shop in Heliopolis; the people whom he used to meet at Abdin and Kubbah, or at Shevikiar's, now saw him behind the counter in his small establishment, called Home Made Cake, in Baghdad Street. Could this inconspicuous figure in a working jacket of grey linen really have been one of the grey eminences behind Farouk? Pulli had put the whole traumatic episode behind him; he had uttered more than enough about that phase of his life. He has maintained that between Farouk and him there was a master-slave relationship; he merely did the king's bidding. When the king left, he, as an Egyptian citizen, began a new career. Pulli covered his tracks so well that few of the Egyptians in Baghdad Street, or in his block of flats in Helipolis realised that this was once Farouk's man-of-all-work.

Thabet and Andraos had died. So had Ali Maher. But Nahas was still alive, a fumbling old man in a great, empty mansion in Garden City, who had outlived his legend. He would survive Farouk and provoke one last riot when he died, in August 1965; a crowd of ten thousand seized his coffin and defied the police in order to hold a special service in Al Husain mosque for the old statesman, before putting his body on a train for Samanoud.

Farouk still held the conviction that the monarchy would be restored in his son's name. But, in his last months, he must have admitted to himself that there was no going back. He would hardly have recognised Cairo; it had changed its way of life, its politics, its voice, and its aspect. A great, trellised radio tower had grown out of the royal palms at Gezirah and along the new Nile corniche stood the concrete monoliths of the Hilton and Shepheard's hotels and the new TV centre; behind them, the streets had been rebuilt and renamed after the fire. Abdin still remained as a museum, though a school and other buildings had eaten into his old playground and tourists wandered among what was left of his belongings. Kubbah had become President Nasser's office, with the spruce, spartan air of a GHQ and its seventy acres of gardens regimented, too. There was no place for Farouk in the new socialism.

His health was failing, and in his last months he grew depressed. 'There's nothing left,' he said when Carlo d'Amelio attempted to cheer him up. 'I've had my time.' In February 1965 he met Farida again; a family crisis brought them together. Fadia, their youngest daughter, had fallen in love with Pierre Orloff, a Christian who had just received a degree of geology at Lausanne. Farida flew from Beirut to discuss the question with Farouk, and there are those who say that, even after seventeen years, the ex-king and his former wife might have been reconciled. But they went their own ways, without resolving the crisis. Fadia went to London and married, without her father's blessing. That saddened him more than most things.

Less than a month later, on the seventeenth of March, he paid a call on Irma Capece Minutolo; he was on his way to the Île de France to dine with his latest girl friend, Annamaria Gatti, a hairdresser. He drove to her flat, picked her up and reached the restaurant an hour before midnight. He had his usual jokes with the waiters and the barman, Elio Piermattei. He ate a dozen oysters, lobster Thermidor, a double portion of roast lamb with fried potatoes and French beans; he refused crêpes because they had put alcohol in them, but took a huge helping of trifle, which he washed down with his second bottle of Evian water. He had lit a cigar and begun to puff on it when the waiters heard a sound and a cry for help from the St Tropez Room; they turned and saw Farouk, slumped against the corner of the alcove, his face purple, his hands reaching for his throat. Elio ran to him and stretched him out; he had seen resuscitation carried out in hospital and began to raise and lower Farouk's legs while a waiter phoned the nearest hospital.

Within minutes an ambulance had arrived at the restaurant. Dr Nicola Massa attempted to revive the ex-king in the dining-room and in the ambulance on the way to the San Camillo Hospital. There, they placed him in an oxygen tent and carried on resuscitation; but Farouk was beyond oxygen, heart stimulants or massage; he never recovered consciousness, and at one thirty a.m. his pulse fluttered for the last time. At forty-five, Prince Farouk Fuad was dead.

His death, like his birth, gave rise to another myth. In Egypt, they said – and keep on saying – that the new régime had finally managed to poison him. There was no autopsy to discredit this rumour. Perhaps the Italian doctors should have performed a post-mortem, but as they maintained, the symptoms were so obvious they needed no confirmation. Farouk had suffered a brain seizure which his physicians predicted might happen; it was not unnatural in a man of his weight with such high blood pressure.

In the pockets of his suit they found a miniature Koran, a revolver and a wallet containing just over sixty pounds in Italian lira. When she heard of his death, his friend, Irma Capece Minutolo, telephoned his children in Switzerland and they motored through the next day to Rome. Farouk's apartment, which he had locked before leaving to pick up Signora Gatti, presented them with a mystery; there was hardly a scrap of paper, and it looked as though their father had sold most of his furniture. Yet, they believed he had kept some form of diary, that he would hardly have cleared out his desk. It appeared that someone had gone through the flat thoroughly before the family got there.

Farouk had left no will. Secretive to the last, he had given no instructions about his belongings or his fortune. Was he wealthy? At the end of his life he was believed to have lost so much by bad investments that he was contemplating breaking the children's trust to enable himself to live. Close friends wondered what had happened to the money he was supposed to have smuggled out of Egypt in his last years as king. They contend that only one man can answer that question: Antonio Pulli. He knew the numbers and the pseudonyms which the king had used for his Swiss accounts. Apart from small investments here and there, the children learned they would have to depend on the trust he had established.

Outside his own small circle, no one mourned his passing. A night or two before he died, he was brooding about how people might react to his death. To a friend, he quoted the proverb, 'When the calf falls...' He was right. Most of the obituarists swallowed the Farouk legend whole; to them it spelled the final act of the rake's progress. What could one expect from a man surfeited with sex and gourmandising? He was the paradigm of cupidity and depravity.

But who can blame them? Farouk devoted much of his life to constructing myths which rebounded on himself. He was, at times, Farouk the Man of the People, Farouk the Pious, Farouk the Omniscient, Farouk the Lion-hearted (defying the British), Farouk the Arab Leader, Farouk the Virile, Farouk the Casanova, Farouk the Great Gambler, Farouk the Playboy, Farouk the Prophet. He might have sustained two, or perhaps three, of these roles, but to attempt to play them all together! ... His minor successes as a king were bound to be overshadowed by the excesses of his private life, for what they were. Here, people had to rely on newspaper interpretation, gossip and Farouk himself for evidence of his sexual exploits. Farouk realised that sex was like murder: few people were caught in the act; he appreciated that an inadequate man who was a king in an oriental country would have become a joke; he knew the fornication legend would shock Egyptians much less than Western moralists. So he invented, desperately, in self-defence; he played out the role to the end. Had Farouk kept his slim figure, his story might have been different. But he began to look the part of the dissolute, depraved character; it seemed that his debauchery was manifesting itself in his gross features and bloated figure. As we have pointed out, all his symptoms indicate a serious endocrine disorder which no one could then have treated.

Accepting Farouk as some depraved ogre, it is easy to underestimate the problems he faced in Egypt. His father had felt the throne tottering several times, and he came to kingship a mature man with the full backing of the British when nationalism was a whisper on the wind. Farouk started with nothing. A sterile childhood in vast, echoing palaces. Hardly a single lesson in the art of ruling. His pleasures identified with stolen hours in the servants' quarters. When he spoke of his boyhood it was never Abdin or Kubbah, but a nostalgic fantasy about spartan days at The Shop or nights in Piccadilly. As Lord Avon (Anthony Eden) has remarked, Edward became a king too late, Farouk too soon. Farouk, however, had to cope with a country which had a feudal outlook, a capitalist economy and a corrupt government in an area which Europe considered a vital strategic bridge between East and West. A boy of sixteen might have turned to his ministers for guidance; but on one hand he met sycophancy, on the other the intransigent Nahas. Is it any wonder that he took refuge first in his own infallibility and later in his divine right to rule as an autocrat. The war discovered his weaknesses. He could not openly condemn the British since he had already manoeuvred himself into isolation from democratic government and needed them; yet nationalism, if not his personal antipathy, forced him into conflict with the occupying power. All he had when the war ended was popular sentiment. That vanished with the Palestine catastrophe, the scandals of his private life and his dependence on the clique of corrupt lackeys. Behind this screen of seedy entrepreneurs, he discerned nothing; the menace of the Moslem Brethren, the disintegration of the *Wafd,* the unrest in the army.

The Aga Khan, a personal friend of Farouk, felt that with proper guidance in his youth, he might have developed into a fine king. His character he summed up thus:

'To me, as to many others, there will always, I think, be something enigmatic in this sad, yet remarkable, man's character. There are many baffling contradictions about him, yet at the back of them all there is great charm and a genuine and compelling simplicity. His father died when he was still a boy. His mother went abroad almost immediately (sic) and the young Farouk was deprived of the influence and love of both parents. He was sent to England to be educated; yet he lived to all intents and purposes a prisoner in a vast house, forbidden to go out and about and mingle freely with the people whom he loved, under orders given by his father in the jealous fear that the boy might not grow up under the lines he had laid down. He had no proper schooling, never went to a university, and spent only a few months attending the Royal Military Academy at Woolwich ... He has, I think, always felt hampered by the lack of the education which both his station and talents merited. This may well have developed in him an inferiority complex when he constantly found himself, as he was bound to do, in the company of highly-educated as well as accomplished men of all nationalities.

'In this unfortunate background lies, I believe, the real reasons for the habits which have earned him criticism at home and notoriety abroad, for the gambling that has been so harshly reprobated and for the long, aimless hours wasted in seeking distraction in cabarets and night-clubs. That they were wasted it is, alas, impossible to deny. Their sad and purposeless vacuity can, however, be explained, if not excused, by his lack of discipline in childhood, and by the fact that nobody bothered to teach him that man's chief capital is time, and that if he wastes time he wastes his greatest asset which can never be recouped.

'Against his defects I prefer to set his good qualities: his piety as a good Muslim, his aversion to alcohol, his courtesy and kindness, especially to the poor, to humble fellahin and servants; and his patriotism and pride in his country ... Each of us, it is said, is composed of many diverse and conflicting elements; seldom in one human being has the mingling been more complex and more contradictory than in this ill-starred yet amiable and talented king ...'

EPILOGUE

And whosoever shall have wrought an atom's weight of good
*   shall behold it,*
And whosoever shall have wrought an atom's weight of evil
*   shall behold it.*   (XCIX: 7 and 8)

His body was anointed and wrapped in eleven winding sheets of
silk, cotton, linen and other materials, after the Moslem fashion;
his face was covered with the Egyptian flag bearing his own
royal emblem; for the time being, he was placed in a walnut
coffin. But where to bury him? He had often expressed his wish
to lie beside his father and most of his other ancestors in El Rifai
Mosque. But Egypt, it seemed, still wanted nothing to do with
him. Nor did the other Arab states which followed Egypt's
lead. On the twentieth of March, the coffin was taken from the
Rome morgue to a chapel where a simple Islamic ceremony
was held. His three daughters and son, Fuad, his former queen,
Farida, two of his sisters and Irma Capece Minutolo – these
and a small, curious crowd followed the hearse, with its coffin
draped in the Egyptian flag. The body was then taken to the
city cemetery in Rome. Would Farouk undergo the final humiliation of burial in a Christian graveyard?

It took his brother-in-law, Ismail Shereen, ten days of pleading
before President Nasser relented and granted permission for
Farouk's body to be brought to Cairo and buried. But it must
be done in secret. No ceremony. No mourners outside the
immediate family. So, on the twenty-seventh of March, Farouk's
body was placed on board a United Arab Airlines Comet; the
plane was delayed in Athens for half an hour and did not arrive
at Cairo Airport until just before midnight. Somehow the news
that it carried Farouk's body had leaked out, and a crowd of
newspapermen and photographers had gathered at the airport.
The Comet did not taxi to the main building but was met on the

runway by a convoy of military trucks, and ringed by an army guard to keep the Press away.

Besides Nasser and a handful of people, no one knew where they had decided to bury the former king. They unloaded the body and placed it in one of the lorries, then the convoy moved off. Some of the lorries were acting as decoys and led the newspapermen a chase through Cairo, coming to a halt at the Ministry of the Interior. The main contingent of this strange funeral procession of jeeps and military trucks sped through the city, taking the back route down past the Citadel and along a mud road to where the Mameluke beys lay buried. There, the lorry containing the coffin drew up.

It was just after two a.m. Troops and officials of the Ministry of the Interior shouldered the coffin into the low building, stealthily so that they would not disturb people in the slums across the road. They bore it to the far corner of the vault covering the thirteen tombs to a gilded, three-tiered tomb which had been opened after dark that night. It was the tomb of Ibrahim, son of Mohamed Ali. The old man had ordered it for himself, but his son had died before him. Mohamed Ali had, so they say, cut off the hands of the designer so that he would never repeat its ornate style.

Now, only three hurricane lamps lit the scene as they removed Farouk's body from the coffin; the only sounds were the weeping of his sisters, Fawzia and Faika, who had come with their husbands, and the whispered burial service from the Koran, read by a local priest, Sheikh Said.

The shrouded body was borne down into the tomb and laid on the sand beside the decayed remains of Ibrahim, buried a hundred and seventeen years before. Farouk's feet pointed towards Mecca; above him he had enough room to sit up when the angels Nakir and Monkir descended on this night to examine him on the sins of his life. The ceremony had taken just over ten minutes; at two thirty, the troops and the civil servants filed out, followed shortly afterwards by the members of the family.

A white-haired old man remained, his grizzled face perplexed by what he had witnessed. All those years ago, Hafiz Khittab

307

had watched Farouk arrive from England as the boy malek, had seen him acclaimed by millions as the saviour of Egypt, had shouted as loudly as the others for him. Now, as caretaker of the Mameluke tombs, he had assisted at the final act of infamy. Could they bury a king like this, even a disgraced king as Farouk had been? In the middle of the night? Like some thief or pauper? With none of the honours due to the dead? He could not believe it. Then, a doubt struck him. Was this really Farouk? He must set his mind at rest. He lifted his lamp and picked his way into the tomb.

Holding the lantern close, he removed the green flag from the face. Like the body, it appeared gross and swollen. Nothing about it reminded him of the face of that graceful youth. But the eyes? The yellow light fell on them. Yes . . . now he could see . . . those were the blue eyes of that marvellous boy.

He left the face uncovered and climbed out of the tomb to prepare for the masons who would seal it that morning.

INDEX

Abbas I, 24, 161, 166
Abbas II, 31, 41, 48, 161
Abbas Halim, Prince, 34, 102, 195, 261, 289
Abbassiah Barracks, 40, 79, 85, 97, 102, 267, 268
Abboud, Ahmed, 262
Abdin Palace, 17, 26, 28, 38, 39–40, 43–4, 48, 50, 53, 54, 66, 72, 79, 80, 87, 90–2, 98, 104, 108, 126, 129, 130–1, 132, 133–8, 146, 161, 163, 165, 173, 174, 178, 179, 192, 212, 235–6, 246, 247, 250, 251, 253, 268, 270, 276, 300
Abdullah, King of Jordan, 197, 201, 205
Abukir Bay, 20
Adli Yeghen, 44
Afifi, Hafez, 252, 254, 255, 263–4, 265
Aga Khan, 48, 226, 239, 304–5
Ahmed, Prince, 34
Ahmed Fehmi, Prince, 34
Ahmed Fuad, Prince (son), 251, 271, 277, 282, 285, 287, 306; birth, 245; as Fuad II, 275; at school, 294, 298
Aida (Verdi), 27
Akif, Hassan, 271, 274
Alaly, Hamed el-, 190
Alamein, El, 139, 152
Aldrich, Winthrop, 152
Alexandria, 16–17, 23, 28, 40, 50, 92–3, 96, 99, 101, 127, 131, 139, 150, 163, 164, 169, 171, 176, 177, 180, 185, 192, 199, 214, 223, 270–1, 272–9, 280
Allenby, Lord, 43–4, 45, 46
Alperovici, Boris, 281, 283

Aly Khan, Prince, 226
Amer, Abdel Hakim, 86, 204, 258, 267–8
Amer, General Husain Sirri, 218, 257, 259, 264, 265, 266
America, 152, 168, 169, 197, 205, 241, 242–3, 262, 265–6, 271, 279
Amery, Julian, 127
Amin, Colonel Abdel Moneim, 269
Amin, Ali, 230
Amin, Mustapha, 96, 167, 206
Andraos, Elias, 172, 189, 214, 228, 229, 255, 262, 264, 265, 274, 300
Anglo-Egyptian condominium (1899), 30, 185, 224, 242
Anglo-Egyptian Treaty (1936), 64–5, 85, 110, 130, 134, 136, 176, 181–2, 185, 196, 205; abrogation of, 222–4, 241, 242
Anglo-Iranian Oil Company, 241
Arab League, 164, 169, 197, 198
Arab Legion, 200
Arab Liberation Army, 198, 199
Arabi, Colonel, 28
Arish, El, 205
Arqero (actor 'double'), 293
Assiut, 194
Aswan, 29, 70, 162
Atallah, Ibrahim, 140, 170
Attlee, Clement, 182, 186, 197
Auberge des Pyramides, Cairo, 121, 141, 181, 215
Auchinleck, General Sir Claude, 129, 130, 131, 139
Azhar, Al, 41, 87, 132, 287
Azzam, Abdel Rahaman, 198
Azziz, Abdel (butler), 264, 265

Baker, Sir Samuel, 25
Balbo, Marshal, 110
Banna, Hasan el-, 84–5, 110, 117, 118, 141, 171, 175, 194, 205–6, 207–8, 213, 289
Baring, Sir Evelyn – see Cromer, Lord
Bassal, Hamid el-, 43
Bastone, John, 47
Beersheba, 200, 201
Ben Gurion, David, 205
Berlin, 236
Berrier, Annie, 215, 226–7
Bethlehem, 200
Bevin, Ernest, 177, 182, 185, 187, 222–3, 224
Biblawi, Sheikh el-, 263
Bitter Lakes, 169
Black Book, 153–4
Black Saturday (1952), 247–56, 262
Blue Shirts, 17, 90
Boy Scouts, 17, 54, 90
Boyle, Harry, 36
British Embassy, 104, 113–14, 118, 132–3, 138, 250–1, 270, 271, 279
Buccleuch, Duke and Duchess of, 76
Buluk Nizam (auxiliary police), 244–5, 247
Bustan Palace, 38, 39, 40

Cadogan, Sir Alexander, 196
Cafazzi, Eduardo (kennelman), 57, 106
Caffery, Jefferson, 242–3, 250, 253, 262, 271, 274, 275, 277
Cairo, 14, 17, 21–2, 23, 26–7, 34–5, 40, 43, 54, 98–9, 113, 122–5, 143–4, 157, 173, 235–6; Farouk's arrival in (1936), 18–19; his accession, 79–81; wartime espionage in, 116–17; British troops in, 124, 134–5, 139, 176, 177; and February 1942 crisis, 134–5, 139, 176; centre for international politics,

169, 171; British troops leave, 177, 185; and Palestine war, 197, 198, 205–6; riots in, 205–6, 244, 245–6; and Black Saturday (1952), 247–56; burning of, 248–54, 257; army coup, 267–70; rebuilding of, 288, 300–301; Farouk's burial outside, 306–8
Cambridge, 76, 77
Camelia (Lilianne Cohen), 180–1, 182–5, 192–3, 199, 202, 215, 226, 227
Campbell, Sir Ronald, 177
Canal Zone, 65, 85, 113, 116, 129, 176, 182, 241–5. See also Suez Canal
Cannes, 225, 238
Capri, 236–7, 281–5
Caro (barber), 57, 71, 106, 119
Casey, R. G., 150
Cavalla, 20
Central Intelligence Agency (C.I.A.), 265, 279–80
Chermside, Anne, 210, 251, 271
Churchill, Sir Winston, 116, 150–1, 168, 169, 171, 182
Cohen, Lilianne – see Camelia
Coin Farouk, 146, 161
Communists, 177, 182, 187, 221, 223, 240, 243, 245, 247, 254, 261, 262, 265, 286
Crabitès, Judge, 25
Craig, James Ireland, 249
Cromer, Lord (Sir Evelyn Baring), 24, 28–31, 35, 36, 48, 89
Cully, 294, 298
Cunningham, Admiral Sir Andrew, 129, 130–1
Curzon, Lord, 44
Cyprus, 182–4, 185

D'Amelio, Carlo, 285, 296, 301
Dairut, 43
Damascus, 199
Darfur, 14, 37, 60
Deauville, 226–7
Declaration of 1922, 44–5, 64, 65

310

Dellawar, Faizi, 158, 160
Denshawi, 29, 30
Derna, 126
Din, Kemal el-, 32
Disraeli, Benjamin, 26
Dokki, 178
Donati, Dr Luigi, 198
Duff Cooper, Sir Alfred and
    Lady, 135, 138

Ebeid, Makram, 153–4
Eden, Anthony (Lord Avon), 15,
    76, 116, 164, 169, 170, 182, 242,
    243, 257, 264, 271, 272, 304
Edinburgh, Duke of, 223
Edward VIII (Duke of Windsor),
    15, 61–2, 105, 166, 275, 304
Egyptian army, 28, 42, 113; and
    Sudan, 29–30, 46; democratis-
    ing of, 85–6; oath of
    allegiance, 88; and Second
    World War, 113, 116; and
    1942 crisis, 140; in Palestine
    war, 198, 199, 200–202, 204–5,
    217, 269; and arms scandal,
    217–18, 264; and Black Satur-
    day, 251–2, 257; discontent in,
    257–61, 264–5; and 1956 revo-
    lution, 257, 265–6, 267–80
Emirghian, 27
Erskine, Lieut-General Sir
    George, 244, 250–1
Ethiopia, 64
Eugénie, Empress, 25, 26, 97
Ezzat, Abdel-Aziz, 64

Fadia, Princess (daughter), 160,
    167, 210, 301
Faika, Princess (sister), 50, 179,
    307
Faisal, King of Iraq, 109
Faiza, Princess (sister), 50, 109,
    210, 277
Fakhry, Gaafer, 47
Faluja, 204–5
Farace, Nicolo, 281–2, 283–4
Farida, Queen (Safinaz Zulficar),
    72, 139, 146, 160, 232, 286; on

European trip, 73–4, 75, 92;
engagement, 92–5; takes name
Farida, 95; her doubts, 95–6;
marriage, 97–8, 235, 236;
births of daughters, 102–3,
124–5; enmity with servant
clique, 106–7; growing
estrangement, 125, 143, 147–8,
165–8; Farouk's wish to
divorce, 165–8, 174, 175, 189;
divorced, 209–10; meets
Farouk again, 301; at his
funeral, 306, 307
Farouk, King: in England, 13–
15, 59–63; told of father's
death, 13–14; arrives in Egypt,
16–19, 64; ancestral background, 20–40; birth, 39–40;
boyhood, 50–58; seclusion and
training, 50–3, 58; contradictory character, 54–5, 69–71,
76–8, 99–102; spoilt by
mother and harem, 56–7, 58,
68; at Woolwich, 61–3; enjoys new freedom under
regency, 65–71; immense
power and wealth, 65–6; collecting mania, 67, 96, 114,
172–4; English tutor, 67–9;
boastfulness and fantasy world,
68–9, 77, 216; shooting, 68,
114; sycophantic entourage,
69, 71, 76, 104–6, 118–19, 120–
2, 180, 262, 264; tour of Upper
Egypt, 69–71, 87; religious
observance, 69–70, 98, 99, 298;
sense of inferiority, 70–71, 102,
126; in love and rejected, 72–
3; visits Europe (1937), 73–8;
indifference to mother, 77,
143; preference for servants,
77, 95, 100, 104–7, 113, 118–
19, 127, 143; accession, 79–81;
clashes with Nahas, 87–90, 131–
4, 137–9, 141, 163–5; autocratic rule, 90, 111, 162–5, 213,
232, 255–6, 260, 262–3; engagement and marriage to

Farida, 92–8; relations with people, 98–9, 124, 171, 172, 194, 202–4, 210, 219–20, 228–9, 232, 236, 263; obsessive eating, 100–101, 158–9, 160, 212, 237, 298–9; corpulence, 100, 101–2, 120, 140, 158–60, 162, 303; lack of virility, 101–2, 125, 149–50, 158–62; birth of daughter Ferial, 102–3; and Arab unity, 108–10, 164, 169, 198; relations with Great Britain, 109–10, 111, 115, 123–4, 129–42, 150–2, 169, 171, 175–7, 181–2, 185–7, 195–7, 223–5, 232, 241–5, 270–2; and Sir Miles Lampson, 111–14, 119, 129–39, 141, 150, 152, 163–4; search for distraction, 120, 125, 143–5, 162, 180–5; night-club haunts, 120, 123–4, 144, 162, 190, 202, 213–15, 225–6; 'Farouk stories', 122–4, 148–9, 216–17; estrangement from Farida, 125, 143, 147–8, 165–8; and February 1942 crisis, 127–8, 129–42, 258; forms new government under threat of dethronement, 137–42; infatuation with Fatma, 145–7, 148, 165–7, 210–11; seeks divorce from Farida, 146–7, 165–8, 174; meanness, 149, 175, 191, 192, 213, 297; myth of sexual prowess, 149–50, 303; pocket-picking, 150–1; car accident, 155–8; sexual impotence, 158–62, 215; restores power to palace, 162–5, 169; steals Persian treasure, 173–4; in Cyprus with Camelia, 181–5; fears for throne, 194–5, 206, 260–1; and Palestine war, 198–202; divorces Farida, 209–10; sybaritic life, 212–17, 226–8, 232, 263–4, 285–8, 294–5, 296–300; erotica and por-

nography, 213, 291–2; and arms racket, 217–18, 219; European holiday (1950), 225–8; increasing hostility to him, 228–30, 232, 237–8, 257, 260–1; 'Treasure Box', 230; marriage to Narriman, 232–9; proclaimed King of Sudan, 242; and Black Saturday, 247, 251–2, 253–6; and corruption, 261–2; claims descent from Prophet Mohamed, 263; army campaign against, 257, 265–6; and *coup d'état*, 267–81, 285; capture and abdication, 272–81; leaves Egypt, 276–9; in exile, 281–8, 294–302; writes memoirs, 286; divorced by Narriman, 287–8; treasures in Cairo auctioned, 290–3; failing health, 298, 301; death, 301–2; character summed up, 304–5; burial, 306–8

Fathi, Colonel Omar, 66, 72, 92–3, 173, 217

Fathia, Princess (sister), 50, 179, 225

Fatma Tussun, Princess, 156, 232, 233; Farouk's infatuation with, 145–7, 148, 165–7; husband's death, 188–9; Farouk's waning interest, 189–90; refusal to marry him, 210–11; marries Prince Juan of Braganza, 210, 212

Fawzia, Princess (sister), 50, 210, 277, 307; marriage to Shah of Persia, 108–9; separated from him by Farouk, 174–5; divorced, 209

Fawzia, Princess (daughter), 124, 298

Fayum, 127

Ferial, Princess (grandmother), 36

Ferial, Princess (daughter), 102–3, 109, 277, 298

Fields, Gracie, 237, 284

First World War, 31–3, 42
Ford, Sir Edward, 67–9, 70, 75, 76–7, 216
France, 20–21, 23, 26–7, 84, 126, 127, 136, 241
Frascati, 285–7
Free Officers' Society, 204, 218, 257, 258; *coup* by (1952), 265–6, 267–80
Fuad I (Ahmed Fuad), 17, 67, 89, 99, 102, 109, 112, 125, 159, 167, 187, 203; death of, 13–14, 64; accession of, 32, 33; boyhood exile, 33–4; marriage to Shevikiar, 34–5; attempted assassination, 35–7; divorce, 35, 37; consolidates rule, 37–8, 41; marriage to Nazli, 38; birth of Farouk, 39–40; autocratic rule, 41, 45, 46–9; and *Wafd*, 43–4, 45, 46–7, 63, 87; proclaimed King, 45; and Zaghlul, 45–6, 53; amassing of fortune, 48–9, 65; and Farouk's training, 51, 52–3, 56–7, 59–61; illness, 53, 56, 58–9; close confinement of queen and retinue, 55–6
Faud II – *see* Ahmed Fuad, Prince
Fuad, Ahmed, 141
Fuad University, 132, 245, 247

Gallad, Edgard, 232, 243
Gallas, Lucien, 294, 298
Gamal, Samia, 226
Garden City, 107, 153, 221, 300
Gatti, Annamaria, 301, 302
Gaza, 199, 200, 201
Gazala, el-, 126
Geneva, 34, 294, 298
George V, 61, 62
George VI, 14, 97
Germany, 31, 32, 85, 109–10, 111, 116, 117–18, 129, 152, 170
Gezira, 107, 300
Ghali, Riad, 225
Gloucester, Duke of, 62, 223

Glubb, Sir John Bagot, 200
Goebbels, Joseph, 110
Gordon, General Charles, 25, 29–30
Gorst, Sir Eldon, 31
Goschen, Major-General A. A., 62–3
Graham, Lady, 38
Graziani, Marshal Rodolfo, 115
Greece, 23, 116
Green Shirts, 17, 90, 171
Greig, Sir Louis, 13, 14

Hadi, Ibrahim Abdel, 206, 207, 290
Hafiz, Suleiman, 275–6
Haifa, 200
Haile Selassie, Emperor of Ethiopia, 169
Hamilton, John, 269, 272
Harb, Salih, 198
Hashem, Zaki, 233
Hassan Tussun, Prince, 145, 146, 188–9
Hassan, Abdel Fattah, 247
Hassan, Dr Ibrahim, 117
Hassan, Mohamed (valet), 126, 212, 233, 264, 274
Hassanain, Ahmed Mohamed, 14, 15, 18, 19, 72, 84, 95, 99, 119, 121, 146–7, 156, 158, 286; explorations, 37, 60; in charge of Farouk's training, 59–61, 70, 71, 77; relations with Nazli, 71, 74, 76, 90–2, 161; increased power, 71, 90–92, 125–6; secret marriage to Nazli, 92, 178; and February 1942 crisis, 130, 131, 134, 136–7, 139, 140; and Black Book, 152–4; plan to oust Nahas, 163–4; and Farouk's desire for divorce, 165–8, 174; death, 178, 180
Haydar, General, 221, 251, 252, 253, 257, 265, 274
Hayworth, Rita, 226
Hebron, 200
Heliopolis, 268, 300

Helwan, 146, 161
Heykal, Mohamed Husain, 198
Hicks, Colonel William, 30
Hilali, Neguib el-, 254, 261–2, 263, 266, 270, 271–2
Hodebi, Hasan el-, 208
Hosni, Husain, 212
Huddleston, Sir Hubert, 186
Husain, Ahmed, 254
Husain, Al-, 87, 300
Husain, General Mohamed Hilmi, 274, 289
Husain, Professor Mohamed Kemal, 47, 155, 156, 157, 158–9
Husain Kemal, Sultan, 32, 41
Husaini, Haj Amin el- (Grand Mufti of Jerusalem), 85, 198

Ibn-Saud, 169, 197
Ibrahim pasha, 22, 23, 24, 161, 307
Inchass Palace, 26, 118, 155, 223
Iraq, 197, 200
Irgun, 197
Islam, 41–2, 83–4, 109, 145, 169, 177, 207, 263, 298. *See also* Moslem Brethren
Ismail pasha, 23, 25–8, 29, 33, 41, 158, 161, 281
Ismail (son of Fuad), 35
Ismail Daoud, Prince, 195
Ismailia, 66, 84, 241, 244, 248
Israel, 197–8, 200–201, 204–5. *See also* Palestine
Italy, 64, 109–10, 111, 114–15, 116, 117–18, 129, 201

Jamal el-Afghani, Sheikh, 42
Jerusalem, 200, 201; Grand Mufti of (Haj Amin el-Husaini), 85, 198
Jordan, 109
Juan of Braganza, Prince, 210–11
Judea, 205

Kafr Abdu, 244
Kamel, Mustafa, 30, 31, 37, 42

Kasr el-Nil Barracks, 134, 177
Kassain, Suleiman, 175
Kassasin, 155–8
Kemal, Brigadier Ahmed, 144, 225
Kena, 162
Kenry House, Kingston, 14–15, 59, 61, 62, 76
Kent, George, Duke of, 15
Khartum, 30, 186
Khittab, Hafiz, 16, 307–8
Kingston Hill, Surrey, 59, 62, 77
Kirk, Alexander, 135
Kitchener, Lord, 31
Kordofan, 14
Korean War, 222, 223
Kubbah Palace, 14, 26, 38, 50–9, 61, 68, 72, 97, 125–6, 165, 172, 179, 210, 212, 260, 276, 292, 301
Kubra Palace, 107
Kubri el-Kubbah, 267, 268

Lady Chatterley's Lover (Lawrence), 291
Lampson, Sir Miles Wedderburn (Lord Killearn), 64, 68, 97, 104, 110, 149, 176, 187, 286; and Farouk's education, 59, 67, 69; sees Ali Maher on outbreak of war, 110; conflict with Farouk, 111–14, 119, 129–39, 141, 150, 152; character, 112–13; demands eviction of Italian staff, 119, 126, 127; Italian wife, 119; urges suspension of Vichy relations, 126, 127; and February 1942 crisis, 127–8, 129–39, 141, 161; supports Nahas, 131–4, 137–9, 162–3; leaves Egypt, 177
Lausanne, 298
League of Nations, 65, 197
Lesseps, Ferdinand de, 24
Libya, 116
Lloyd, Lord, 46, 48
Lorraine, Sir Percy, 54
Lowdon, Dr Andrew, 155

314

Lugano, 237
Luxemburg, Prince Felix, Duke of, 62
Lydda Airport, 201
Lyttleton, Oliver (Lord Chandos), 129–30, 135, 137, 138, 150, 151

McDonald, James G., 205
Madi, 261
Maher, Ahmed, 46, 89, 167–8, 169, 170, 176
Maher, Ali, 71, 87, 97, 104, 119, 133, 176: as prime minister, 15, 18, 64, 109–10, 255, 261, 269, 273–5; and Moslem Brethren, 84–5; sees Egypt as leader of Arab world, 85, 109–10; conflict with Nahas, 88–90, 152; helps to draft constitution, 89–90; Axis sympathies, 109–10, 114–15, 116, 127, 196; 'rusticated', 118; and Black Saturday, 255; and 1952 *coup*, 269, 272, 273–5, 276, 277; gives ultimatum to Farouk, 274–5, 276; resigns, 288; death, 300
Mahmud, Mohamed, 43, 45, 46, 48, 90, 104–8, 109, 122
Maletto, General, 116
Mamelukes, 21–2, 307, 308
Manshyat el-Bakri, 267
Maraghi, Mortada el-, 261, 264, 268, 279
Maraghi, Sheikh Mustapha el-, 69, 87, 97, 108, 109, 119, 127, 147
Marg, 145
Marie, Queen of Rumania, 53
Marnham, Sir Ralph, 155
Masri, General Azziz el-, 60–1, 114, 116–17, 273
Massa, Dr Nicola, 301
Mawawi, General Ali el-, 201
Maxwell, General Sir John, 60
Mazzolini, Count, 115
Mena House Hotel, 150, 252–3
Mersin, 184

Military Academy, 85, 172, 202, 258
Milner, Lord, 25, 43
Minutolo, Irma Capece, 295, 301, 302
Moassat Hospital, Alexandria, 214, 264, 289
Mohamed Abdu, Sheikh, 42
Mohamed Ahmed (the Mahdi), 29–30
Mohamed Ali (founder of dynasty), 20–4, 29, 161, 307; end of dynasty, 288
Mohamed Ali, Prince, 64, 132, 195, 234
Mohamed Khosrev, 21
Mohamed Reza Pahlevi, Shah of Persia, 108–9, 173–5, 209
Mohamed Tahir, Prince, 107
Moheddin, Zakariah, 86
Mohsen, Murad, 70, 92
Monaco, 294
Monckton, Sir Walter, 132
Montazah Palace, 50, 54, 59, 67, 68, 94, 101, 199, 212, 263–4, 266, 270–1, 277, 291
Montgomery, Lord, 139, 150, 177
Montreux Convention (1936), 65
Moslem Brethren, 84–5, 110, 116, 117, 170, 171, 177, 187, 194, 196–7, 198, 205–8, 221, 238, 240–1, 245, 247, 254, 258, 286, 289, 290, 304
Mossadeq, Dr, 241
Mosseri, Helene, 144
Mountbatten, Lord Louis, 223
Moyne, Lord, 170
Mukhtar, Alahadin, 145
Murray, Sir Charles, 22
Mussolini, Benito, 64, 110

Naguib, Ahmed, 214, 230, 232–3, 235
Naguib, Suleiman, 92
Nahas, Mustapha el- (Nahas Pasha), 44, 64, 83, 84, 157, 176, 227–8, 229, 304; chairman of *Wafd*, 46–7; prime minister,

315

47–8, 79; leads delegation to Britain, 64–5; signs 1936 treaty, 65; and Farouk's popularity, 86–7; attempts to limit Farouk's power, 86, 88; increasing distrust and friction, 87–90, 162–3; dismissed, 90; and February 1942 crisis, 127, 130, 131–4, 137–9, 141; forms new government, 138, 141; and Black Book, 152–4; dismissal, 163–5, 169; prime minister again, 220–3; treaty negotiations, 223, 236, 241, 242; and Moslem Brethren, 240–1; hate campaign against Britain, 241, 244; abrogates 1936 treaty, 241, 242; and Black Saturday, 250, 251, 253, 254; dismissed, 253; arrest and acquittal by revolutionary tribunal, 288, 289; death, 300

Nahas, Madam Zeinab, 86, 153–4, 222, 229, 239, 242, 288, 289

Nahas Institute, 162

Nakib, Dr Ahmed, 289

Naples, 281, 295

Napoleon, 20, 21

Narriman, Queen: Farouk's first interest in, 233–4; betrothal and marriage, 234–6; honeymoon, 236–9, 287; and 1952 *coup*, 271, 277; in exile, 282, 284, 285, 287; divorce, 287–8

Nasr, General el-Yel, 274

Nasser, Gamal Abdel: at Military Academy, 85, 117, 171–2, 258; on February 1942 crisis, 140–1, 258; on use of terrorism, 171–2; and Palestine war, 202, 204; and Free Officers, 218, 257–60, 265–6, 267–9, 279–80; early career, 257–8; and 1952 revolution, 267–9, 273, 275, 279–80; urges exile for Farouk, 273, 275, 281; as President, 288, 301; allows

Farouk's burial in Egypt, 306, 307

National Socialists, 254

Naylor, Mrs Ina (Ninzi), 51, 53, 54, 55, 57, 60, 62, 66

Nazareth, 201

Nazli, Queen, 13, 15, 36, 66, 72–3, 87, 108, 122–3, 125, 144, 286; marriage to Fuad, 38; birth of Farouk, 39–40; and his boyhood training, 51, 52, 55, 56–7, 59, 68; dotes on him, 55, 56–7, 77, 161; virtual prisoner in harem, 55–6, 76; kidney complaint, 56, 179, 195–6; in love with Hassanain, 71, 74, 76, 90–2, 161; and Farouk's accession, 80; secret marriage to Hassanain, 92, 178; and Farouk's engagement to Farida, 94–5; leaves Egypt, 178–9, 180; refuses to return, 195; deprived of titles, 210, 225

Negev, 201, 205

Neguib, Ali, 251

Neguib, General Mohamed, 49, 124, 263, 286; first meeting with Farouk, 100–101; on February 1942 crisis, 140; and Palestine war, 202, 204; on 'kitchen cabinet', 212; on arms racket, 217–18; and Black Saturday, 251; and Free Officers, 257, 260, 264–5, 268–70; and 1952 *coup*, 268–70, 271–4, 277–8; and Farouk's departure, 277–8, 280

Nile river, 17, 22, 42, 69–70, 81

Nile Valley, 17–18, 23, 24, 41, 82, 162, 175, 195, 196, 221

Nokrashi, Mohamed Fahmy el-, 46, 104, 176, 177, 182, 190, 195–6, 197–8, 199, 202–4, 206, 207, 209

O'Connor, General Sir Richard, 115

Officers' Club, Cairo, 257, 259, 260, 265
Omar Tussun, Prince, 32, 145
Omdurman, 186, 252
Orloff, Pierre, 301
Osman, Amin, 170

Palestine, 85, 170, 196–7; war with, 197–202, 204–5, 209, 217, 224, 264, 269, 304
Parker, Sergeant, 63
People's Party, 37
Philosophy of the Revolution, The (Nasser), 259
Piermattei, Elio, 301
Pilbeam, William, 47
Prevention of Sin, Society for, 84
Pucci, Emilio, 284
Pulli, Antonio, 57–8, 67, 71, 96, 100, 106, 118–19, 120, 122, 124, 146, 155, 165, 172, 175, 181, 183, 193, 212, 236, 264, 270, 271, 274, 275, 296, 299–300, 302

Qusum mosque, al-, 109

Rafah, 205
Raif, Major-General Ahmed, 245
Rainier, Prince, 294
Rapallo, 237
Ras el-Tin Palace, 16, 50, 199, 212, 266, 271–2, 273–9
Rashad, Dr Yussef, 274
Red Crescent Society, 32, 37
Richmond Park, 13
Rifai mosque, El, 18, 306
Roda, 64, 259
Romanoff, Sonia, 299
Rome, 285, 286, 294–9, 301–2, 306
Rommel, General Erwin, 116, 126, 127, 139, 150, 152
Roosevelt, Franklin D., 168, 169, 171
Rostum, Abdel, 282, 294
Royal Automobile Club, Cairo, 112, 144, 158, 189, 190, 199, 202, 260, 266
Royal Military Academy, Woolwich, 15, 59, 60–1, 62–3, 304, 305
Russell pasha, 114
Russell, Richard B., 151
Russia, 23, 116, 175, 236, 241, 243
Rutherford, Lord, 77

*Saad*ist party, 169, 182, 228
Sabri, Abdel-Rahim, 38
Sabri, Wing Commander Ali, 269
Sabri, Cherif, 64
Sabry, Hasan, 115
Sadat, Colonel Anwar el-, 86, 116, 117–18, 140, 170, 258, 265, 269–70, 272, 274, 288
Sadek, Assila, 287
Sadek, Husain Fahmy, 233
Sadek, Mustapha, 271
Sadek, Colonel Yussef Mansur, 268
Said pasha, 23, 24–5, 26, 161
Said, Nuri es-, 164
St Moritz, 74–5
Salah, Abdel Meguid Ibrahim, 190–1
Salem, Wing Commander Gamal, 272–3
Salem, Saleh, 86
Salih Magdi, 27
Sami, Salib, 127
Samiha, Princess, 147, 148
Sanhuri, Abdel Razek, 276
Sarwat, Abdel Khalek, 44
Saudi Arabia, 109, 201
Second World War, 60, 110, 111–71, 304
Seif ed-Din, Prince Ahmed, 34, 35–6, 47–8, 143
Serag-ed-Din, Fuad, 191, 221, 229, 239, 241, 242, 244, 245, 250, 251, 261, 288, 289
Sergeant, Lucy, 39
Sève, Colonel Joseph (Suleiman pasha), 23, 38

Shahin, Dr Mohamed, 39, 40, 56
Shawki, Ahmed, 31
Shawki, Colonel Wahid, 271, 272
Shepheard's Hotel, 122, 252
Shereen, Ismail, 266, 306
Sheviakar, Princess, 60, 167, 172, 194–5; marriage to Fuad and divorce, 34–6, 37, 38; and corruption of Farouk, 143–5, 146, 147, 190; death, 195
Shone, Terence, 127, 129
Sidi Barani, 115, 116
Sidki, Ismail, 43, 45, 46, 47, 48, 114, 176, 177, 178, 181, 182, 183, 184, 185–7
Simpson, Joseph, 275
Sinai, 23, 199, 205
Sirry, Husain, 115, 117, 119, 121–2, 126, 127–8, 129, 210, 221, 264–5, 266
Siwa, 37, 60
Slim, Sir William, 223
Smart, Sir Walter, 129, 138
Smuts, General, 151
Sotheby's, 290–1, 292–3
Stack, Sir Lee, 45, 89
Stansgate, Lord, 182, 185
Stern Gang, 170, 197
Stettinius, Edward, 169
Stevenson, Sir Ralph, 223, 241, 250–1
Stohrer, Dr Eberhard von, 33
Stone, General R. G. W. S., 130, 135–6, 137, 157
Sudan, 23, 25, 29–30, 45–6, 65, 182, 185–6, 187, 196, 222, 223, 224, 241, 242, 243, 262
Suez Canal, 24–5, 26–7, 64, 97, 111, 129, 130–1, 176, 182, 187, 205, 223, 241, 242–5, 295. See also Canal Zone
Suleiman pasha (Joseph Sève), 23, 38
Syria, 129, 140, 200, 201

Tabeh, Mohamed el-, 74, 281
Taha, Colonel Sayyid, 204

Tahar, Lieutenant Abdel Kadar, 259
Tahir pasha, 21
Taormina, 236
Tedder, Air Marshal Sir Arthur, 129
Tel Aviv, 200, 201
Tel el-Kebir, 28, 244
Tewfik pasha, 27, 28–31, 41, 161
Teymour, Ismail, 134
Thabet, Karim, 120–1, 126, 180–1, 183, 189, 190, 194, 201–2, 204, 207, 212, 213, 220, 221, 223, 229, 230–1, 232, 233, 234, 235, 238, 255, 262, 264, 265, 266, 274, 289, 300
Tobruk, 116, 126, 150
Transjordan, 197
Truman, Harry S., 197
Turf Club, Cairo, 248–9, 250
Turkey, 20, 21, 23, 27, 31–2, 184, 241

Umma party, 186
United Nations, 186, 195–6, 197, 199, 200, 242

Valle, Pietro della, 57, 71, 106, 118, 119, 284, 300
Venice Lido, 237
Verdi, Giuseppe, 27
Verrucci, Ernesto, 57, 67, 105, 106
Vichy France, 126, 127, 136
Victor Emmanuel III of Italy, 285
Vienna, 34
Villa Dusmet, Frascati, 285–7, 294

Wafd: founded by Zaghlul, 42–3; feud with Fuad, 43–4, 45, 46–8, 53, 63, 87; elections, 45, 46; and 1936 treaty, 65, 85; corruption, 86, 111, 153–4, 164, 171, 224, 229, 239–40, 261–2; conflict with Farouk, 86–8, 90, 109, 127–8, 129–42, 152–4, 162–

318

4, 176, 206, 251, 254–6; youth Blue Shirts, 90; and British, 111, 129–32, 137–9, 141, 163, 175, 185–7, 223–4, 241–2; and February 1942 crisis, 129–32, 134, 137–9; forms new government, 131–2, 138–40, 141; and Black Book, 153–4; out of office, 164, 167; and 1946 treaty negotiations, 182, 185–7; and revolutionary elements, 187, 245, 247; 1950 elections, 220–1; economic crisis and maladministration, 239–42; and Black Saturday, 247, 251, 254–6

Wassef, Willa, 47

Wavell, Field Marshal Sir Archibald, 116

Western Desert, 110, 111, 144, 152, 169

Wilson, Sir Henry Maitland, 116, 139–40

Wingate, Sir Reginald, 32, 42

Woolley, Sir Charles, 183

Woolwich, Royal Military Academy, 15, 59, 60–1, 62–3, 304, 305

Yad Mordecai, 200

Yalta Conference (1945), 168

Yehia, Abdel Fattah, 58

Yemen, 109

Young Egypt, 17, 170, 176, 187, 221, 245, 258

Yussef, Ahmed, 20, 52

Yussef, Hassan, 158, 185, 189, 211

Yussef Kemal, Prince, 32

Yussri, Wahid, 147–8, 195

Zaafaran Palace, 26, 35

Zagazig, 132, 241

Zaghlul, Saad, 31, 38, 41–6, 53, 84, 106

Zaki, Selim, 206

Zamalek, 107, 178

Zog, King of Albania, 214

Zulficar, Squadron Leader Husain, 117

Zulficar, Safinaz – see Farida, Queen

Zulficar, Said, 58, 97, 113

Zulficar, Judge Yussef, 73–4, 92–4, 97

Zulficar, Madam Zeinab, 52, 59, 72, 73–4, 93, 96, 125, 160